Belonging

Edwin Muir, aged 17, 1904

Belonging
A Memoir

Willa Muir

Introduction by
Aileen Christianson

Kennedy & Boyd
an imprint of
Zeticula
57 St Vincent Crescent
Glasgow
G3 8NQ
Scotland

http://www.kennedyandboyd.co.uk
admin@kennedyandboyd.co.uk

First published 1968 by The Hogarth Press, London
This edition Copyright © Kenneth Ross 2008
Introduction © Aileen Christianson 2008

ISBN-13 978 1 904999 70 6
ISBN-10   1 904999 70 0

Note
The extracts on pages 240, 243, 270 and 276 are taken from Edwin Muir's *Collected Poems*, by courtesy of Messrs Faber & Faber, Ltd.

Dedicated to
EDWIN MUIR
with love

Contents

Wilhelmina Anderson, 1910, St Andrews

Illustrations

Edwin Muir, 1917, Glasgow

Introduction[1]

> Yet when he died in 1959 I became aware that I had been
> assuming we should die together, when it came to dying, hand in
> hand. I could not believe it possible for me to be alive and for him
> to be dead. It did not make sense. We belonged together.
>
> *Willa Muir,* Belonging

Willa Muir was born Wilhelmina Anderson, 1890, in
Montrose; she was educated at Montrose Academy and University
of St Andrews where she took a first class degree in classics, 1911,
followed by a further year's study with the Berry Scholarship, 1911-
12; she had a one year assistantship in the classics department, St.
Andrews University, 1914-15, then taught Latin and educational
psychology at Gypsy Hill Training College, London. She met
Edwin Muir[2] in Glasgow, 1918, and married him, 1919. They lived
in London till 1921, then, beginning their peripatetic married life,
they moved from Prague to Germany, Italy, Montrose, and France,
1921-26; their son Gavin was born in 1927 and they mainly lived
in England, 1927-35. The Muirs financed their life translating
works from German, such as Lion Feuchtwangler's *Jew Suss* (1926)
and Franz Kafka's *The Trial* (1937). In *Belonging* (1968), Muir's
memoir of Edwin (that also acts as a memoir of her own life and
opinions), she indicates that sometimes most of the translation
was done by her, at other times they split it in half. She also
translated alone under the name Agnes Neill Scott. Her own first
published work, *Women: An Inquiry* (1925)[3] was a short discussion
of ideas, many now outdated, about male/female differences. She
described her first novel, *Imagined Corners* (1931; written between
1926 and 1931),[4] as 'Quite pre-Marxian! But a good picture of the
world I grew up in';[5] it was reviewed as 'a memorable contribution
to the cartography of Scotland' (*Glasgow Herald* 1931).[6]   Her
second novel, the powerful *Mrs Ritchie* (1933),[7] was darker and
less autobiographical. Muir's non-fiction study, *Mrs Grundy in
Scotland* (1936),[8] her exploration of Mrs Grundy, that archetype of
female sanctimony and social hypocrisy, and the repressions Muir

saw as inherent in Victorian Scotland, was commissioned for a series of works on Scotland devised by Lewis Grassic Gibbon and Hugh MacDiarmid. Muir also wrote two unpublished novels, *Mrs Muttoe and the Top Storey*, completed 1940, and *The Usurpers*, 1951-52.[9] The Muirs lived in St Andrews, 1935-42, Edinburgh, 1942-45; after the war they lived in both Prague, 1945-49, and Rome, 1949-50. Muir continued her own writing, mainly short pieces, including radio talks, doggerel verse, and her journals. They lived at Newbattle Abbey, Dalkeith, where Edwin was warden, 1950-55. Because her parents were from Shetland, Willa saw herself as a 'displaced person': 'I grew up not fitting into Angus tradition and therefore critical, resentful, unsure. Hence my secret desire to *own* a house';[10] after 1955 the Muirs mainly lived in Cambridgeshire where they bought a house in 1956. Edwin died in 1959. Willa took up his contract for a book on the ballads, writing most of *Living with Ballads* (1965)[11] herself. From 1963 she lived mainly in London, moving back to Scotland in 1969; she died in Dunoon in 1970.

Willa Muir's feminism and her intellectual interests are apparent in all her writing, published and private. The reprinting of her two novels and some non-fiction in 1987 and 1996 made possible a reassessment of her work in both Scottish and European contexts. Intellectual, passionate, insecure, inextricably connected with Edwin Muir during her adult life, Muir can now be assessed in her own right, author of two very different novels, and a professional writer who wrote to contract, but with much of herself apparent in that writing and in her many journals and letters, leaving extensive details of an intellectual European life as well as detailed and moving information of growing up female in Scotland. *Belonging*, her memoir of Edwin, can be read in counterpoint to her other works, as source of both information and commentary. But read separately from them, it is a moving reconstruction of two lives in the twentieth century and an illuminating analysis by a particular feminist of those two lives, of Scotland, Europe and that century. It is both informative and creative, her last great work.

Belonging

Muir began planning *Belonging: A Memoir* (1968) early in the 1960s. It was always intended to be her memoir of Edwin and to interpret it as her own autobiography would be to misunderstand her purpose. But she also intended it to be a memoir of her life with Edwin, exploring that shared life in a way that Edwin himself had been incapable of doing in his own *An Autobiography* (1954).[12] *Belonging* begins with their first 'unlikely' meeting in Glasgow in September 1918 when Willa was a lecturer in London and Edwin was a 'costing-clerk in a Renfrew shipbuilding firm' (*page 1*). Unlikely as their friends thought it that the marriage (which followed nine months later in June 1919) would last, Muir records in the first paragraph of *Belonging* that, when Edwin died in January 1959, she realised that she had assumed they should die together, 'hand in hand. I could not believe it possible for me to be alive and for him to be dead. It did not make sense' (*page 1*). The rest of the memoir is Muir's narrative of their life together. Before Muir met Edwin, she found a paragraph in his *We Moderns* (1918; published under the pseudonym of Edward Moore), headed 'Love and Innocence', which reminds her of her childhood feeling of being floated 'out and up into . . . the Universe' (*page 4*). In another paragraph, headed 'Love and its Object', he writes of lovers generating 'such wealth of life that it overflows, enriching their friends, their enemies, all the world',[13] and Muir wonders if this 'sense of overflowing feeling' was 'essentially the same' as her own feelings of 'Belonging to the Universe' (*page 4*). Shortly after this thought, Edwin is introduced to her. At their second meeting in December 1918, they talk about his origins in Orkney and hers in Shetland, and where they felt they belonged. Edwin told her about his displacement from Orkney to Glasgow and the 'shocks he suffered' (*page 8*), while Muir spoke of her first shock being in relation to language, 'my first words were in the Norse dialect of Shetland' and, age two, she remembers being mocked outside in the Montrose street by older girls squealing 'in delighted mockery' at her dialect (*page 9*). She records her reflections in the train after the meeting that her interest in language dated from that moment 'when my intelligence came to the rescue of my hurt feelings and told me that I could learn to "belong" by speaking Montrose' (*page 10*). She could speak 'Shetland, Montrose and the kind of English used at the small private school in Bridge Street' by the time she was four (*page 10*). Her thoughts about her early trilingual skills are placed retrospectively. She concludes the first chapter: 'About the great shock in my adult life, the 1914 war, which knocked me to pieces for a time, I did not think at all'; her thoughts 'lingered comfortably within the lesser ambience of personal displacements' and 'compared with [Edwin] I had been let off lightly' (*page 10*). Muir thus positions herself equally with Edwin from the first chapter of *Belonging*. The 'great shock of her adult life', world war one, remains unexplored; she writes about it only in her fiction, directly in *Mrs Ritchie* but only obliquely in *Imagined Corners*.

In 1938 Edwin was working on *The Story and the Fable* (1940)[14] while Willa was working on *Mrs Muttoe and the Top Storey*. He wrote to Sydney Schiff about it:

> I am taking notes for something like a description of myself, done in general outline, not in detail, not as a story, but as an attempt to find out what a human being is in this extraordinary age which depersonalises everything. Whether it will be a success or a failure, I can't say; it may be that I have found at last a form that suits me; it may be that I haven't found a form at all, but merely a collection of fragments. I have begun to note myself, anyway, and I find that in doing that I am noting other people too, and the world around me. That is bound to have some value: the problem is to discover what you are, and then what your relation is to other people: I am starting from that and it takes me in ever so many directions, inwards and outwards, backwards and forwards: into dreams on the one hand, and social observation on the other; into the past by a single line, and over the present by countless lines. At any rate I am learning in the process, whatever the artistic result may be.[15]

The Story and the Fable became the first section of Edwin's *An Autobiography* (1954) and the process he describes above was continued there. Willa herself is far less central in his story than he in hers, however much she might have been ever present in his daily life; the index lists her only eleven times, although he does write 'My marriage was the most fortunate event of my life'.[16] It was when he was preoccupied in 1952 with extending *The Story and the Fable* in Newbattle that he so annoyed and depressed Muir by failing to read her typescript of *The Usurpers* and by admitting that he would leave out from his autobiography the painful episode in their marriage when he told her about Gerda Krapp (later Liebrecht) and his intention to leave her and return to Gerda. Muir headed the entry in her Journal recording their long discussion '*Why I am to be described as a mess*', taking her pain into herself. She describes her anguished feelings in 1923 on the shores of Lake Garda in *Belonging* (*page 78*). As he had acknowledged, Edwin makes no reference to the episode in *An Autobiography*. This difference illustrates Willa Muir's central positioning of her own self and feelings into *Belonging* and shows Edwin Muir's intense concentration on aspects of himself rather than on a narrative of his life. However important Willa was in his life, he writes the kind of autobiography which foregrounds intellectual and artistic development over any exploration of his emotional life with his wife. There is a clear contrast between *An Autobiography* with its interest in the symbolism and allegory of his life rather than its detail, and Muir's memoir of him in *Belonging*, grounded as it is in the details of their lives together, as well as in her interest in psychology and her own feminist perceptions of a patriarchal world. For Muir, the memoir is part of her 'never-finishing performance of the female self' rather than 'the definitive, significant male-history', in Sabine Vanacker's phrases about other modernist women writers.[17] Edwin's *An Autobiography* is too interested in the story and the fable behind his own 'male-history' for it to be 'definitive' as a life history, with its attention to the inner, the poetic and philosophical. Muir's memoir of Edwin in *Belonging* resists a reading of it as 'definitive, significant male-history' by placing herself so firmly as part of the story, ensuring that she, even though it is not *her* autobiography, produces a 'never-finishing performance of the female self' where her constructed self acts both as narrator and narrated.

Lumir Soukup discusses the differences between the Muirs'

life-writing in his short memoir, 'Belonging'. He calls Willa Muir's *Belonging* 'her memoirs'. He believes their 'autobiographies' should be read together as they are 'complementary'.[18] His comparative judgment on their works trusts Muir's accuracy over Edwin's:

> From our countless encounters after many events experienced together, I can vouch for Willa's recollections as the more accurate. She was more down-to-earth, a factual, relevant observer; a recorder, whereas Edwin was concerned with atmosphere and the impressions made on him. Occasionally . . . he did not see or remember certain things, because he had withdrawn into a dream and a search for formulation. He was an interpreter. To give just one example, Willa's operation and recovery as described in *Belonging* . . . and in *An Autobiography* . . . , one almost wonders whether they were writing about the same event. Knowing Willa, I believe her unsentimental account. (L. Soukup. p. 30)

But this is a preference based on Willa the 'recorder', whereas Edwin achieves the artistically superior role of 'interpreter'. Lumir Soukup thought 'Edwin's additional chapters', written while at Newbattle Abbey, were 'uneven', lacking 'firmness of thought and judgment', and thought it 'likely because he felt that his real writing was poetry' (L. Soukup. p. 30, p. 31). Thus both Edwin's successful early chapters and (in Soukup's view) less successful later ones, are described and justified in relation to Edwin's artistic role as a poet, and Willa's success is related to her 'accuracy', even though Soukup concludes that '*Belonging* is her long poem, the Story written in prose' (L. Soukup. p. 32). Sherry Simon in *Gender in Translation* thinks Muir 'a talented writer'; defining *Belonging* as Muir's 'memoirs', Simon sees them as 'a remarkable demonstration of the fluidity of her style and the acuity of her perceptions';[19] Simon's reference to Muir's 'fluidity of her style' implies artistic capacity but Muir herself writes defensively in her journal of her attitude to style: 'In writing a book I attend far more to the construction, the sequence of incidents, the feeling conveyed, than to the style, although I am not aware of neglecting the style'.[20] This description seems to corroborate Soukup's view of her as a 'recorder' even though this list of what she pays attention to in her writing (at that time *The Usurpers*) implies artistic choices. Muir herself, in an opposition between Scottish and English baking, categorised *Belonging* as 'very like a Scotch bun . . . because it has a bit of everything in it, not classified into layers like a respectable English cake'.[21] This opposition implies solidity and completion, with Muir for once taking Scottish as positive and dismissing the respectability of an English cake's layering.

Most commentators on Muir's work take *Belonging* as 'straight' memoir, using parts of it to give biographical information or to discuss Muir's feminism. David Robb certainly uses the passage about the Muirs' respective studies in Hampstead as straightforward information about her position which indicates 'an occasional twinge of resentment without which she would not have been human'.[22] What Muir does in *Belonging* is to show the contrasts between their two studies in ways that more than hint at gendered divisions, with Edwin as the austere, privileged poet whose study's peace and separation is sacrosanct while Willa's work space is constantly intruded on by the household:

> In his study at the top of the house which contained only a table, a chair, an ink-pot and a fine view over roofs and tree-tops, Edwin now and then produced a poem. The bareness of his study was how he liked it; my memory may have exaggerated that, but slightly. Ten poems, some composed in Crowborough and some in Hampstead, were published in 1934 by Dent, with the title: *Variations on a Time Theme.* // My study on the ground floor was neither so bare nor so secluded. Here I was intruded upon at all hours by household staff, the weekly washerwoman, any casual caller ready for a gossip, and Gavin whenever he came home from school. . . . Toys, picture-books and hoards of Gavin's were in my study, an upright piano, a wicker wash-basket for laundry, a sewing-machine, a small sofa for visitors and goodness knows what else. I envied Edwin's power of sitting down immediately after breakfast to concentrate in solitude on what he wanted to do. // Yet there was always a press of work, and so I reverted to a student habit of mine, working at furious speed late at night into the small hours, after the vibrations of the day had died down. (*page 158*)

Edwin was also working on novel reviewing for *The Listener* from January 1933 for several years ('an article of about 1500 words about once a fortnight, dealing usually with three novels' which provided their most regular 'small, but assured' income), [23] as well as any contribution he made to their translating of Sholem Asch, Kafka's *The Great Wall of China* and 'another Broch' (*page 157*); Muir acknowledges all of this work immediately before the study passage, but still manages to imply in the passage itself that all that Edwin had to do in his study was write his poems, concentrating 'in solitude'. She, meanwhile, at the centre of their domestic / work space is 'intruded upon at all hours', busily entertaining visitors ready for gossip, mothering, housekeeping (in an organising rather than a doing sense) as well as translating and completing her second novel, *Mrs Ritchie*. She ensures that a reader's sympathy should be with her not Edwin, providing an example of what Sidonie Smith calls 'both the process and the product of assigning meaning to a series of experiences . . . by means of emphasis, juxtaposition, commentary, omission'.[24] This trope of male / female writing conditions is not an unusual one. Virginia Woolf's *A Room of One's Own* (1929) may be the most famous and extended of the contemporary explorations of the female lack of private writing space and its effect on a woman's chances for literary productivity, with its conclusion that 'it is necessary to have five hundred a year and a room with a lock on the door if you are to write fiction or poetry'.[25] But in 1934 Winifred Holtby makes a comparison between two unrelated Victorian writers who, in their respective houses in Chelsea and Manchester, were enacting the same trope as the Muirs in Hampstead fifty years later:

> While Carlyle was shutting himself up in his sound-proof room, and sacrificing his wife to his dyspeptic or creative agonies, Mrs. Gaskell was writing her novels at the end of a dining-room table, among a constant whirl of children, servants, draughts and callers. Carlyle's achievement, considered by purely intellectual standards, was the more impressive; but the author of *Mary Barton* and *North and South* had an alert intelligence and imagination which, had they been adequately respected, might have raised her literary work from competence to greatness.[26]

This employs the identical feminist suggestion to Muir that the intrusion of domestic concerns undermines any possibility of 'greatness' although Muir also implies her own competence is undermined because of the demands of her surroundings. Undoubtedly accurate in its analysis and implied criticism of the privileged position of the male, Holtby does not take account of the capacity of some writers (such as Jane Austen) to produce works of 'greatness' in the midst of domestic activity. It works best as an interesting trope in the history of feminist analysis of male / female relations, rather than as an explanation or excuse for the 'success' or otherwise of particular kinds of literary production.

While I would not assert that all Muir's work constitutes autobiography (and would think it a reductive assertion to make), certainly Muir's works, all of which interknit her own experiences and concerns to some extent, could be interpreted in this way if Sidonie Smith's widest definition was adopted: 'Since all gesture and rhetoric is revealing of the subject, autobiography can be defined as any written or verbal communication' (Smith. p. 19). To some degree Muir certainly follows this idea, every piece of written work (published or not) including some reflection on her self and experience. Elphinstone, while understanding the complexity of Muir's relationship to 'autobiography' and that *Belonging* is not Muir's autobiography, nevertheless uses the concept of autobiography to underwrite her analysis of Muir's works:

> Willa Muir's autobiography is an elusive text; ostensibly it was never actually written, but that need be no deterrent to making it the starting point of this examination of self, gender and society in her work. On the contrary, the location of autobiography as a hidden subtext, both in the novels and in the late works *Belonging* and *Living with Ballads*, is exemplary of Muir's analysis of marginality and identity'.[27]

Muir's works are also exemplary of Sidonie Smith's view that the autobiographer joins 'together facets of remembered experience—descriptive, impressionistic, dramatic, analytic', constructing 'a narrative' as she works on 'self-interpretation' (Smith. p. 45). What underlies Smith's analysis of the genre is the clear point that autobiography or memoirs are necessarily artistic constructions using memory (itself both selective and creative) and that non-fiction texts are as much constructs using literary skills as are fictional texts. No more than history can memoirs or autobiography be taken as 'truth' and any attempt to use *Belonging* as narrative 'truth' about the Muirs has to be accompanied by awareness of Willa Muir's creative capacities in interpretation and use of her material. For me, *Belonging* represents a pulling together of all Muir's concerns: Edwin, gender and feminism, the patriarchy, Scotland, the unconscious. It is a final writing of Edwin, herself and their joint story, re-mining her past work (published or unpublished), using her experiences and her interpretations of past life with Edwin, to construct her memoir of him in *Belonging*, ensuring that she is strongly present both as the narrating 'I' and as the narrated 'I' that accompanies Edwin's 'he'.

Aileen Christianson

1 Muir, W. *Belonging* (1968) London: Hogarth Press; rpt. (2008) Kennedy & Boyd. This introduction is closely based on my discussion of *Belonging* in Christianson, Aileen. (2007) *Moving in Circles: Willa Muir's Writings*. Edinburgh: Word Power Books. pp. 177-85. I have drawn on that chapter by kind permission of Elaine Henry of Word Power Books, Edinburgh.

2 Edwin Muir (1887-1959), born in Orkney; poet and critic.

3 Muir, W. (1925) *Women: An Inquiry.* London: Hogarth Press; rpt. in Kirsty Allen (ed.). (1996) *Imagined Selves*. Edinburgh: Canongate.

4 Muir, W. (1931) *Imagined Corner.* London: Martin Secker (first pbd. June 1931; second printing Aug. 1931); rpt. (1987 and 1996) Edinburgh: Canongate.

5 Willa Muir's journals are in the extensive archive of her manuscripts in St Andrews University Library; (18 March 1948) 'The Putsch, and after' journal, Jan.-May 1948; St Andrews MS 38466/5/4.

6 Anon. review. (1931) *Glasgow Herald* (2 July). p. 4.

7 Muir, W. (1933) *Mrs Ritchie*. London: Martin Secker; rpt. (1996) in *Imagined Selves*. Edinburgh: Canongate.

8 Muir, W. (1936) *Mrs Grundy in Scotland*. London: George Routledge & Sons; rpt. (1996) in *Imagined Selves*. Edinburgh: Canongate.

9 Muir, W. (1938-40). *Mrs Muttoe and the Top Storey* (typescript, St. Andrews, MS 38466/1/2) and (1951-52). *The Usurpers* (typescript, St. Andrews, MS 38466/2/9 and 10).

10 Muir, W. (n.d. [1947]) 'Dirty work', Prague journal, 1947-Jan. 1948; St Andrews MS 38466/5/3.

11 Muir, W. (1965) *Living with Ballads*. London: Hogarth Press.

12 Muir, E. (1954) *An Autobiography*. London: Hogarth Press.

13 'Moore, Edward' (pseud. Edwin Muir) (1918). *We Moderns: Enigmas and Guesses*. London: Allen and Unwin. p. 210 and p. 211.

14 Muir, E. (1940) *The Story & the Fable: An Autobiography*. London: George G. Harrap & Co.

15 Muir, E. Letter to Sydney Schiff. (17 May 1938) in Butter, P. H. (ed.). (1974) *Selected Letters of Edwin Muir*. London: Hogarth Press. p. 100.

16 Muir, E. (1993) *An Autobiography*. Edinburgh: Canongate. p. 147.

17 Vanacker, Sabine. (1997) 'Autobiography and Orality: The Work of Modernist Women Writers' in Broughton, Trev L., and Anderson, Linda (eds.). *Women's Lives / Women's Times. New Essays on Auto/ Biography*. Albany, NY: State University of New York Press. p.198.

18 Soukup, Lumir. (1992-93) 'Belonging', *Chapman* 71. p. 30.

19 Simon, Sherry. (1996) *Gender in Translation Cultural Identity and the Politics of Transmission*. London: Routledge. p. 76.

20 Muir, W. (14 April 1952) Journal, Jan. 1951-Sept. 1953. St Andrews MS 38466/5/5.

21 Muir, W. Letter to Tom Scott (22 March 1968). NLS MS 19703.

22 Robb, David S. (1990) 'The Published Novels of Willa Muir' in Schwend, Joachim, and Drescher, Horst (eds.). *Studies in Scottish Fiction: Twentieth Century*. Frankfurt am Main: Peter Lang. p. 149.

23 Butter, P. H. (1966) *Edwin Muir: Man and Poet*. Edinburgh: Oliver and Boyd. p. 130.

24 Smith, Sidonie. (1987). *A Poetics of Women's Autobiography*. Bloomington: Indiana University Press. p. 45.

25 Woolf, Virginia. (1925; rpt. 1945) *A Room of One's Own*. London: Hogarth Press; Harmondsworth: Penguin Books. p. 103.

26 Holtby, Winifred. (1934) *Women and a changing civilisation*. London: John Lane. p. 104.

27 Elphinstone, Margaret. (1997) 'Willa Muir: Crossing the Genres' in Gifford, D., and McMillan, D. (eds.). *A History of Scottish Women's Writing*. Edinburgh: Edinburgh University Press. p. 400.

Edwin Muir in Vienna, 1923-4

Chapter One

1918-1919

I first met Edwin Muir in a Glasgow flat sometime during September 1918. On the face of things our meeting was unlikely; he was a costing-clerk in a Renfrew shipbuilding firm and I was a lecturer in a London training college for teachers. It was still more unlikely that having met we should get married less than a year later and most unlikely of all that our marriage should last. Edwin's Glasgow friends, who thought they knew him, prophesied that it would not last six months; my friends in London, who thought they knew me, were of the same opinion. Yet when he died in 1959 I became aware that I had been assuming we should die together, when it came to dying, hand in hand. I could not believe it possible for me to be alive and for him to be dead. It did not make sense. We belonged together.

*   *   *

The Glasgow hostess in whose flat we met was a handsome widow known to her friends as Mam. Her daughter, E., had been my close friend at school and at the University of St Andrews. In 1908, ten years earlier, Mam had launched a campaign against me in our home town, Montrose, Angus, insisting that I was not unintelligent but had no originality, nothing but an excess of vitality, so that I always pushed E. into the background and hogged any credit that should have been hers. In the course of these ten years she had not modified her version of my character; she prepared Edwin for our meeting by repeating almost word for word the description she had broadcast in Montrose, leaving out only the imputation that I stole all E.'s credit. I did not know about this until after Edwin and I were married, when he told me, quoting Mam with enjoyment: 'Mam kept insisting that you were not unintelligent. Not stupid, you know, but with no sensibility, nothing fine, just a lot of vulgar energy. Not unintelligent, mind you!'

Having coated him with the proper repellent, Mam was ready to introduce Edwin to me. I suspected her of wanting to show him off, her latest acquisition, a young man who had written a book, but I feel now that she must have known how frustrated he felt in Glasgow and may have hoped that I, the aggressive thruster, could help him to a job in London. She did not tell me this and it did not enter my mind. Quite likely I was lacking in sensibility, as she believed, for when I met Edwin I did not perceive that he was in a state of quiet desperation, needing help.

I had no inkling of what the future had in store for him and me, nor any expectation of it. I was now twenty-eight and in my own opinion quite grown-up, an independent woman with a career ahead of me. And I thought I had been cured of falling in love. At the age of twenty I had fallen blissfully in love with a medical student, a famous player in my university's Rugby team, and got engaged to him, a glamorous man not unlike Jane Austen's Henry Crawford, with 'countenance' and 'address', a lively eye and an impressively broad chest. Out of doors he was a delightful companion; he taught me to waltz on skates, he swam magnificently, he drove a gig with style; indoors he had little to offer but petting except for the clean breast he insisted on making about his recurrent peccadilloes with other girls after I had gone away to England, teaching Classics. Rather more than two years later, taking his ring off my finger—a pretty ring of diamonds and sapphires—and saying: 'Watch this!' I threw it into the sea off St Andrews pier where we were standing.

In the late afternoon I now arrived at Mam's flat and almost at once she put Edwin's book into my lap. *We Moderns*, it was called, published under the pseudonym Edward Moore. He had written it, she said, on slips of paper hidden among the pages of his ledgers; it was made up of paragraphs and aphorisms which had appeared in the *New Age*. Aphorisms? Scaffolding for a book rather than a book, I decided. But I began to look through the longer pieces and felt increasing surprise as I read. *We Moderns* was not only an unusual work to come from a costing-clerk's office, it was not at all what one would have expected from a friend of Mam's.

What Mam asked from life and from the books she read was material that could be turned into amusing stories. She was concerned with appearances, with show business, and cared little for truth. But this book, *We Moderns*, was written by a young man trying to lift himself by his boot-straps beyond his ledgers into a world he accepted as noble and true, inhabited by figures he thought noble and true, such as Goethe and Ibsen and Nietzsche. 'Edward Moore' seemed an earnest, occasionally solemn, young man of a kind that I could have sworn Mam would find boring.

I felt impatient with him myself, here and there, as I read. His extreme admiration for Nietzsche put me off. When thou goest to Woman forget not thy whip, said I to myself with scorn. I laughed inwardly when he denounced camaraderie between the sexes and asserted that realism in art and comradeship between the sexes were two aspects of the same misunderstanding. I wondered why he should pay so much attention to G. K. Chesterton, and why he should bother himself so much about Original Sin. And yet he had a feeling for words and a pleasure in manipulating them. 'Fate has dealt ironically with Mr Wells. It has turned his volumes of fiction into prophecies and his volumes of prophecies into fiction.' Sometimes the wit was more than verbal. 'Sympathy is Love bereft of his bow and arrows—but still blind.' Behind the mannered style I could sense a yearning for love, innocence, poetry and mystery. I wished he had not used the word 'creative' so frequently, yet the section on Creative Love began to hold my attention and awaken my sympathy, blind as he might consider that to be. There was one region in Man, he said, where innocence and a good conscience still reigned, in the unconscious. The very well-spring, the central ego of Man, he called it.

Now at this time I was altogether fascinated by the unconscious, but I did not care for Edward Moore's description of it as 'the central ego of Man'. I was inclined to think of the ego as a construction which had been over-developed until it weighed like a burden on the unconscious. All my hopes lay in the unconscious itself. For years I had been probing more or less ignorantly into the underworld of feeling, ever since I discovered Jane Ellen Harrison's *Prolegomena to Greek Religion*, which I carried in my bosom during my first university summer, and I was now exploring Jung—after all, I was lecturing on Psychology in my training college—so I went on reading what Edward Moore had to say.

I chanced then upon a paragraph entitled: 'Love and Innocence', which moved me unexpectedly because it brushed against an experience of my own that was of great and secret importance in my life. I had not told even E. about it when we were intimate, nor had I mentioned it to my Rugby player. My first awareness of it came at the age of two, when I was being pushed high in a swing, a small wooden chair slung from the branch of a tree. At the top of my swing I looked up and saw a pattern of green leaves against the blue sky. Boundless delight floated me for one moment up into that sky beside the green leaves, a moment I have never forgotten. My mother later identified the occasion for me, since I remembered also a fast river of brown bubbling water with a narrow, teetering suspension bridge on which ladies of our party stood and shrieked, and that memory pinned down the day for her: it was the day we went on a church outing up Glenesk, near Edzell, she said, when I was about two and a half. This 'floating' experience recurred at odd times, always with an uprush of joyousness; I recognized it when it came upon me but took it for granted; there was no need to put it into words. Yet one evening when I was sixteen it broke over me so strongly and lasted so long that I was awed into giving it a name.

I was sitting alone in a boat beached at the back of the island in the throat of the tidal lagoon, called the Basin, behind Montrose; the sun was setting before me and the Basin was full. Except for a distant curlew's call there was no living sound. The 'feeling' came upon me like a tide floating me out and up into the wide greening sky—into the Universe, I told myself. That was the secret name I gave it: Belonging to the Universe. Like Thoreau, I felt myself 'grandly related'.

Did Edward Moore mean the same kind of experience when he wrote of a feeling of universal comprehension arising, he said, out of Love? I had not associated my 'feeling' specifically with Love. But he was so sure of it that he even contradicted Nietzsche, who argued that Love is narrowly egoistic, isolating two people. Edward Moore insisted: 'Only lovers can generate such wealth of life that it overflows, enriching their friends, their enemies, all the world. To love one is to love all.' This sense of overflowing feeling, was it essentially the same as mine?

I was thinking about it when Mam came in. I shut the book, for I could not discuss these resonant words with her.

'How do you like Edwin's book?'

'He enjoys putting words together, doesn't he? That makes him quite witty sometimes.'

'Oh, he *is* witty. He can be very amusing. Have you looked at the epigrams in the Appendix?'

I had not, so Mam took the book into her own hands and read them aloud, chuckling. Every now and then with all her force, which was considerable, she pushed at me the suggestion that I must tell Edwin Muir how much I liked his book. I privately determined to say nothing about it unless he did, and even began to stick derogatory labels on him, such as 'Nietz-schean!' I was not going to add anything to the size of the fish in Mam's net.

But when he came in and was introduced the labels fell off at once. As I usually did when meeting young men for the first time, I looked at eyes and mouth. I had too often met well-shaped foreheads and clever eyes spoilt by ill-shaped mouths, tight-lipped or foolish, the mouths of men whose intellects had been educated but not their feelings. Edwin Muir's eyes and mouth promised well; his brow was an intellectual's, disproportionately wide and high, very noticeable above the slight, even meagre body, yet his eyes were dreamy-looking, sea-blue, with a hint of distance in them, and his mouth was well cut, with full, sensitive lips. A little later I noticed that one of his thin shoulders, the left, as if cramped with too much leaning on an elbow, was held stiffly above the level of the other. But when he laughed two blue flashes shot from his eyes and one forgot the cramped shoulder. His voice, too, was pleasantly soft and gentle.

He was not like a satellite of Mam's to look at, more like the Edwin Muir I had chanced to hear about in London towards the end of that summer term. A Scottish girl, Mary Robertson, newly come to teach in Walthamstow, had walked me up and down Kensington Gardens one evening to hear the story of her love-affair in Glasgow with a certain Edwin Muir, an attractive and gifted young man. It was a melodramatic story ending in a grand renunciation scene when Mary gave him up for his own good. This was the first time I had heard the name Edwin Muir. The coincidence struck me when Mam and E. urgently invited me to stay a night with them on my way back to London in order to meet the same young man, and out of sheer curiosity I accepted.

As usual at Mam's, there were plenty of sallies and pleasantries while we ate one of her famous casserole dishes. But she did not mention Edwin's book and he himself made no reference to it. Perhaps I was supposed to throw that stone into the pool. I did not do so; as it happened, I stirred up the pool with a stick instead. Listening to Edwin's soft voice I remembered that he was an Orkney-man and I turned to him and told him that my people came from Unst in Shetland. We began to exchange Orkney and Shetland words and phrases and to discuss the habits and temperaments of the Islanders. From Mam's point of view this must have seemed grossly unfair; she deflected me by asking me to sing some student songs at the piano. I had not what is called a singing voice, but I could half-croon songs in a not unpleasant contralto. Now, instead of roaring the usual student choruses with E., I crooned one or two Gaelic songs I had heard Patuffa Kennedy Fraser sing in Tobias Matthay's house. These songs enchanted Edwin, as I could tell. He left shortly afterwards.

Mam looked tired and vaguely dissatisfied.

'Why didn't you tell Edwin how much you liked his book? You should write and tell him so when you get to London. Oh, do write to him.'

I did not write to him, wary as always when urged by Mam to do something. To my surprise in about six weeks' time he wrote to me, apologizing for what he called a 'career-y' letter, begging me to tell him if I thought he had any chance of finding work in London. He made the appeal as lightly as he could, but now it did occur to me that the writer of this letter was in a state of quiet desperation, although he had tried hard to suppress it. The very handwriting bore witness to the effort of suppression, it was so secretive. The lines were neat, the script small and self-contained, though cramped, but every letter was so like every other letter that the words were difficult to decipher—the handwriting of a man accustomed to hide his inner self, to keep it from being read by others' eyes, perhaps even by his own.

I answered the letter warmly. From personal experience I was sure that London provided opportunities to develop one's interests, and I said so. I had myself been drawn into the stream of interest in education and was then involved with people who were hoping to organize Day Continuation Schools for youngsters employed in shops and factories. In my club, too, the 1917 Club, there was constant discussion about the psychology of the unconscious. We all believed that a new liberal-minded era was about to dawn. So I wrote gaily to Edwin, with cocksure optimism, and we exchanged several letters. In a burst of high spirits over the Armistice I even sent him some doggerel couplets in the Unst dialect. The upshot of all this was an appointment to meet one evening in Glasgow when I went north for Christmas; we could then, it was supposed, talk things over.

When we did meet I was slightly taken aback to be ushered into Miss Craig's restaurant for a High Tea, having temporarily forgotten about this Scottish habit. But the High Tea made an enjoyable meal, for there was no constraint between Edwin and me. During the three months' interval since our first meeting the acquaintance had apparently grown into friendship without our knowing it.

We exchanged confidences about jobs. Edwin told me stories of his shipbuilding office, which was much more easygoing than any others he had been in. The elderly manager did not believe in 'new-fangled gadgets' for saving staff, and there were so many clerks that they all had time to spare although the work was efficiently done. They had a daily rota for escaping to the lavatory, where each man smoked a cigarette or two and read for about twenty minutes. Edwin usually took a volume of Nietzsche with him, he said.

I told him about my factory girls, packers from Bryant and May's and Knight's, whom I used to teach during wartime in the Mansfield House University Settlement, Canning Town. On discovering that none of them had been farther west in London than Aldgate, I had a hilarious afternoon escorting a dozen of them to Westminster, which I described to Edwin. It took me more than half an hour, for instance, to get them off the escalators at Liverpool Street Station, since they had never seen escalators before and abandoned themselves to the ecstasy of rushing up the Down and down the Up. I told him too about the women I was in charge of in my hostel, all older than myself, uncertificated primary teachers taking their last chance of getting a teaching certificate; a few of them were rather odd, like the Manchester woman who startled me by saying: 'I have one of my bad heads, Miss Anderson, and what I need is de-magnetising. Can you de-magnetize me?'

We Moderns was never even mentioned. We got on to Orkney and Shetland speech instead. I commanded a fine flow of Shetland abuse and kept Edwin laughing at the bad little Shetland names my grandmother used to call me. Around us in Miss Craig's a genteel decorum was prevalent; people at the other tables did not speak above a half-whisper, let alone laugh aloud. I saw a woman screening her mouth with the palm of one hand to keep her neighbours from hearing what she said. This reticence at the other tables reminded me too much of the more troubling reticence in Edwin's handwriting, and I did my best to entertain him. I wanted to see the blue flashes from his eyes when he laughed.

As we explored the background of our common Norse inheritance I did not think we were doing anything but cementing a friendship. I liked Edwin Muir much better than Edward Moore, his pseudonymous self. Our exchanges became more personal and intimate. Instead of talking things over with an eye on possible London jobs for Edwin, we were now talking ourselves over.

Edwin told me a little about his Orkney upbringing and a lot about the shocks he suffered on being shifted to Glasgow at the age of fourteen. In Orkney he had taken his world more or less for granted; in the urban noise and dirt of Glasgow he became at once a displaced person. His parents, especially his father, suffered in the same way. Both his parents died, so did two of his brothers, and the family home was broken up. The uncertain years of adolescence became more than ever uncertain and precarious for him, in his solitary lodgings.

What he told me was enough, I thought, to account for the hidden unhappiness I had sensed in him. I did not, I could not, guess at the horrors and despairs he had lived through since his adolescence. He did not disclose them on that evening. The most extreme horrors, his experiences in the bone-factory, were never disclosed at all until he set them down in his Autobiography years later—until, that is, he was at last able to contemplate them.

'Do you feel now that you belong to Glasgow?' I asked. The question of 'belonging' had preoccupied me nearly as far back as I could remember.

Edwin hesitated and then said that if he belonged anywhere it must be to Orkney.

I did not feel that I belonged whole-heartedly to Montrose. Well before I was three, I explained, I had discovered that I did not really belong to the Montrose way of life. My people spoke Shetland at home, so my first words were in the Norse dialect of Shetland, which was not valid outside our front door. I remembered standing in Bridge Street, where we lived, fingering my pinafore, dumb with embarrassment, while four or five older girls squealed in delighted mockery of what I had been saying and urged me to say it again.

'Maybe it's better to have that kind of shock very young and not wait for it till you're fourteen,' I suggested. 'You learn more easily to adapt yourself.'

'Did you adapt yourself?'

'Well, I learned to speak broad Montrose.'

I did not tell Edwin then about my Belonging to the Universe.

'I've been good at languages ever since,' I added, trying to be humorous.

As Edwin paid the bill, I noticed how thick and strong his wrists looked. His hands were small, fine-boned with tapering fingers, scarcely bigger than mine, but his wrists were nearly as thick across as his knuckles.

We arranged to meet again at Easter. A member of the Glasgow Guilds group, a fellow-student of mine at St Andrews, was planning to give an Easter dance and meant to invite me. Edwin was to be invited too, and we looked forward to seeing each other there. Despite Edward Moore's disdain for 'the camaraderie of the sexes' we were now on Christian-name terms.

In the train I thought more or less idly about the value of getting over one's shocks at a very early age. When one was two or three the slightest push was enough to send one in any direction at all. My interest in languages was awakened at the moment when my intelligence came to the rescue of my hurt feelings and told me that I could learn to 'belong' by speaking Montrose. By the time I was four I could speak Shetland, Montrose and the kind of English used at the small private school in Bridge Street we three children attended until our father died. And that, I decided, was why I became good at Greek and Latin as I grew up.

I was luckier than Edwin, too, in the displacements I had had to undergo. At first they were only displacements from one local shelf to another, from private school to Board School, from Board School to Academy. By the time I went with a bursary to St Andrews University I was already used to moving from one shelf to another.

About the great shock in my adult life, the 1914 war, which knocked me to pieces for a time, I did not think at all. Edwin had said nothing about it, and so my thoughts lingered comfortably within the lesser ambience of personal displacements, remembering that St Andrews had been a pleasure to me, as Glasgow was not to Edwin, and that compared with him I had been let off lightly.

Chapter Two

Easter 1919 – June 1919

The elder of my two cousins in Cambuslang, by Glasgow, Dora Anderson, was like a sister to me. We were born in the same year and as children had always spent part of our summer holidays together. Dora had abundant auburn hair and eyes of the same colour with a temperament to match; she was fiery, easily kindled and generous. Just before the Easter dance, when I went to stay with her, I found to my amazement that on this occasion she was blazing with ardour for nothing less than a crusade to save Edwin Muir from being swallowed alive by Mam. The Glasgow Guilds group was losing sleep over him, I gathered, and holding agitated conferences about how he was to be rescued. He was in Mam's house every night, said Dora—well, several times a week, anyhow. I was told what various members of the group had said, and how distressed they all were, and how unaware Edwin seemed to be of his danger. The group seemed to regard him as a kind of White Hope. What was to happen both to him and to them if he fell into Mam's maw did not bear thinking about.

Remembering those strong wrists of his I remarked that Edwin might not be so helpless as the group feared. And why shouldn't he spend his evenings in Mam's?

'Mam's a good cook,' I said, 'and good company. What she hasn't read in French literature isn't worth reading. Of course Edwin likes going where he's made welcome and given a good supper.'

My disbelief was flouted. I was reminded that I knew very well myself what Mam was like. I did, certainly, but I could not be persuaded that Edwin's danger was real. We argued the toss back and forth, but there was a dance to get dressed for, and we were on top of a tram careering towards Glasgow before I said to Dora, using what had become a formula of ours: 'Bet you a bob.'

This code-phrase went back to 1905, the year Dora and I won a shilling from a cousin of hers, a sceptical young man, on a bet that we would sing 'Clementine' in the High Street of Stirling at ten o'clock on a Saturday night. I now betted Dora the usual bob that I could detach Edwin Muir from Mam. I was to win this bet but it had ceased to matter by the time I won it.

In the dance hall we greeted E. and Edwin who had just arrived together, but it was some little time before I was free to dance with him. He led me out for a waltz. The floor was good and our steps matched so well that we floated rather than danced round the hall. I had never had so light-footed a partner, nor, perhaps, had he, for as the evening wore on it became understood between us that we should partner each other for all the waltzes. As the evening wore on, too, we became more and more wordless. I think we both fell into a trance. I do not know how otherwise to account for the fact that Edwin, leading me to a sit-out place after a waltz, took me into the men's lavatory before we noticed where we had got to. At the end of the dance we went off together in the most natural manner in the world. I did not remember that Edwin should have taken E. home, nor did he.

The park Edwin guided me into was near the University. He must have been accustomed to use it as a trysting-place; he made directly for it, with no hesitation. There we sat on a park bench for hours, in bliss. At one point of time a policeman shone a bull's-eye lantern on us and enquired: 'Is this love or lunacy?' It was both, we assured him and relapsed again into our trance. I do not know how or when I got back to Cambuslang.

The feeling which rose up and overwhelmed me that evening, obliterating my conscious self, was like the feeling of Belonging to the Universe but stronger, even more joyous, more full of wonder. It seemed inexhaustible. I suspect that Edwin was having the same experience, for we inherited, each of us, a primitive simplicity from our Orkney and Shetland forebears which was likely to be wide open to vibrations from our tribal unconscious. Behind our more or less civilized frontages Edwin and I each had a large area of primitive feeling, a greater proportion of simplicity than is usual in Britain, a simplicity which more sophisticated people call naivete. We had inherited it from islanders who practised co-operative not competitive ways of living, and so in each of us that simplicity was keyed to general goodwill. Each of us had the personal problem of consciously controlling floods of primitive emotion, but on this night the strength of our feeling for each other swept us right out of ourselves beyond consciousness.

Edwin must have turned up in Cambuslang very soon afterwards for he reported that he had just got an angry letter from Mam informing him that he was no gentleman. Poor E. had had to make her way home from the dance alone. Of course he was no gentleman, said Edwin, but how little that mattered! I do not remember going home to Montrose. Before I left, Edwin and I arranged to join a small party of my cousins and some friends in a long weekend at a St Andrews hotel.

I arrived in St Andrews before the Glasgow contingent, so went down to the station to meet them. And here I took a long look at Edwin as he came down the platform. He was wearing a grey suit of material so cheap that it was creased like paper from having been newly cleaned, and a pair of shoes as scuffed and worn as if he had gone to school in them years ago. In either side-pocket of his jacket a volume of Nietzsche was stuffed. Beneath his chin was a bow tie of his favourite colour, daffodil yellow. His eyes were sending out blue flashes more radiantly than ever and my heart turned over with sheer love of him, paper-thin suit, scuffed shoes, volumes of Nietzsche and all.

I think it was on the last day of our long weekend that something happened to which I attached little importance at the time. On the East Sands Edwin and I were sitting apart from the others, being, as I thought, very contented. Edwin was digging his fingers into the sand. All at once he looked at me and said: 'You know, this isn't going to do.'

'What isn't?'

'You and I.'

This struck me as such an absurd statement that I had to laugh. In a moment or two Edwin also began to laugh and no more was said about it. I would have forgotten the incident had Edwin not reminded me of it, later, in London at Whitsun. In defending his threatened individual self, he said, he had developed in Glasgow a technique to keep under control his susceptibility to girls. When one of his 'affairs' had gone on long enough for him to feel his independence encroached on, he got a last-ditch feeling that enabled him to say: 'You know, this isn't going to do.' If the girl wept, as often happened, he wept too, but his will to stop the affair remained inflexible. In a moment of panic he had tried the same technique on me, but instead of weeping or arguing I laughed, such a genuine laugh that he was disconcerted. And suddenly he felt how ridiculous he was with his willpower and his precious personality, and he could not help laughing too.

He then recounted the long tale of his various affairs, beginning with Katie Swan, an Orkney girl, and finishing up with my predecessor. I could not but smile as I noted how completely Mary Robertson had turned her story upside down; she had been cut off with the same gentle ruthlessness as all the others. Edwin enjoyed telling me these stories. It was with glee that he recalled an incident which happened while he was squiring Jessie Roberton, a daughter of Sir Hugh Roberton's. Sir Hugh was making a speech on some public platform in Glasgow, in a theatre, I think, and in the middle of denouncing various enemies of society, Exploiters and Parasites, he paused, shot an accusing glance up at the side-box where Edwin and Jessie sat and added, with intent, 'and Philanderers!'

In his Autobiography Edwin was concerned to show how these rootless love-affairs sprang from the bad psychological state he was in at the time and he did not admit that he much enjoyed them, but I am sure, from his manner of recounting them, that there was a good deal of enjoyment. What impressed me most as I listened was the speed and coolness with which he had practised 'breaking it off'. Breaking off my early engagement had taken me a long time to achieve and cost me much anguish. Edwin's power of detaching himself from emotional experience was clearly much greater than mine; whenever he felt his deeper feelings in danger of coming up he could shut a door on them at once. I might have recognized this repression of feeling as a danger signal, but being head over ears in love I did not.

On the East Sands of St Andrews, meanwhile, quite unaware that an intuitive reaction had saved me by a hair's-breadth from disaster, I relapsed into my happy dream. That evening, our last, Edwin proposed that we should spend the weekend in London together when he came up at Whitsun for the National Guilds League conference. To my own great surprise I felt unwilling and found myself arguing that if we had any children I shouldn't like them to be bastards.

Until that moment Edwin and I had been assuming that our being in love was our private affair and nobody else's business; possible bastards were an intrusive complication which we did not like the look of. Then and there it was decided that we should get married at Whitsun. I say 'it was decided' because I cannot now tell which of us first brought out the word 'marry'. I undertook to put up the London banns, or whatever one had to do; we could get married quietly at a register office and have the long Whitsun weekend together, interrupted only by a tiresome Guilds conference. What was to happen after that we did not bother about. Our whole lives were to be spent together and ways and means would doubtless discover themselves.

We were indeed naive creatures. As a basis for living, to feel that one Belongs to the Universe can prove misleading, especially if one takes for granted, as I then did, that the run of the Universe corresponds to one's own needs and aspirations. As a subjective experience Belonging to the Universe feels natural and right, but once it is framed as an intellectual concept it may begin to look absurd. I did not frame it as a concept; to me it seemed natural and right. My love for Edwin and his for me Belonged to the Universe and so things were bound to work out well. Naïve as it was, this assumption of mine was sustaining.

I went back to London with a photograph of Edwin which I put under my pillow each night. I also bought a copy of *We Moderns*. Some belated streaks of common sense then began to appear in my actions. I wrote to my mother telling her that I was going to marry a man called Edwin Muir, and I provided the Principal of my training college with the same information. She seemed interested and sympathetic. I am not now sure whether there was still at that time an ordinance forbidding female teachers in training colleges to have husbands, but I was quite certain that if the Principal and the patroness of this college, a rich old lady, Miss Belle Rennie, chose to approve, I could have a husband and go on lecturing, since the Principal herself had just got married with Miss Belle's blessing. I gave her *We Moderns* to look at and went back to my hostel without any misgivings.

Nothing out of the ordinary happened for a few days and then I was summoned to a special interview with the Principal and Miss

Belle. They both wore shocked faces, and Miss Belle, picking up with obvious distaste my copy of *We Moderns*, said: 'Miss Anderson, do you know that this man you are proposing to marry doesn't believe in God?' They made it clear to me that if I persisted in marrying 'this man' I must give up my post as lecturer and Vice-Principal. It seemed pointless to argue. I said that I would resign my post on the spot, rescued that godless book *We Moderns* into my own loving hands and stalked out.

This was not the first time I had thrown away something valuable for the sake of True Love. When I first got engaged to my Rugby champion I had just won a University scholarship at St Andrews, the Berry Scholarship in Classics, and my professors, two distinguished scholars, John Burnet and W. M. Lindsay, offered to secure for me in addition an open Scholarship, the Ferguson, if I would use the proceeds to go to the British School at Rome and do research. It was the chance of a lifetime, and I refused it because in the ecstasy of first love I could not be so widely separated from my sweetheart. Then a couple of years later when I had discovered that my sweetheart was not really my True Love I threw his ring into the sea, the only diamonds and sapphires I have ever owned. And now that I had at last found my one True Love I threw away an excellent lecturing job.

I had sometimes wondered with regret how different a life I might have had, doing classical research in Rome. But I never regretted leaving my training college because of Edwin. I left it at the end of term with a light heart, and I also stopped, once and for all, regretting those other throw-aways.

My mother ignored my announcement about marrying Edwin, having probably acquired a habit of discounting anything I said. I had to write again and insist that I was really going to get married. This time she reacted, pleading that I must come home and be married properly by a minister of the Kirk. How like my mother, I thought; she meant well but she did not understand. To get married in Montrose, properly or improperly, in a social context to which neither Edwin nor I belonged, would not make sense at all. The St Pancras Register Office was much more suitable. I had been offered, through a friend, the loan of a flat in Hunter Street,

W.G., over Whitsun; for the purpose of marriage I was domiciled in St Pancras, and that became my official address. I filled up the needful forms, booked a couple of good seats at Diaghileff's *La Boutique Fantasque* and was ready for the wedding.

Chapter Three

June – September 1919

I do not know how Edwin felt on his way to London. I ought to have realized that new experiences were being rather crowded upon him, but I was too happy to have misgivings. He had not been married before, but then neither had I. Yet London was familiar to me, since I had lived here and there in it since 1915, while to him it was entirely unknown. I had seen many Diaghileff ballets; he had never seen a ballet in his life. He was booked, as a Scottish delegate, to make a public speech at a National Conference the day after his wedding; I was a practised lecturer and did not think that making a speech was an ordeal; not until I heard him speak did it occur to me that he might find it so. Looking back now at the seventh of June 1919, our wedding day, I feel that he might well have been weighed down by the burden of events. On the contrary, like me, he was carried through everything on a wave of exhilaration—everything, that is, except the speech. As for the ballet, that lifted him clean out of himself. He had never imagined such magic to be possible, he said; how he wished he could have been a ballet dancer! Russian ballet always intoxicated me too and we were both drunk with sheer elation when we went back to Hunter Street. Then in bed together we were as well matched as on the dancing floor.

We went off serenely to the Conference next day. I should have thought that we were both confident. My acute embarrassment during Edwin's speech, however, was probably greater than his, since in Glasgow his style of speaking may have been taken as the norm; 'Mr Chairman—eh—I have the pleasure of —eh— bringing greetings—eh——' For the first time in my life I suffered vicariously from the performance of a public speech and, my cheeks burning, stared at the floor. Privately I made up my mind to help Edwin to become a more fluent speaker, but as helping one another to develop our potentialities was taken for granted in my notion of what marriage meant I did not then bother to say so. Edwin admitted to having been 'a bit nervous'; that was all.

A friend of mine had booked us in at a hotel in Sheringham for three days, insisting that we must have a honeymoon. It was not the kind of place we would have chosen but it was on the sea, and the sea attracted us with a strong pull, then and for years afterwards. We bathed and I discovered that Edwin could not swim; he was never able to stay in the cold North Sea long enough to learn how. He lay in the sun instead and scorched the fair skin across his shoulders until it was red and angry. In spite of that discomfort I think he went back to Glasgow serenely enough. He had been a little shaken to find that I was going to lose my job in the training college but I was so certain that the Universe was on our side that if he had apprehensions he did not voice them.

Astonishingly, the Universe did seem to be looking after us, for I found us a house to live in. A fellow member of the 1917 Club, Barbara Low, had an option on half a house in Guilford Street, W.C., and wanted someone to share it with her. Guilford Street had been allowed to run down, but the firm of lawyers who administered the Georgian houses had set out to rehabilitate them; each house was re-pointed, done up with fresh paint and divided into an upper and a lower 'maisonette'. Barbara Low and I became joint tenants of the lower maisonette at number thirteen. She had the two upper rooms, I the two ground-floor rooms; we had to share the bathroom upstairs and the big basement kitchen. She had secured her option because the number was supposed to be unlucky, but thirteen was my lucky number, since I was born on a thirteenth of March, and I was not deterred. Even had I known more about Barbara Low's character I should not have been deterred, for housing was scarce after the war, Edwin and I needed somewhere to live, and Guilford Street was central. About Barbara Low I shall say only that she was a Freudian psycho-analyst, that we thought her an unhappy old woman, and that she said to us one day, with scorn, that we were the kind of people who expected everyone to like us. D. H. Lawrence used to visit her occasionally; she boasted that he once threatened her with a bread-knife. Probably he did.

Most of my savings went in furnishing our home. The front room, the living-room, had an Adam chimney-piece, and behind the bedroom at the back there was a small paved yard which I bordered with African marigolds. A week after we set up house an uncle of mine on his way to America presented us with an old wheel-back armchair, hand-carved, and two small chairs to match: we had also two blue pouffes from my college sitting-room and a Morris armchair, so that we felt luxuriously outfitted. The rent came to forty-five pounds a year and I paid the first quarter of it before going north.

My interest in the training college had been receding since my interview with the Principal and Miss Belle, so that I was rather fagged by the struggle of forcing myself, against the grain, to finish my term's work in style. But now the examinations were over, all certificates signed, even farewell parties accounted for. I stumbled into the train at Euston with a sense of relief, clutching a copy of *The Young Visiters*, a parting gift from a colleague. The nearer I got to Glasgow, the more I came alive, and I forgot my fatigue when I saw Edwin on the platform.

He had been lent a flat for us to live in until we should leave for Montrose, belonging to a friend of his, George Thomson, who was away on holiday. The stone stairs leading up to it did not surprise me, nor the solidity of the front door with its brass plate, like Mam's. But I was surprised to find a large coal range in the kitchen. Fortunately, there was also a gas ring, a kettle and a frying pan. The gas ring, I told Edwin, would do well enough for the few days of our stay. And then I had my big surprise. Edwin, looking embarrassed, on the defensive, said that he had not given in his week's notice at the office.

It strikes me now that he may have felt himself overborne by my providing and furnishing our new home, that his old apprehensions of having his personality encroached upon were stirring again. But as I had no intention, no thought of dominating, as I had merely done what seemed to me the natural thing since I was the partner on the spot in London, this explanation did not occur to me at all. I was simply bewildered.

'But you said you didn't want to be a clerk all your life, and that you wanted to get out of Glasgow.'

'But I'm earning three pounds seventeen and six *a week*.'

He emphasized 'week' as if it were the last word in reasonable

Edwin and Gavin Muir
in Dormansland, 1928

Gavin in Orkney

common sense. Yet a reliance on reason and common sense did not seem to me to provide the last word on anything. Had I been asked whether I believed the Universe to be run on lines of reason and common sense I should have said: No.

'In London we'll soon earn more than that between us.' I assured him. 'It isn't really a leap in the dark. And we'll be *together*.'

A shadow of fear touched me, lightly, but enough to make my heart sink a little. This was a new Edwin. There was much in him that I did not know. Perhaps the magic word 'together' did not mean so much to him as to me. I began to remember the coolness with which he could cut off personal relationships, and I became aware that I was very tired.

'Let's sleep on it,' I said.

Next morning, still undecided but less on the defensive, Edwin went to his Renfrew office and I was left alone to reflect. I was not really able to do this, because I was too deeply involved. I did not then see, for instance, that my being at a loss about Edwin made me feel at a loss about most of my surroundings. I was only aware that the coal cooking-range in the kitchen, with all its dampers, seemed as incomprehensible as Edwin, since I did not know what to do with either of them; that George Thomson's flat looked ugly and gloomy, despite its lofty ceilings, with the dark heavy mahogany furniture and large dark oil paintings; that the wooden bunker full of coal which stood waiting in the hall was somehow a reproach to me, since I had not one single apron in my suitcases.

I slipped out to do some household shopping and went badly astray before I found my way back. Then I decided to risk taking a tram into the country, among the heather hills which Edwin had said were quite near at hand. The majestic trams with their coloured headlights and unfamiliar destinations bamboozled me; I found myself being taken into even more unknown suburbs instead of into the hills. When I got back to the flat all I could do at first was to sit down and cry.

The bout of sobbing cleared me up. I remembered that I Belonged to the Universe. To Belong to the Universe did not mean lying back in tears and making no effort; it meant rather that when you wanted to do something, to follow a 'hunch', you could be certain that it would be worth doing, that your 'hunch' corresponded somehow to the run of the Universe. My unconscious, in which I was putting my trust, had told me that our marriage was in accordance with the run of the Universe, and I believed that to be true. Edwin had only to become fully himself and I had to become fully myself; we should then move in harmony with each other and with the Universe.

After sitting for I do not know how long, feeling my way rather than thinking, I came to the conclusion that the passage from known, familiar Glasgow to unknown unfamiliar London was a Rubicon Edwin had to cross of his own accord. I did not myself like being pushed into things and I must not push Edwin, or bring any pressure to bear upon him. He knew that I had had to give up my job because of getting married, but I must not let him know that I was virtually sacked because I insisted on marrying the author of *We Moderns*. Nor should I expatiate on the delights of our home in Guilford Street. He must feel free to make up his own mind.

This conclusion lightened my heart a lot. When Edwin on his return met me with the same searching, eager look I remembered from the day he told me about Mam's angry letter, it drew up an answering smile from inside me. I made him laugh about my blundering into the wrong streets and the wrong trams. I asked if we could not go to see one of the close friends he had told me about, Denis Saurat or F. G. Scott, but they were both away on holiday. Even my Cambuslang cousins were holidaying in Sutherland. It began to dawn on Edwin that Glasgow was a strange place to me, full of strangers, and that the day had seemed endless without him. He suggested that he should play truant from the office and himself take me to the heather hills, to Strathblane, not next day but the day after, so that he would have time to get beforehand with his work.

On the day appointed we did play truant, feeling like children giving school a miss. I rang up Edwin's office in a feigned Glasgow voice, pretending to be his landlady, and reported that Mr Muir had a very bad cold and had better stay indoors for the day. In no time at all we were in Strathblane, among the heather hills as he had foretold. Glasgow seemed very far off. We spent some time at a burn launching little boats of wild flag-leaves, with a bit of folded leaf for a sail, just as he had done in Orkney as a boy, and we began to say 'thu' and 'thee' to each other instead of 'you' in good Orkney fashion. Away from his office Edwin grew visibly happier and we came back to the flat in high spirits.

But here another problem presented itself. 'Thu's freckled like a troot!' I said, half in dismay, half in mirth. The tale of his having been cooped indoors by illness would hardly be swallowed in the office next day. In the morning I had to ring up again and say that Mr Muir was not yet recovered. Again we had a day of truancy, but this time we had the foresight to keep out of the sun and I rubbed Edwin well with anti-freckle lotion. On this day he decided, with apparent lightness, to give the shipbuilding firm a week's notice. He was duly provided with testimonials to his efficiency as a costing-clerk which said that Mr Edwin Muir was neat, methodical and could be trusted with the cash.

Next Easter he went to look up his old office-mates and found that the easygoing manager had been laid off shortly after his own departure and an up-to-date manager installed. Some clerks had been sacked and the survivors felt harried. There was no longer a rota of leisurely intervals in the lavatory. 'See what the unconscious did for us, getting thee out at the right time,' was the comment I made.

When we reached Montrose my mother took to Edwin at once, as she had never taken to my Rugby player. I knew that she had been disappointed at my marrying a mere clerk instead of a minister of the Kirk or a university professor, but Edwin was an Orkney-man, a sound recommendation to her. In a day or two she was inclined to favour him rather than me, for she valued men more than women and would have been sorry for any man I married. He would never have a button on his shirts, she told him, or on his trousers, or a pair of whole socks to put on his feet, poor Edwin.

Poor Edwin, meanwhile, spent one afternoon in our garden roaring over some tragic short stories I had once written and now dug out of a cupboard. I was both vexed and infected by his merriment. Through his eyes I could see how funny was my offhand treatment of whole hours of mental agony suffered by my characters, and yet I felt he need not have laughed at my efforts quite so heartlessly. One of my agonized heroines, Dagmar, a Viking maiden whose sweetheart became a Christian and turned the other cheek, especially delighted him; he kept teasing me by repeating with hoots of mirth: 'Dagmar strode by the sea till dawn.' If I had had any doubts about Edwin's power of detaching himself from personal feeling they should have been resolved that afternoon.

Yet when at last we entered our Guilford Street home early in September, his personal delight astonished me by its intensity. After his many years of dingy lodgings our two rooms seemed like heaven to him, the doors and windows were so well proportioned, the furnishings so gay. We began to apply the tender Northern adjective 'peerie' to nearly everything around us, and to ourselves. 'Peerie' is used to describe what is lovable as well as small: it is a very affectionate diminutive. I became 'peerie Willa' and Edwin reverted to his mother's name for him, 'peerie Breeks'. As time went on we shortened these pet names into P.W. and P.B., in the private Orkney language we spoke to each other for the rest of our married life.

Although I knew that I was no longer Miss Wilhelmina Anderson, although I had gladly become Peerie Willa in an atmosphere of tenderness and unanimity, I did not yet recognize myself as Mrs Muir; people could almost shout 'Mrs Muir' at me and get no response. Nor did I often wear my wedding ring, which was much too big. It fell off my finger into crevices, into butter, into the fireplace, and seemed safer left in a drawer. Edwin might as well have married me with a curtain ring, I said, smiling to myself as I pictured the scene in the Glasgow shop where he must have shyly asked for a wedding ring, standard size. We got it shrunk to fit me and were given fourteen shillings along with it, the price of the gold that had been taken out minus the cost of shrinking. Another windfall came from the sale of superfluous wedding presents, such as a pair of silver entree dishes and a claret jug of green glass, two feet high, with an ornate silver lid. We economized on food but we could not do without cigarettes, then twenty for a shilling, so I became gaily expert at withdrawing a shilling or two from the gas meter in the basement. Once in a while we treated ourselves to tea in Kensington Gardens. Exactly two weeks after our arrival in London we each got a stop-gap job, on the same day. Edwin was engaged nominally as a clerk in an engraver's office, but found that he was mainly occupied in packing and tying up parcels of engraving blocks. He became skilled in parcel-tying; for the rest of our married life all parcels from our house were professionally tied by him. I was taken on by a cramming institution in Red Lion Square to teach précis-writing. Between us we now earned just enough to live on until something more suitable should turn up. That September the weather was still and golden, making a peaceful ambience for us, and the Rubicon, I felt, had now been safely crossed. I ought to have known better, perhaps, but my experience of horror and despair, even in the 1914 war, had not schooled me enough to learn that a habit of horror and despair deeply stamped through eighteen years in a sensitive nature like Edwin's could not be grown out of so easily.

Chapter Four

September - December 1919

Our home in Guilford Street was a warm refuge for Edwin where he felt secure, but the rest of London outside our front door might have been an ice-field, so coldly did it make him shrink into himself now that he had to walk alone to his work in Farringdon Avenue. Until we landed our jobs we had gone everywhere together and Edwin had shown no sign of fear, but now he shivered with apprehensions. Sometimes he felt that buildings were going to crash on his head as he passed them, sometimes he cowered beneath the conviction that he barely existed, being an anonymous unit in a crowd of anonymous units, and, even worse, a very small anonymous unit. In Glasgow, he told me, he had been reckoned a tall man, since he was above the average height for that city—he was about five foot eight—but in London he found that he was below the average. By night he slept peacefully enough yet by day he was often hag-ridden by these obscure fears. They must have been present in Glasgow, but he had, I supposed, managed to check them, buttressed as he was by a familiar routine of daily work and the armature provided by Nietzsche.

The way he walked showed how rigidly he had been repressing some part of himself. His whole left side was somehow cramped, the left shoulder unevenly higher than the right and the left arm, never allowed to swing free when he walked, held stiffly close to his body. The pressure on him had now been loosened, partly by our marriage, partly because the familiar Glasgow framework was missing, partly because Nietzsche's inward armature was breaking up, and the repressed forces in his unconscious were beginning to assert themselves as fears. I had an idea that what he needed was to be loosened up still more, so I tried to multiply the friendly, warm spots in which he could relax, taking him to visit friends of mine in the evenings. He also went round now and then to see Orage at the *New Age* office in Cursitor Street, which became a very warm spot. A football match on Saturdays had been part of the Glasgow routine—for many years to come Edwin retained an interest in football, which he had himself played until he began to wear glasses—so on our free Saturday afternoons we took a twopenny tram to Hampstead Heath and watched up to a dozen football matches. On the Heath Edwin became an absorbed spectator, calling out: 'Well played, sir,' and turning on his heel with a quick flirt of one ankle to catch sight of a goal being scored behind him; his fears were apparently non-existent there, his movements as spontaneous as when he was dancing. John Holms and Hugh Kingsmill Lunn turned up in Guilford Street one afternoon; it must have been very shortly after our advent, for they came by daylight and we were both at home, not yet having found work. There were chairs to offer them, too, so their visit must have happened during our second week, after my uncle's gifts had arrived. Holms was in military uniform, Hugh in a civilian suit. I say Holms, not John, because I never came to like him well enough to think of him as John. Holms, then, and Hugh sat down in our sitting-room and at once the air grew dense with embarrassment. I could not think why, for I felt kindly towards these friends of Edwin's; I had not met them before but I knew how much he liked them. Apparently they did not welcome my kindness. If I said anything, Holms fiddled with his moustache, stared fixedly at Edwin with round, red-brown eyes that matched his hair and made no answer. Hugh gave me a quick, sideways glance and made no answer either. Their conversation was addressed exclusively to Edwin, so I fell silent. Clearly my presence incommoded them. Would they have been equally embarrassed, I wondered, had I been a man they were meeting for the first time, or was it my being a woman that bothered them? Of course, they were not long out of prison in Germany where they met no women, and before that they had grown up in English public schools without feminine company in the daily round; was it possible that they did not know what to say to a woman or what to do with her unless she was for going to bed with? In that case I was simply Edwin's woman to them, a *femme couverte*, with an invisible label: keep off the grass.

There was more to it than that, I thought, for I was being pointedly and rudely excluded from the slightest social courtesies. Here my upbringing caused me to jump at once to a conclusion that was partly false. I had been too often roused to resentment in my youth by the bland assumption around me that men were superior to women in all ways, especially where intelligence was needed. These two visitors, Edwin had previously told me, were men who had thought long and deeply about literature and life during their years as prisoners of war. If they did not want to talk to me, it must be because they considered me, a woman, incapable of conversing on their usual level. For them I was a non-person, unconversable, a mere woman.

Not entirely so for Hugh, I decided, after catching several uneasy glances from him. But entirely so for Holms, whose eyes remained steadily fixed on Edwin. He was intent on blotting me out, and Hugh was being dragged willy-nilly in his wake.

Quietly I pushed my chair back, away from their little triangle, got out a darning basket I had, selected the thickest sock I could find, the largest darning needle, settled myself on a pouffe where I could catch Edwin's eye and began with exaggerated movements to draw my formidable poker to and fro through the sock, using a very long tail of wool. Edwin caught the idea quickly enough: I saw his lower lip beginning to tremble. (He never knew what his lower lip was doing; it trembled with amusement or curled with contempt quite involuntarily.) Holms and Hugh got the idea too, but my manoeuvre instead of amusing or embarrassing them soothed them wonderfully. I had now become what I should have been all along, an undemanding bit of background, a proper wife darning a sock. They began to quote Shakespeare, interrupting each other freely. Their embarrassment vanished. Holms started a long monologue.

After they had gone I told Edwin that these two had brought in with them the same fog of ignorant prejudice about women that had been thick around me when I was growing up, and that I did not like having a pocket of that fog in my own sitting-room. Edwin said mildly that they were probably only shy. And yet we were both wrong, as I now see, for Holms was simply jealous, wanting to keep Edwin to himself. He had had a blissful heart-to-heart talk with Edwin one day that summer near Glasgow and was hoping for a renewal of the experience. It seems odd to me that I did not realize this at the time. But I never quite got away from my first impression of Holms as someone who had tried to blot me out of existence; although I learned to put up with him, I never came to like and admire him as Edwin did. On the other hand, I did grow fond of Hugh.

One of my friends, in whose house Edwin and I had been dining, was a Russian, Alexis Gregorievitch Chodak, who had fled from Moscow in 1905 after the rising in which he had been involved as a student. In the course of getting a medical degree, before going on to London, he had turned up at St Andrews University and become attached to my circle of close friends. Alexis was a small, well-built man, spontaneous, attractive and very charming. He married one of his tutors, a distinguished and delightful woman; they set up a joint practice in Bloomsbury not far from Guilford Street, and Alexis became Dr Chodak Gregory, an easier name for British tongues to get round. When Edwin and I were laid low by the so-called Spanish influenza that was sweeping through London, I sent an S.O.S. to Alexis, who saved both our lives, as we felt at the time.

During that virulent illness Edwin grew a beard, a ginger beard, although the hair on his head was quite black. As we became convalescent he began to insist that he was going to keep it, not shave it off, because he admired Ezra Pound's beard and he longed to look like Ezra Pound, whom he had met in Orage's office. He had described Pound's appearance to me: the neatness of the little beard, the knee-length Norfolk knickers, the black stockings and patent-leather pumps that contrasted so delightfully with the poetic freedom of the wide-open shirt collar and lavish black silk bow worn instead of a tie. This, Edwin felt, was how a poet should look. He was not himself a poet as yet, but some inklings of vocation must have been stirring in him. After the stick-up collars of Glasgow Pound's flying silk bow and large, wide-open collar were irresistibly attractive. So was the beard.

The difference between his beard and Ezra Pound's had to be brought home to him. Pound's beard was presumably clipped and trimmed, if it were, as Edwin said, neat. Edwin's beard, unbrushed and untrained, grew sticking out at all angles, sprouting ginger horns up, down, out and sideways. I showed it to him in a hand-glass. I pled that I loved his mouth, the way his lips were shaped and folded, and that I could not bear to have it hidden in a ginger jungle. Wide-open shirt collars, yes; flying silk bows, yes; but this beard, no.

Here Alexis unexpectedly reinforced me. We must go into the country to finish our convalescence, he insisted, and it was nonsense for us to say we could not afford it, since it would cost us nothing. He would himself send us to a hotel he knew of in Crowborough, and all we had to do was to go, except that Edwin had better shave his beard off first.

So the barbaric beard came off and, pale and tottery, we went to the Crowborough Hotel, where we took walks, daily longer, into the countryside, a little way into the Ashdown Forest. I then discovered that except for The Tree in the middle of Kirkwall trees were just trees to Edwin; not having known them in childhood he did not know pine from fir, beech from elm, oak from ash. At first when he came to Glasgow, he said, he felt that trees in a landscape were suffocating and intrusive, preventing him from seeing the great round of sky to which he was accustomed in Orkney. In Crowborough he began to share my love of trees: later on he came to love them himself.

Shortly after we returned to London Orage invited Edwin to be his assistant in the *New Age* office; three days' work at three pounds a week. Edwin gladly accepted the offer and there was no more parcelling of engraving blocks. He joined the weekly *New Age* conferences in the Kardomah Cafe, Chancery Lane, where he got to know AE and saw a little more of Ezra Pound, who was then extemely poor, he told me, and might have starved had it not been for what Orage paid him. He also got to know a Yugoslav, a Serb called Dmitri Mitrinovic who was trying to 'influence' people in London, including Orage, and finally helped to sink the *New Age* by the dead weight of the columns he contributed under the pen-name of M. M. Cosmoi. Deadly as he was to the *New Age* he was a source of joy to us when he came visiting at 13 Guilford Street. After discovering that empty beer bottles were as good as currency, since we exchanged them for coppers at the corner pub, he never arrived without two quart bottles of beer crammed into the pockets of his frock-coat, which, from the look of it, served as dressing-gown as well as calling kit. He would appear about six o'clock, saying that he had an urgent appointment at seven, but at ten or eleven o'clock he would still be sitting beside our fireplace entrancing us with his speculations—the evolution of Sex, for instance, through various grades of animals. We finished up, I remember, with Pan-Man, Sex harmonious. As for Scorpio, why was he set in the zodiac as the sign of Sex? Because he made an effort of will and turned himself Inside Out with one great convulsion, and so the vertebrates were born.

This brand of nonsense was novel to us and we enjoyed it hugely. Mitrinovic made a plummy mouthful of every word he used. He did not say: Albion, he said: 'All-bion, Word of Mystery, Name of Strength.' Feeling gay, he would imitate Serbian bagpipes with zest. The only thing that irked him was the success of Ouspensky, his rival as a seer, and behind Ouspensky, farther away but more menacing, the magnetic force of Gurdjieff. Too many clever men in London, he complained, were throwing up their jobs and migrating to Fontainebleau because Gurdjieff had promised that he could raise into full bloom the merest bud of a soul. Yet after melancholy shakings of the head Mitrinovic would then gurgle with laughter and cry: 'London is Looney-bin, no?' He had an eye for a pretty woman, too; he told us that Ezra Pound's wife was like a cherry tree. We found him an entertaining companion because he was such an egregious nonsense-monger, which, we suspected, he was aware of himself. Two years later when we set off for Prague he gave us a farewell present, a postcard on which he had drawn a diagram guaranteed to solve any problems we might meet. It was a reproduction of the Seal of Solomon.

Another Yugoslav whom Edwin got to know through the *New Age* was Janko Lavrin, a different kind of Yugoslav from Mitrinovic, as he would have been the first to insist. He was no Balkan type but a Slovene, highly educated in many universities all over Europe. His conversation was just as heady as Mitrinovic's with the great advantage of being based on actualities, and he radiated even more charm, so that he trailed clouds of friends around him and was the means of introducing us to I do not know how many painters at I cannot tell how many studio parties.

In this way, two months after coming to London, Edwin had become a member of a small group centred on Orage; his circle of acquaintance was widening and he was no longer an utter outsider, although in general the literary men of London were as unacquainted with him as he was with them. He had none of the usual connections with friends from family school or college which most young literary men coming to London can take for granted. Looked at with a cold eye he would have been seen as an unknown provincial clerk with literary leanings, quite outside the ambience of current literary fashions or movements, and he was aware of this, as his fears and diffidence implied. He would not have nerved himself even to call on Middleton Murry, which he did, asking for books to review, unless Orage had prodded him. He went to see Murry at Hampstead Heath and told me when he came back that 'a fairy-like creature' had opened the door to him, and when he said 'Mrs Murry?' she pirouetted on one leg and answered: 'I'm not Mrs Murry, I'm Katherine Mansfield.'

Murry did give him books to review and presently so did others. Various literary figures penetrated to the *New Age* office, including the Sitwells, who arrived one day, flanked by Aldous Huxley, to make mincemeat of Orage, since in an article referring to them he had used the word 'blind', which they chose to interpret as an imputation on their sobriety. It was Edwin they found behind the editorial desk, looking young and defenceless, no doubt, for his youthful appearance belied his thirty-two years and he told me that he quaked inwardly as these four tall figures advanced upon him. In his gentle voice he invited them to sit down and then managed to allay their wrath.

None the less, he was still in a disturbed state, although his involuntary fears were fading, and Orage, an ultra-sensitive man, was aware of it. Pulling together was what Orage thought he needed, so that he could make a more positive impact on people, and so, very kindly, Orage produced his own recipe for achieving concentration and inner power, the practice of yoga and meditation on abstract virtues. Edwin was given the proper formulae for recitation which we were supposed to practise together, he and I, morning and evening. I recoiled from the suggestion, pleading that I should feel a fool standing up to recite the stuff. My attitude discouraged Edwin from following the discipline and he gave it up. In any case, I still had a notion that loosening out was what Edwin needed rather than pulling together. I think now that I was instinctively repelled by the doctrine of accumulating deliberate power, either power over oneself or power over others, and that I was probably right in refusing to accept it.

Edwin himself may have felt that what he needed was to be left alone, but he was not left alone. Maurice Nicoll, prompted by Orage, invited him to look in one evening and persuaded him to start being psycho-analysed, just for the interest of it, without payment. The psycho-analysis, as Edwin tells in his Autobiography, proved a very painful process; it both shocked and stimulated him so that he began to have vivid dreams. I had no misgivings about these, being a persistent dreamer myself, and I sympathized with whatever Edwin told me about them, until the exciting evening came when he had his first waking visions. These were of the highest importance to us both.

I am not going to describe the visions, as Edwin has done so himself, in his Autobiography and in some of his poems. They came of their own accord, not induced by alcohol or opium or any drug, nor by any incantation or ritual. Edwin had come home feeling out of sorts and simply lay down on the sitting-room divan with his face to the wall. How long afterwards it was when he sat up and began to tell me what he had seen, I do not know, for I was absorbed in correcting précis and had lost count of time.

His excitement communicated itself to me like an electric current and I sat thrilling while he unrolled the pageantry that had been projected on the wall before him. He spoke at great speed, for the visions had come so fast, episode upon episode, that he was anxious not to omit or forget any part of them. I was, like him, filled with wonder at what had happened. The last episode of all, when he and I on one wing apiece flew hand-in-hand through the sky and settled behind the back of an antique Jehovah figure, where we kissed, lit me up with happiness as well as wonder because it showed that in the deeps of Edwin's unconscious we now belonged unquestionably to each other.

Apart from the interest of the episodes themselves, the most important aspect of the visions for Edwin was that they had apparently come to him from outside. Throughout the spectacle he had been consciously aware of the ordinary light in the room, my presence at the table, the rustling of the papers I was correcting, and none of these perceptions had any relation to what he saw, which presented itself unpredictably as if he were watching it in some theatre, not knowing what was to happen next, except that he himself was involved as an actor, indeed a protagonist, in every drama, so that a succession of three-dimensional dramas was played out around him. These dramas, coming unsummoned, were even more exhilarating to watch, he said, and more magical than a Diaghileff ballet. He felt that these visions were a revelation of some kind, if he could only interpret them, perhaps a myth of man's destiny.

We sat far into the night trying to find possible meanings for the visions, since the release of so much emotion—rage, fear, horror and triumph—had entirely cured Edwin of the malaise that had made him lie down and turn his face to the wall. He was in such an illuminated state that I did not quibble at his arguments and restricted myself to suggesting that the myth, if myth it was, came from the Collective Unconscious. Even as I uttered the words I feared that they did not explain anything, for what was the Collective Unconscious, after all? An accumulation of human vibrations, perhaps, through many, many centuries, hanging in our air like invisible clouds and fogs, making climates of opinion and belief and tradition, which we breathed in daily and daily helped to form, usually without knowing it? That did not account for the dynamism of the visions, but I did not want to speculate any farther. Edwin wanted to go much farther away, both in space and in time, for the source of the dramas he had been playing a part in. Even then, I thought, the mystery remained a mystery and a wonder which could not ultimately be explained. We always lived in a cloud of unknowing, I said, and we should just have to go on living in it. Then, remembering that kiss behind Jehovah's back, I added: 'But not in a cloud of unloving!'

One conclusion at least was certain: that Edwin possessed an uncommon power of communicating with forces from the unconscious. If the channels could be kept open, he would have the imagery of the unconscious at his command and something uniquely worth while to communicate. And these visions were such a massive break-through that inspiration might go on welling up.

It did go on welling up; he had more visions, waking visions all of them, all different from each other. Maurice Nicoll was alarmed and told him to stop them, if he could, for his own good. Edwin felt that he could stop them and did so, shutting the door on the underworld of feeling with his usual skill.

Not being steeped in Nietzsche, as Edwin was, I did not think that human life needed the transcendental justification he was looking for in his visions. I shied away from cosmic explorations. I felt that I Belonged to the Universe, yet I believed that the human mind, because of its inborn limitations, could not grasp the mystery of the Universe I belonged to. Any alleged explanation, in my opinion, was bound to be wishful thinking, or, if it claimed to be impersonal, was likely to be merely arid system-making. This difference between my attitude and Edwin's could be traced back, I think, to early experience in both of us. As a child in Orkney, which was then not very far from the Middle Ages, Edwin had lived in an atmosphere saturated with legend, myth, ballads and Bible stories. There was some kind of accepted story to account for everything. It was natural for him to look for a great story, an all-encompassing myth, to explain the mystery of life as he later found it, especially in what seemed the chaos of Glasgow. Scottish Presbyterianism, Scottish argumentative rationality, confined him to criticism when he was searching literature for clues but did not satisfy him; he was much closer to the Middle Ages than the people around him and he needed poetic myths. In Nietzsche, especially in *Thus Spake Zarathustra*, he found the poetic content and the wide cosmic sweep of story he wanted. Now, although he was beginning to distrust Nietzsche's Super-Man, he still looked for some great story, some cosmic pattern that would assign a place to every experience in life, relating it to an inclusive whole and justifying it. He was looking for that in his visions, and he kept on looking for it as long as he lived, until he thought he had found it.

As a child I too lived among legends, fairy stories and Bible stories, but only the Bible stories were accepted in the ambience of Montrose; the others were a private indulgence confined to my home—more precisely, centred on my father who told them to me. When he died and went to heaven, which endured, I was told, for ever and ever, amen, I tried to follow him there in imagination, and that involved trying to grasp imaginatively the meaning of the phrase: for ever and ever, amen. It drove me nearly insane. Night after night for some weeks I struggled in sleep with images that represented eternity. A vanishing perspective of hedged fields lay before me, each crammed with halfpence sitting up on their rims and lying down again, which I had to count interminably; there was no end to them and I woke up screaming in terror. This beating of my mind against its human limitations at the age of nine left me with a strong sense of these limitations. When it came to the facing of cosmic immensities I winced away and shrank from trying to grasp in imagination what had no beginning and no end; finally I did not believe that the human imagination was capable of doing so. Consequently my mind played much more round the 'how' of Edwin's visions than round the 'whence'; his mind did exactly the opposite.

Although Maurice Nicoll ridiculed transcendental explanations for these visions, Edwin did not abandon them, and they gave him a new access of self-confidence. I found him one day in the sitting-room with discarded scribblings around him, scoring out again what he had just written. 'I'm trying to improve my style,' he said, and from that day set himself to practise writing clearly and simply without Nietzschean rhetoric. In my slap-dash way I had never supposed that one sat down consciously to improve one's use of a mother tongue, believing as I did that words welled up on a flood of inspiration; the stronger the inspiration, the better the style. I was therefore much impressed. This was another of the lessons in conscious discrimination that I was learning from Edwin. I remember saying to him, as we came down from the Heath one Saturday: 'I think I've made thee more human, and thu's made me more discriminating.' Both statements had some truth in them.

I half expected the great loosening-up of these visions to have immediate results—a lessening of the cramps on Edwin's left side, for instance. They did lessen, but at a slower rate than I looked for. They had vanished by the time we went off to Prague, as also had his trick of furtively buttoning a book beneath his jacket every time he went to the bathroom, an automatism dating from his office days in Renfrew, but that was nearly two years later. Nor was it until after we went to Prague that he became consciously aware of his need to write poetry, since he could not rightly get into prose the full sense of the imagery that haunted him.

The psycho-analysis was never completed. Maurice Nicoll was leaving England; I have an idea he was going to Gurdjieff at Fontainebleau; he turned Edwin over to a colleague of his, James Young. For some reason, or impulse, or prejudice Edwin could not make the transition with confidence. I know that he was put off by James Young's telling him that a man set more value on something he paid for than on what he got free, so he would charge a shilling or two for each session. This, I believe, was current psycho-analytical doctrine but it seemed misconceived to Edwin, who paid the token shillings with, I fear, a curling lower lip. Whatever the cause, he became more and more irregular in his attendances and the psycho-analysis petered out.

Chapter Five

January 1920 – August 1921

Edwin's reaction from Nietzsche, which was bringing a new sobriety into his style, was part of a general reaction from what he felt to be the false personality he had hidden behind in Glasgow. He was now less on the defensive and wanted to live without being on the defensive at all; he was beginning to repudiate Edward Moore and would have liked to cancel *We Moderns*. No longer did he wish to deride and attack and ram home debating points with exclamation marks. Nor did he want to make an impact on people, as Orage had discovered, who tried to train him to do that, the only result being that Edwin continued to write articles for the *New Age* in his own way, not in Orage's. It was about this time that he told me he had always wanted to keep his forehead serene and unfurrowed.

Meanwhile he quietly refrained from reviewing books with which he was not in sympathy. This liberation of what he felt to be his true self did not proceed without setbacks; he had many relapses which he felt to be Original Sin, and he was never quite free of a preoccupation with the story of the Fall. I was aware of this and wished that he would take it less seriously, since I thought it burdened him. But I was completely in sympathy with his desire for serenity.

I did not at all want Edwin to attack or to project himself at anyone, yet I hoped he might at least throw his voice towards an audience when he gave a lecture. He had been asked to give a talk on 'The Novel' to a branch of the English Association, and with his soft voice, which did not carry well, he would not achieve the reciprocal flow, from speaker to audience and from audience to speaker, that a good lecture needs, unless listeners beyond the front rows could hear what he said. I persuaded him to get in a little practice at speaking out, in our sitting-room, where I sat at one end and commented on his delivery as he stood at the other. He then prepared a good script, on 'The Novel'. At that time lecturing without a script was a bee in my bonnet, but Edwin was not yet ready to do that. I went to the lecture-room with hopes of his acquitting himself well. I should sit at the very back of the hall, I told him, and he was to look for me and pitch his voice straight at me.

Nearly every word he said was audible. But I had quite failed to allow for the effect of an Orkney upbringing. In Orkney, as in Shetland, all j-sounds are softened into -ch; jam becomes 'cham' and genius 'chenius'. People from Orkney and Shetland also feel uncertain about their 'o's' when they come south, like my mother, who always called soda 'sodda', and in Edwin's script lurked a danger I had not perceived; he had picked on Tom Jones as a key-novel in his discourse. The first time he mentioned it he said 'Tom Jones' and everyone knew what he meant, but as he got more absorbed in his subject he kept referring to 'Tome Chawns', and I doubt whether his other listeners followed him.

In time he mastered even the 'o's' in English speech, although our habit of speaking Orkney together in private did not help. How deeply rooted Orkney was in Edwin could have been deduced from the length of time he took to become sure of those 'o' sounds. Even seven years later, after our son was born, when we were looking for somewhere to live in the country, we turned down a house called 'Broad Oaks' because both Edwin and I knew that he would find himself saying 'Erode Awks' as often as not.

It may have become apparent that I rather nattered myself on being aware of ambiences, yet I now ignored an ambience I should have attended to in the new job I was offered just before Christmas.

The job came to me out of the blue, thanks to three young women whom I had earlier been helping to train for Day Continuation School teaching. They were all Oxford graduates and had come regularly to Canning Town during the war to try coping with the factory girls. Without my knowing it they had now persuaded a group of West End drapery stores to start a Day Continuation School for their own employees and to appoint me its headmistress, at £400 a year. This seemed wealth to Edwin and me; we now felt well provided for. But in concentrating on what my young pupils were to be taught, and what staff I should engage to teach them, I forgot to attend to the wider ambience in which they moved, the atmosphere of the business world.

In Canning Town I had not needed to attend to that. My girls there were all packers, a low form of labour, from Knight's soap factory and Bryant and May's match factory; they came to Mansfield House for their instruction, and the management of Knight's, or Bryant and May's, once having been persuaded to let some packers have two afternoons' education a week, did not bother about the kind they got. The ambience the girls brought with them was that of their private lives, not of their daily work. In itself that was unexpected enough to occupy me fully, for these rough-handed, gentle-hearted girls were bound by the conventions of a punctilious etiquette usually found in weapon-bearing societies. Their boyfriends all carried razor blades to fight with, and especially at dances each girl had to watch her step if bloodshed was to be avoided. So my interest in the girls who laid their difficulties before me did not extend to the work-a-day world in the factories; it remained personal and private.

As for the work-a-day world in the big drapery stores, I thought I had attended sufficiently to that when I decided to build my school programme round textile materials, starting as it were from the known and proceeding to the unknown. If I were in these youngsters' shoes, I thought, I should be fascinated by romance and colourful adventure along the great silk road from China, or a story about merino sheep in Spain, or the waulking of tweed in Harris; and I asked everywhere in vain for films to show scenes of that kind. My three graduates and I then talked over how to use their special subjects, history, geography and English, to light up the youngsters' imagination, beginning from textiles, if possible. English, we decided, was not to be manipulated in that way. It would be better to begin enjoying English Literature from love poetry and dramatic love stories, which would take one easily into Shakespeare. But history could be taken from the unusual angle of cloth-weaving or lace-making, if one concentrated on presenting the whole context of a region actively at work. Geography could range farther afield and supply the excitements of the silk road from China, Kashmir shawls, Egyptian cotton, Indian muslins, Australian wool.

Something like that, in fact, was done in the school. I added instruction in practical work, hand-loom weaving, fashion-drawing, pattern-designing, colouring. All this accounted for three-quarters of the time-table; the rest of it was given to eurhythmics, dancing and singing. For the eighteen-year-olds I took a class myself called 'general psychology'; they asked me questions about anything at all and I did my best to answer. We had a hundred youngsters in the school at a time, they each had one morning and one afternoon's schooling weekly, eight hours in all, and were divided as nearly as possible into classes of twenty-five.

My first difficulty struck me as comic, and I solved it in what might be considered a comic manner. Each batch of a hundred girls contained young ladies from the showrooms, in black satin and pearls provided by the firm, solid secondary-school girls from the clerical side, mostly spectacled, and dowdy little trotters from the workshops. The showroom ladies despised all the others, the clerical girls despised the trotters and the trotters looked to be very downtrodden. I did not propose to allow a pecking order in my school, so I got over a hundred gymnastic tunics of varying sizes, and each batch of girls was put into them. The result was admirable. I had, in fact, no more difficulties from the girls; I think they enjoyed their schooling too much to make difficulties. All the trouble I had came from the wider ambience of the business firms.

As I had been accustomed to do, I took every girl who came to my room as an individual case. When a girl arrived distraught and sobbing because she had been severely dealt with for being unpunctual, I could not feel that she had committed an unpardonable sin and did my best to comfort her by minimizing her offence. The Welfare Workers on the staff did not approve of that, nor of my smoking cigarettes at my desk. They thought I was a subversive influence. Then forewomen from various departments began turning up, some of them friendly, delightful women, others not friendly at all, since they had heard shocking rumours that the girls spent their time in school dancing and singing, and were even more shocked to find the rumours true. Was this what the girls were let off work for? I was accused of wasting their time and the firm's time.

My idea that schooling should be fun scandalized them. So I was a stumbling block and an offence to many, who all laid complaints with the management. The upshot was that after a year of running what I considered a successful school I was politely asked to resign and given a sum of money in compensation.

A new headmistress was appointed. But soon enough the school was closed, because Parliament had not passed the expected law making Day Continuation Schools compulsory, and Excess Profits Duty was altogether abolished.

My compensation money allowed me to stay at home for a while and practise cooking, before I began lecturing to L.C.C. evening classes. One other immediate advantage I had; being closely associated with these fashionable shops, I had bought myself some good clothes, including an elegant cloak. When we went up to Scotland at Easter that cloak provoked comment. Some members of the Glasgow Guilds Group, I was told, could not abide what they mockingly Anglified as 'Mrs Muir's clowk'. It was felt that Edwin and I were getting a bit above ourselves, though the censorious voices blamed me rather than him.

On the Easter visit I was introduced to Edwin's eldest brother Jimmie and his eldest sister Lizzie. Jimmie was in charge of a department in a Glasgow furnishing warehouse. Edwin and I went up in a goods hoist to a large barn-like room where the three of us presently stood in a corner, Jimmie leaning against one wall, Edwin at right angles to him leaning against another, and I in the open between them. Jimmie and Edwin never let their eyes meet after the first hand-shake; their remarks crossed each other in the air, passing me where I stood. The brothers were not at all unfriendly, but spoke to each other across a psychological distance. I did not know whether it was Jimmie's business surroundings that made him so remote, a self-defence acquired in the context of Glasgow, or whether remoteness was a family characteristic of the Muirs. When I commented on it to Edwin he laughed and said that Jimmie was only distantly related to him anyhow, being twelve years older. 'Wait till you see Lizzie,' he added, 'she's even farther away from this world.'

When I met Lizzie, I saw at once what he meant. She was small, spare, gentle and reticent, with a face very like Edwin's except for the brow. Edwin had told me that several times she had dreamed beforehand the winner of the Derby, but had never betted on her knowledge; looking at her, I could well believe it. There was a wary pride in Lizzie; she was not going to be patronized by any stranger. I was pleased to find that she laughed easily, but even when relaxed she still had the same quiet, withdrawn dignity. Remoteness was a family characteristic, I decided; the Muirs had a built-in power of withdrawing into some inner fastness of their own. Edwin had come farther out of his shell than his sister or his brother; compared with them he could be called an extravert. I told him that, and he was much amused. Lizzie had been very ambitious as a young woman, he said, and Jimmie as a young man had been 'a great lad for the girls'. I wondered if Edwin too were going to shrink into himself as he grew older, or if it were only a discouraging ambience that made the sensitive Muirs beat a retreat. Lizzie, according to Edwin, had had a hard life, and Jimmie had been more or less conditioned into respectability by his wife. I could not imagine my conditioning Edwin into respectability, and I hoped that his hard times were now at an end; presumably he would not need to withdraw into remoteness, sensitive though he was.

Our life in London became busier and busier. Edwin was made dramatic correspondent for the Edinburgh *Scotsman*, which meant going to shows three or four times a week, dashing off immediately afterwards to the *Scotsman* office in Fleet Street, writing a *critique* as fast as possible and getting home not earlier than one in the morning. By an inescapable law of London life the busier we got the more we were invited out and the more people dropped in to see us. My recollection of this period, which tells me that every time Edwin came back from Fleet Street he found our sitting-room crammed with people drinking Russian tea out of tumblers, may be somewhere at fault, but the impression remains that we were crowded out of any leisure time. It could happen that we were too tired to go to some concert or show we had meant to attend together. It surprised me to discover that people, friendly, intelligent, lively people, could be exhausting. It might have been London we were drowning in, but I felt we were drowning in a flood of people, and if one is drowning it does not matter whether the water is clean or dirty, the people pleasant or nasty, one drowns just the same.

But a way out now offered itself. Van Wyck Brooks, the literary editor of a new American weekly, *The Freeman*, asked Edwin to contribute one or two articles a month, at sixty dollars an article. I think that H. L. Mencken had brought Edwin's *New Age* writings to his notice. The prospect of so many dollars was more than bright, it was dazzling. From our painter friends we already knew that living in Europe was cheap, and our imaginations were fired by Janko Lavrin's stories of European adventure. Neither Edwin nor I had ever been out of Britain and we were already in our thirties. It was high time, I thought, that we should see a bit of the world; why not drop everything in London and go abroad? We could easily live on the *Freeman* money, not to mention stray articles for other weeklies.

To Edwin and me Europe was an imaginary region, a never-never land, for our knowledge of it was gathered from books, except for newspaper reports of fighting during the war. I knew about ancient Greece and the Roman Empire: Edwin was well versed in translations from German writers like Nietzsche and Heine; we both had a fund of scrambled information, drawn entirely from fiction, about France and Russia. In any schools we had attended contemporary European history had not been mentioned at all; we were unthinkably ignorant of actual conditions beyond our own country. Europe was simply one large, romantic blur to each of us.

We turned to Janko Lavrin for advice. He supported the project with enthusiasm, saying: 'Why not go to Prague to begin with?' Prague was in the very middle of Europe; it had the best ham in Europe and the best beer. These arguments seemed compelling; we decided to go to Prague, knowing nothing about the Czechs and Slovaks except that they had got a country for themselves out of the Great War. I believe we were aware that Czechoslovakia had been a constitutent part of the Austrian Empire, but that was the limit of our knowledge.

Breaking up the home was easier than I expected. Some furniture we gave away to needy friends; the pieces we wanted to keep were parked among other friends who promised to give them back on our return; our books and our cat we took to my mother's house in Montrose. At the end of June 1921, the end of a quarter, we left 13 Guilford Street for ever. Allowing ourselves enough ready money to get to Prague, we had thirteen pounds left in our bank account—my lucky number—which we instructed the bank to forward to Prague. In August we embarked at Leith for Hamburg.

Chapter Six

PRAGUE

August 1921 - March 1922

In London Edwin had already been trying to break the defensive pattern of living that had been hardening on him in Glasgow, and we could not have gone to a better place than Prague for inducing him to come farther out of himself. Czechoslovakia was a brand-new republic and its capital city, Prague, was sizzling with hope and experiment and enthusiasm. We could not be unaware of the lively 'feel' of the air in Prague, and the fact that we did not understand it, having no clue at all to the Czech language, only challenged us the more to make efforts to understand. Yet the difficulties were formidable, since in any case Prague was unlike anything we had been accustomed to, and the incomprehensible language made it appear not only unfamiliar but wildly unfamiliar.

As soon as we got out of the train in the large station, a mathematically symmetrical station, we were faced by identical stairways at either end. One stairway was marked Vchod, the other Vychod. 'Now, which of these?' we said to each other, but at once abandoned visual aids and followed the rest of the passengers, who all trooped up Vychod; thus we began to learn the only practical method of discovering Prague, through our foot-soles, through our skins, through our noses as much as through our eyes.

Emerging into a hot, dusty promenade we saw a rank of one-horse open carriages, such as we had already met in Berlin, and made for one of them. The driver perceived without difficulty that we were foreigners and indicated by gesture that he knew where to take us. After being carried past mosaic paved sidewalks and fine shops with unreadable signs we were decanted not at a hotel but at a Büro. Here luck was on our side, for this was the office set up to provide accommodation for foreigners visiting the Trade Fair then being held in Prague, and our wily driver got us registered as visitors to the Fair, which procured us a hotel address and a title to a room. Our hotel was in the very heart of the Old City, near the mediaeval Powder Tower, and the room struck us as being grand indeed. Later on we were to take it for granted that hotel rooms in Czechoslovakia should be lofty, with large double doors, well-spaced tall windows and still taller porcelain stoves; when we eventually went into Austria, we perceived that this style of room was typically Austrian, and still later discovered that 'typically Austrian' buildings took their inspiration from Italy.

In the restaurant downstairs we then had the first of many games with a Czech menu hand-written in purple ink. Guessing that the top few items might be soup or fish, the middle items meat dishes and the section at the foot probably sweets, we each put a finger against something and waited to see what would come. Had we been travelling separately in this strange country either of us might have been daunted; we might have crawled right into ourselves. As it was, because there were two of us, we came out of ourselves instead of crawling in, feeling gay and irresponsible, called to adventurous living.

The food that came was mostly excellent. We soon learned to avoid bulls'-knees or the rather rank-tasting mutton and, after one horrified trial, Olomoucky cheese, which was justly kept caged under a glass bell. It occurred to us, after that experience, that the queer smell in some of the narrow old streets which we had surmised came from mediaeval drains was probably Olomoucky cheese. Among the sweets we discovered *palačinky*, delicious thin pancakes, and avoided puddings compounded with poppy seeds.

Outside the hotel there were many problems to solve. In the big post-office hall about twenty wickets had each a collection of improbable consonants above it; which of them sold stamps? Having solved that one, we then found out how to order tea with lemon or rum, where to get Pilsener, how to ask for a tram ticket and where to climb up on the Small Side of Prague across the river, the Malá Strana, away from the heat and the drifts of white dust into gardens with spectacular views over the city. Prague was crammed tight between two high cliffs carved by its river in the course of centuries and sprouted towers, spires and domes as thickly as an English garden sprouts delphiniums and hollyhocks. We were enchanted by the sight, and spent hours cooling off on cafe benches halfway up the heights, drinking a mixture of white wine and mineral water.

Meanwhile we were learning about contemporary Prague and some of its past history as well, mostly through our foot-soles. We could not climb up the hill of the Malá Strana without becoming aware that Prague once housed a king, for his castle was at the top, just where a king's castle should be. His nobles, we realized, must have been ambitious and probably turbulent, for they had each tried to outdo their peers in getting their palaces up the hill as near to the king as they could, striving to build more grandiose edifices than their neighbours. One of them, we were told, had bankrupted himself building the huge Czernin Palace which was now the Czech Foreign Office. On our side of the river, in the Old Town of Prague, there were ancient nooks and corners that gave us inexplicable shivers down our spines, so that we remembered the existence of books like *The Witch of Prague* and thought that we understood why they had been written.

Our new gay boldness finally gave us the courage to use Paul Selver's letters of introduction and so we met and at once took to Karel Čapek, who was a focus for much of the heady excitement in the city. He and his brother Josef, who also drew, painted, wrote poetry and plays, and Josef's wife Jarmila, who wrote children's books, lived together in a pleasant old house in the Malá Strana where we always felt welcome, although our conversation had to be carried on in a wild farrago of French, German, Czech, English and gesturing. Edwin's tendency to withdraw a little into Muir-family remoteness when he met strangers earned him at first the nickname of The Spanish Grandee which did not long survive the gentle teasing he got. I suppose I was naturally more foot-loose than he was; at any rate they called me The Gipsy. And now we were really hurled into Prague life. We had ventured once to the National Theatre to see Bajazet, not realizing that it would be presented in Czech of which we understood only three words at the end of the play announcing that Bajazet was dead, but now Karel Čapek urged and insisted that we must see every new production at the Vinohrady Theatre where he had recently been made a *regisseur*.

Francis George Scott

Hermann Broch, 1935

Čapek's Robot play had already been done, but the Vinohrady was seething with new ideas for plays from all countries. Almost at once we found ourselves attending a performance of *Troilus and Cressida*, presented in Czech and clothed in versions of what the producer, Kvapil, guessed to have been the anachronisms likely in Elizabethan times. Pandarus was got up in ruff, jerkin, and padded breeches; Ajax came straight off a Greek vase in a brief kilt and a large helmet; Achilles was the perfect nancy in a sculptural cloak bordered with a Greek key-pattern, carrying a small metal hand-mirror which he frequently consulted. Cressida herself was 'a fair, hot wench in flame-coloured taffeta'. We did not understand a word, but we understood the action very well and enjoyed it extravagantly.

All this happened within the first three months after we came to Prague. We found that we were expected also to attend the operas, hear all the incomparable string quartets, haunt the cafes and, of course, set ourselves seriously to learning Czech. Karel Čapek's urgency was not to be resisted, and he showered free tickets for the Vinohrady upon us although he did not know, I think, that we were getting into financial difficulties.

Our money troubles had begun early. We could not afford to stay long in our luxury hotel, and about a week after arriving set out to find our bank and draw out our capital. Adventurous as we felt, we regarded looking for the bank as a very minor difficulty. What we did not expect was the frustration we encountered inside it. Edwin wrote down his name and presented it to the nearest of about six clerks, each in a glass cubicle of his own. The paper was passed from cubicle to cubicle and presently passed back with head-shakings. No money for anyone of that name was in the bank. Disappointed, wondering what could have gone wrong, we hunted up the British Consul, a friendly Aberdonian, the first of our countrymen we had troubled to meet, since it had not occurred to us that we should call officially on our Ambassador. After an exchange of Aberdeen jokes we told our story: our bank account, presumably transmitted from London as we had been assured, had not arrived in the Prague bank. What was to be done?

The Consul was very helpful and concerned. He would at once get in touch with our London bank and make sure the money had been transferred. 'By the way,' he said, taking notes of our case, 'how much money is in your account?' 'Thirteen pounds,' said Edwin. The Consul nearly fell off his stool. We had to soothe him and dispel his fears, the nightmare, I believe, then haunting every Consul, that he was going to have on his hands bankrupt British subjects to be sent home at government expense, with, we gathered, a passport black-marked and probably confiscated. His fears about us were, I think, never quite dispelled. We patted him on the back and promised that we should never come to him bankrupt. Nor did we.

Yet it was a near thing. The Mystery of the Missing Bank Account was at length unravelled. Our thirteen pounds had been sent to Prague all right, but the name Muir seemed to the Czech bankers highly improbable; they decided it must be some clerk's mistake for Meier, a name everyone knew, and so our money was booked in the name of Meier. When that was cleared up we went to the bank and sat down on a bench like other applicants for money, waiting till the name Muir should be called out by the cashier, not realizing that Muir pronounced in Czech style becomes Mooeersh. Naturally we never heard the name Muir being called. One by one all the other clients departed, leaving us alone on the bench. Then the cashier glared at Edwin and in a loud, impatient voice shouted: Pan Mooeersh! All at once we became aware that he had been uttering that sound at intervals for the past half-hour. 'Can this mean me?' said Edwin and went up to the cubicle. Yes, he was Pan Mooeersh.

This delay did not incommode us much: what seriously inconvenienced us was the frequent non-arrival of cheques from *The Freeman* owing to thefts in the Czech Post Office. Czechs in the United States were sending many dollar notes to their people at home, and it was a paying business to open the American mail and extract the dollars. Unusable cheques, we supposed, were merely torn up; two out of every three due to us failed to arrive. Czech currency was rising in value all the time, except when unaccountable flurries occurred on the exchange, as when something called the Kapp Putsch happened—what it was we never really understood, not knowing anything about Kapp nor why he was Putsch-ing. But as the exchange was mostly going against us we came off badly by the time we had confirmed that a cheque was missing and secured a duplicate. Someone explained that Czechs had for so long regarded it as a virtue to cheat the Austrian Government that they could not learn all at once not to cheat their own government. Every two months or so there was another purge of the Post Office staff; before we left Prague our cheques were coming along regularly. In this way we got a lively understanding of what the Czech attitude had been to the Hapsburg Empire. We also discovered how much easier it was to be poor in Prague than in London. Excellent Pilsener lager was less than a penny a litre, and in some small low-browed shop one could always buy a pennyworth of roast goose—usually a leg—wrapped in newspaper. In the large cafes, for the price of a cup of coffee, about twopence, one could sit undisturbed for a whole evening enjoying a good cabaret performance. We could not understand much of the satirical political couplets but we could and did enjoy the antics of the 'funny men', especially one who was expert in wriggling his trousers down to danger-point and up again. So we did not starve or lack entertainment.

But by Christmas-time, as it happened, we were almost penniless, and could not afford to have a hole mended in one of my street shoes, the only pair fit for outdoor winter wear. The winter was more severe than we had looked for; temperatures were sometimes thirty below zero, centigrade; the whole countryside was covered with what I came to regard as the idiot blankness of snow. For the first time in my life I went down with bronchitis. I do not know how we could have avoided troubling the Consul had not a Czech friend, a delightful man called Vojaček, lent us a considerable sum of Czech crowns.

In this memoir I do not wish to repeat incidents mentioned by Edwin in his Autobiography, so about the English-speaking Austrian doctor from upstairs who attended me I shall say only this: after hearing from us that we did not believe in hatred or violence of any kind, he shook his head with a smile and remarked that we were a pair of over-valued neuropaths.

A pair of ignorant fools was what he meant. Central Europe was steeped in memories of violence and hatred: it was no Garden

Willa Muir, official identity card, Prague, 1945

The new Ph.D. and students, 1947

of Eden. Hatred for the German language was so rabid in Prague that it dumbfounded us. I had long ago picked up a few scraps of German, enough to ask my way politely in a street, and the first time I approached a kindly-looking Czech and asked if he could direct me to the Post Office I got a shock. His smile vanished, his face stiffened, his eyes narrowed, he shot out a couple of Czech sentences and spat on the pavement at my feet. I now know that he said: 'I don't understand German, I don't speak German,' and that it was probably a lie, since all Czechs had been technically Austrians until not so long before and could nearly all speak German. After that I tried a new technique for asking my way; I said in German, very quickly: 'Excuse me, but do you perhaps speak English?' This gambit evoked instant courtesy and all the help I needed.

We were so busily involved in Czech doings, private parties as well as public shows, that we never knew about the German life still going on in pockets here and there in Prague. We never got even a hint that Kafka or his friends had ever existed in the city. An invisible but unyielding barrier cut off German-speakers from Czech-speakers, and it was only the Czech-speakers that we came to know.

A lodging, in which we stayed only a couple of days, introduced us for the first time to bed-bugs, slow-moving creatures that loved the dark and, as we soon discovered, grew bemused in the light. A Czech friend whom we told about it explained something we had found rather puzzling, that in all the private houses we had entered there was no wall-paper, merely flowery wall-paper designs stencilled in colours on bare walls. During the war, he said, Prague became infested with bugs, and it was supposed that they lived on the paste behind the wallpaper, so an order was issued that all wall-papers must be stripped off. But he wasn't surprised to hear that a few bugs still survived, there had been such a plague of them. This was an aspect of the war in Central Europe which we had never thought of, and we were touched by the solicitude with which the Praguers had replaced their missing flowers.

Although the doors of German-speakers were hidden from our knowledge, many doors of Czech-speakers were opened to us, even although we were not able to invite them back. Our landlady,

Pani Mala, fed us at breakfast and luncheon time, and we made tea for ourselves in the afternoon on a picnic kit I had; supper we ate in cafes or at home, where and how we could afford. When we got to know the English residents in Prague, through joining their Club for the sake of the dancing, some of them used to haunt our room about tea-time, especially two young men, one a devotee of Dorothy Richardson, the other a devotee of Erica Cotterill, who did not much like each other yet apparently enjoyed our company. But afternoon tea was not a Czech habit, as we discovered the very first time we got an invitation to tea. Punctually at half-past four we turned up, respectably clad in our best day-time suits, only to discover our hostess, the wife of a university professor, in the middle of baking petits-fours for the party, delicious crescents and stars that melted in the mouth. Czech tea-parties did not begin until six o'clock and ended at nearly midnight. One arrived in evening or semi-evening dress. After tea there were liqueurs, after liqueurs cards, after cards dancing and more liqueurs with sandwiches and a cold buffet supper. Czechs believed in doing entertainments thoroughly.

They were all purposive and eager, with energies seemingly inexhaustible. Our obvious lack of purposefulness must have puzzled many of them. An incident which rather shook me at the time suggested that we might be suspected of being spies. In a cafe a total stranger rushed up to me crying 'Lisa!' and overwhelmed me with a torrent of speech, perhaps Russian, since I knew it was not Czech. My bewilderment enraged him; he began to scowl and sound threatening. Even when Edwin produced our passport and pointed me out on it as his wife, the stranger was not mollified; probably he thought the passport a fake. As far as we could make out, with the help of a kindly interpreter from the next table, he insisted that I was Lisa So-and-so whom he had once known very well in Russia, and surmised treachery when I denied knowing him. In the heady political excitement then current in Prague I suppose anything in the way of double-crossing may have seemed likely.

We sensed the political excitement, knowing that the people we met were striving tooth and nail to make this new Republic work, but we could not really enter into it; the language was too

Formal opening of Kaunic Palace, Prague,
for the British Council.
Edwin Muir speaking

great a barrier. We had to make an effort, sometimes a severe effort, to understand even partly everyone and everything, except for the music we heard in chamber concerts and at the opera. This brought a sense of strain. There was an alien quality in the life around us that prevented us from ever being quite relaxed, and I thought it came largely from the language.

I had buckled down to learning Czech and acquired a fair reading knowledge; Karel Čapek gave me a copy of his *Insect Play* when I had proved that I could read it; yet I could not speak Czech fluently. There were too many consonants and too few vowels for my liking. Unlike a Czech I could not easily manage to pronounce six separate consonants next to each other in one word. Then there was the Czech 'r', a very canine letter; at or near the beginning or at the end of a word it turned into something like rzh; we found it almost impossible to pronounce when it came after a p or a t, as it very often did. Edwin had to answer to Mooeersh and sometimes to say it on occasion, but he never mastered the r, because his natural r was the French r. He took refuge in averring that Czech was a language you couldn't believe in; the very look of it in print was incredible. I took refuge in sticking to a reading knowledge, noting that the curious sound of the Czech 'r' perhaps corresponded to the rough breathing over an initial 'r' in ancient Greek, and that Němec, the word for German, meant 'the one who can't speak', the dumb one who is literally unspeakable, so that the barrier between Czechs and Germans was actually built into the language.

Yet if we did not divine the inwardnesses, the nuances of Prague, we were able to understand something of it. Except in the matter of hating the German language, the Praguers struck us as being anything but hidebound, ready to improvise and adapt and experiment at the drop of a hat, willing to try anything. It was in Prague that we first heard Schoenberg, in a performance of *Pierrot Lunaire*. And the theatres were noteworthy: we guessed that in Prague at that time they were more alive than anywhere else in Europe, even Berlin. For instance, when it was decided to put on the whole cycle of Molière plays, someone got the notion that the cabaret star, the trouser-wriggler, was the very man to play the protagonist in all of them, and after some argument this was arranged. He was a spectacular success. We first saw him in *Le Médecin Malgré Lui*, which was embellished by a ballet of doctors in black cloaks and steeple-crowned hats, each carrying an outsize clyster, or enema. The theatre producers of Prague were not only open-minded, they had a wicked sense of fun.

This talent for improvisation had its disadvantages, especially in the Post Office. Parcels arriving in Prague were thrown pell-mell into the large stable-arches of a palace, I think Wallenstein's; when one arch was full, the next was requisitioned. The recipient got a chit advising him that a parcel had come for him and would he please visit the parcel depot and dig it out for himself? We had already warned friends at home not to send any parcels, but my mother, filled with pious sentiment about New Year celebrations, had posted us a solid Scottish black bun for New Year, in a cardboard box. Early in March we got the chit for it and spent three days clambering over the heaps of parcels, accompanied by a Post Office guide, until we found it, uneatable, of course, by then. This last brush with the Post Office gave a fillip to our growing restlessness. We were getting impatient with the severe, prolonged winter, which was wearing us down. People assured us that Prague in spring, bowered in fruit-blossom, was enchanting, and we did not disbelieve them, yet spring even in March seemed still far away. The river, frozen solid since November, was only beginning to break up and we felt a need to see brown earth again. Perhaps we had had as much of Prague as was good for us, since it had kept us on the stretch; at any rate, in a sudden fit of impatience, we decided to go to Dresden for a weekend, to see what it was like.

Curiously enough, we seemed to have absorbed the knowledge that crossing a frontier was an easy thing to do. Sailing from Leith across the North Sea, which must have been a psychological as well as a geographical barrier, we had felt we were setting out momentously into the unknown; in Prague we now climbed carelessly into a train without thinking much about crossing a frontier.

And in Dresden spring was really in the air, even although it lay farther north than Prague, for Dresden was less deeply embedded in the continental land mass and was not so far from the sea.

Sometimes in Prague we had felt very far from the sea, despite the numerous seagulls flying and crying over the river-bridges. In Dresden we met the breath of spring and were joyously surprised. The sense of relaxation was wonderful. The German language, too, compared with Czech, was generous with clues to its meaning. 'Czech is as spiky as the Tyn Church,' I said to Edwin. 'It's like a diet of fish-bones without much fish.' We had a half-awed and wholly unexpected sense of being more at home in Dresden than in Prague. There was no doubt about what we should do. We went back to Prague, packed our suitcases, said goodbye to everyone we knew and vanished into Germany.

Chapter Seven

DRESDEN AND HELLERAU

March 1922 - May 1923

In Prague we had taken our first plunge into 'abroad' and found that we had gone in at the deep end, a strenuous experience. Perhaps because of this, once left alone with each other and released from the strain of peripheral attention to the unfamiliar, we were aware of a pervasive sense of well-being. It was more than physical well-being. A glow of joyous feeling enfolded us, whether strolling in the autumn river-valley among geese and bright red cherry trees, or feeding blackcaps and tits in the winter Kinsky gardens, or merely resting in our room. When we came to Dresden this glow of feeling accompanied us all the time, since the atmosphere of Dresden was altogether relaxing after Prague.

Not that Dresden was a sleepy city, only its rhythm of life was less hustling than Prague's. The city seemed self-complacent and both had and gave plenty of elbow-room. The river here was flowing through flatter, wider country, and Dresden spread itself at large, not crowded, as Prague was, between eroded heights. What lingers most in my memory of the months we spent in Dresden before going to Hellerau is the fragrance from avenues of blossoming lime trees which went to our heads as we sat in the open eating ices in mindless peace.

Yet although we were in a state of gentle dreaminess we noticed what seemed streaks of incongruity in the Saxon set-up. To begin with, although Dresden had produced Meissen tea-services, including tea-pots, some of its people did not understand tea. In the Old Town we asked for it in a café, expecting tea with sugar and lemon slices as served in Prague, but we got two large earthenware bowls each full of a pale liquid with an enormous blob of whipped cream floating on top. Then we learned that some pastries almost delicate enough to make silk purses were called 'pigs' ears'. And at the little hotel we stayed in for a week, where the cooking was good, we found to our dismay that the great treat for dinner on Sunday was beer soup, a horrible concoction.

Table manners in that hotel were a strange blend of delicacy and coarseness. The burly Saxons who came in from outside during the week for their midday meal never failed to greet the residents as they sat down, but when they began to eat shovelled their food in anyhow. They ate hugely, putting away portions fit for labourers after a day in the harvestfield, and when offered a third helping said, with comfortable belches: 'Danke, ich bin satt', which we took to mean 'full to bursting'. They were not self-conscious at all, giving an impression of collective simplicity that might well harbour incongruities of all kinds.

We found the same unself-conscious simplicity in the couple whose flat we lodged in. Just inside the New Town of Dresden, in an unfrequented square near the river, we got two rooms on the top floor of a long yellow-stuccoed insurance building filling one whole side of the open space. The official caretaker and his wife, whose daughter spoke English, took us on as lodgers after saying that they were strictly forbidden to let rooms and would we mind passing ourselves off to the Insurance Herrschaften as cousins of theirs from Scotland on a visit? Our spacious rooms looked over tree-tops to the Elbe and were furnished in high style with leather armchairs, an enormous flat desk at which we could both sit, and in the bedroom a Himmel-Bett adorned with cherubs. For all that we could see, the old, comfortable burgess life was still going on in Dresden and the 1914 war might never have happened. Nothing in our daily routine ruffled our peace. If there were any ferment in Dresden, it remained very secret. The one small sign of uneasiness we were aware of was our landlady's half-humorous insistence that we must find a British or American husband for her pretty seventeen-year-old daughter; we had the impression that the foreign passport was longed for even more than the husband.

As the air grew warmer we idled for hours on the shore of the Elbe. The river was chillier than the air—perhaps Prague was still sending blocks of ice into it—but Edwin could splash about while I swam a bit against the current. The first time we decided to try the water I had a sober British bathing-suit and Edwin had none, so he went off to buy one while I strolled down to the beach. I had to pick my way among recumbent monsters, fat men like walruses in drab loin-cloths, with sausage-rolls at the back of their necks, tanned a deep mahogany colour that made them look like bronze images, replicas, say, of the Chinese God of Prosperity. All at once they began to turn their heads and some even sat up with amazed expressions on their faces; when I also looked up I saw a streak of moonlight flickering past the bronzes and coming my way, an incredibly slim, incredibly white-skinned figure in daffodil-yellow trunks, Edwin, stepping jauntily among the walruses.

In this mellow peace we both found our imaginations beginning to stir. As Edwin himself has said, he felt as if he were recovering from the long illness that had seized him when, at fourteen, he came to Glasgow, and he was now looking back over his life with new eyes. He was being the reverse of teleological; he was looking at everything back to front for the sake of undoing in imagination all that he felt had been wrongly done in the past. This backward movement, going against the flow of time, gave him great pleasure and he made a practice of it, as comes out clearly in his poetry. I took it to be part of his private technique for surprising his unconscious unawares.

In Dresden he was looking as far back as the personal unconscious would take him, back to his childhood, and he was not doing so out of simple nostalgia for past innocence. He was beginning what was to be his life-long task, exploring within himself the extraordinary dramas that his London visions had made him aware of, because he believed that they came ultimately from a transcendental source and had a meaning for everyone. But he had to learn how words should be arranged to convey poetic meaning, and his childhood setting provided an apparently simple starting-point. In Prague he had already tried to catch a mood here and there, without much success; he felt that the fresh immediacy of a child's impressions would be more rewarding. His first poems, published in 1925 by the Hogarth Press, were those that he now began making.

The Orkney of Edwin's childhood, into which he was returning against the flow of time, was, as I have already remarked, close to the Middle Ages. Edwin himself used to say that he was born at least two hundred and fifty years before the present age, and, with so much leeway to make up, that was why he was fascinated by

Time. Thus the childhood's setting he was reviving belonged to a far past age. This may not have been immediately obvious to his first readers, since every child begins life in an age well before twentieth-century consciousness, but when they read his later poems they may have wondered at the prevalence of legendary monsters, heraldic lions, dragons and sea-creatures, symbols which came, as I believe, from the almost mediaeval unconscious to which Edwin had access through his dreams and visions. It is convenient, though arbitrary, to divide the unconscious into personal, collective and, perhaps, cosmic unconscious; elements from all of them could be identified in Edwin's poetry. From the cosmic unconscious, he himself believed, came his overruling positive yearning for harmony rather than discord, for gentleness rather than violence, for tolerance, compassion and love rather than hatred and punishment.

Only after experiencing his visions in London did he begin consciously to shape his life according to this pattern, which he felt corresponded to his true self, but there are hints of it in *We Moderns*, although he came to reject that premature work. When he wrote there about a feeling of universal comprehension arising out of Love, when he insisted that to love one was to love all, he was expressing an aspiration of which he then had an inkling but as yet no clear awareness. The longer he lived the more sure he became that cosmic radiation from far outside conveyed this aspiration to mankind, from an unknown source to which one's unconscious gave access and which he called 'The Fable' of one's life. Much less decisive was 'The Story', the sum of conscious happenings from day to day on earth. His poetry, he was sure, came ultimately from The Fable.

The extraordinary sources from which he drew his poems, visions from The Fable, made it necessary for him, he felt, to use simple, traditional language in shaping them, and that brought an extra difficulty with it, for the current fashion in England had been setting towards changes in verbal technique, craftsmanship in poetic texture, concentration on poetry's medium, language, rather than on its content—a quite different mode of extending conscious awareness. Had he not been essentially tough Edwin could not have persisted in writing his own peculiar poetry for the rest of his life.

In Dresden I did not perceive this even so tentatively as I do now. But I liked the poems he made, appreciated the difficulty he had in framing them and felt vaguely the significance of what he was trying to do. We were both happy in the glow of feeling that enfolded us and I had no doubt that whatever came out of it would be worth while.

In my happiness I accepted without demur the recurrent presence of the Holmses. Holms had left the Army, and his father, an Anglo-Indian martinet, then sent him to Oxford, from which he was presently sent down, whereupon his father cut him off with an allowance of two hundred and fifty pounds a year on condition that he never returned to Britain. He persuaded Dorothy Jennings, a pretty red-head, to share his fortunes abroad; they were not yet married, but it is easier to refer to them as the Holmses. They turned up now in Dresden and with them we went to concerts and various shows or ate in cafés and restaurants of an evening. Apart from monologues addressed exclusively to Edwin, Holms's conversation consisted of dissertations on what was and what was not a good wine or a good dish, or who was and who was not a Great Man in Literature and the Arts. I developed the habit of listening with only half a mind.

At this time I was thinking of writing a play. Apparently I had been so steeped in theatre during the winter in Prague that my imagination turned to play-writing as a way of embodying the making of a new world. My idea, which I must have picked out of the air, was to dramatize in modern terms the situation in which Noah and his family found themselves once the floods had gone down and the world had to be made over again from the beginning. In my mind I sketched important parts for Mrs Noah, Mrs Shem, Mrs Ham, and Mrs Japhet, but I was still trying to decide precisely what kind of man each husband should be. Shem, the father of merchant adventurers and bankers, might be a prospective City man; Ham, according to S. Augustine, the father of Zoroaster the Magician, was surely an ancestor of gipsies, musicians and artists; while Japhet, the father of land-grabbers and fighters, looked to me like someone in plus fours with a reddish face. But when at last I broke silence and spread my idea out before Edwin, to my dismay he did not like it at all; worse than that, he was shocked by it. The mere suggestion of putting Japhet into plus fours distressed him. He objected that it simply should not be done. I did not understand why this way of using an old story should raise all his hackles, but I realized well enough that he thought it vulgar.

Edwin had often enough been shocked by gay doings of mine in the past, at my taking shillings from the gas meter in Guilford Street, for instance; I had usually laughed at him and gone my own way, telling him that it was good for him to be shocked every now and then. But here I could not laugh, for I was on new ground where I felt uncertain. I had never before tried to write a play and Edwin was more experienced in writing than I was, so that his disapproval and my inability to understand it discouraged me profoundly. I am sure he did not expect me to be so downcast, for despite his gentleness he was much tougher inside than I was; had he decided to write a play, disapproval from someone else might have influenced but would not have stopped him. Yet the conviction that he found my notion outrageous did stop me. Much later on, someone else picked that notion out of the air, or something very like it, and made it into a play; today the transformation of old stories into modern terms has become a commonplace. Later on, too, Edwin turned the story of the Flood into a ballad, which he thought a more proper way of handling an ancient theme.

Whether or no I might have eventually gone on with the play I cannot tell, for at this juncture we ran into A. S. Neill at a tram stop, a chance encounter that changed the course of our lives. Neill and I were equally surprised to meet each other and cried simultaneously: 'What on earth are *you* doing here?' Neill, it appeared, was starting a school in a place called Hellerau, some miles out of Dresden, an international school; as soon as he set eyes on me he made up his mind that I was the very person he needed to help him.

Edwin had barely met Neill before and knew little about him. I had not seen him since leaving my training college; at that time he was teaching in the King Alfred school at Hampstead, but since then had been working, he said, with an organization called 'The New Era'. We had been good friends since 1912, when he was a student at Edinburgh and I at St Andrews—a brotherly and sisterly relationship which has lasted through the years. It was, I suppose, a foregone conclusion that I should yield to Neill's entreaties and go to Hellerau, although on the spot I made no promise. It was also a foregone conclusion that I should take for granted Edwin's willingness to adopt my friend Neill as a friend of his, although no two men could have been more different in their make-up.

Next day we went out to Hellerau in a tram through six miles of birch-scrub to see the place. Both of us at once liked the look and the feel of Hellerau, a village planned for craftsmen and artists, the original model for places like Letchworth, with pleasant houses set irregularly on the slopes of a sandy hill among pinewoods and hedged in everywhere by fragrant sweet-brier. The buildings erected in it for Jacques Dalcroze, the originator of Eurhythmies, had lain derelict since the 1914 war, but the owner, who lived in Hellerau, wished to have them put to use again and for that purpose had formed a limited liability company to run them, made up of Hellerau residents and Neill.

It was Frau Doktor Neustätter who had persuaded Neill to join the venture. She was an Australian who had gone with her sister (the novelist Henry Handel Richardson) to study music in Leipzig and there married a Bavarian eye specialist now living in Hellerau and working for a Ministry in Dresden. Neill and she had become friendly during the war, which caught her unawares in England when she brought her son to be educated at the King Alfred school.

She liked the way Neill dealt with her son and was fired by his educational ideas. When the Hellerau project was mooted, she saw in it a heaven-sent chance to begin the very a.b.c. of international understanding in a school run by Neill, since there was a spare wing among the Dalcroze buildings. The whole scheme took shape much as she had envisaged it. The central complex, with its theatre, sun terraces and practice rooms, was the Eurhythmic college; Neill had one of the two substantial wings for an international school, while the other became a German school for the village. A separate building, the Schulheim, was a residence for Neill and his pupils as well as a meeting-place for everyone at a midday meal shared in common by the Eurhythmic students and all staff. Frau Doktor, as everyone called her, had appointed herself housekeeper-matron for the Schulheim and everything was now in train.

Edwin and I liked Frau Doktor, who gave us an excellent tea and promised, if I were willing to help Neill, to lodge and board us very cheaply in her own house. Our midday meal we should have, like the others, in the Schulheim. It seemed to me an attractive offer. Among the pine trees behind the house Edwin and I talked it over. I pointed out that he would be able to do what he liked, since he need not bother about the school; he could share in the life of the little community or stay out of it, as he pleased. I did not think that he would stay out of it, but I put it that way since by this time I knew how shy he was of letting himself in for anything unless he were sure he could get out of it again. He was well aware that I felt almost bound to answer Neill's call for help, and both of us were pleased by the idea of an international school: the upshot was that Edwin agreed to the plan and we moved into Frau Doktor's house towards the beginning of June.

The community we joined made a European international enclave in the German village of Hellerau. The Eurhythmic students, young women from seventeen to about twenty-three years old, came from all over Europe, and so did Neill's pupils. Every country in Europe was represented except Spain, Italy and Russia. Three of Neill's pupils came from England, two little brothers and a girl in her early teens. In the schools and at the Schulheim dining-table the common language simply had to be German. Edwin and I soon became fluent in German since every word we learned was on active service. In Neill's school the English children and a couple of Belgians who wanted to practise their English could be dealt with in English, but the others, who, like me, were also learning German, had to be addressed in the common tongue.

The atmosphere was genuinely international. No racial, political or national prejudices interfered with the many new friendships now formed, Nushi, a gay young sprite from Hungary, for instance, easily became the bosom-friend of Margit, another gay young dancer from Yugoslavia. No one country had a preponderance in numbers and each young student was met and treated as an individual person, not as a Finn or a Czech or a Belgian. Many of these girls were hoping to become professional dancers; some of them did do so; a few became well known and won European reputations.

Frau Doktor, who never gave away any secrets, became a confidante and mother-figure to all the Eurhythmic students as well as the younger pupils in Neill's school. Neill was to some extent a father-figure for all of them, but he and a handsome young Bavarian assistant in the German school, the only two bachelors among so many girls, became also emotional centres for the 'hopeless passions' which young girls seem to need for practice. A Swedish girl who like us boarded with Frau Doktor nursed her 'hopeless passion' for the conductor Furtwängler, to whom she had never even spoken, while Nushi, the enchanting young Hungarian, presently attached her dreams to a curly-headed Southerner from the United States who used to visit Frau Doktor from time to time. It was a Czech girl, Jarmila, who was successful in transforming her dream into reality; towards the middle of our year she married the young Bavarian, Dr Schirer. As far as we could tell, neither Czech nor German national prejudices caused any trouble between them.

This youthful effervescence made an enjoyable ambience to live in. I think Edwin had never been so carefree in his life. The burden of earning a living had taken wings and flown off his shoulders, since Frau Doktor charged us a derisory sum for our keep. He had found, too, a dear friend in Ivo von Lücken, an impoverished elderly Junker who was a poet and lived in the basement of the Schulheim on the food he got from people to whom he taught Spanish; together these two wandered in the pinewoods reading and meditating on Ivo's two favourites, Hölderlin and Kleist. To Edwin Hölderlin's gods sitting on their mountain tops became very dear; he did not take to Kleist with the same enthusiasm. In the evenings we sometimes joined a group going down to the local inn, the Waldschänke, where one drank lager, danced in the earthen court-yard to a couple of guitars and sang the latest German popular songs.

Behind the fun, serious work was going on. The dance-mistress for the Eurhythmic students, Valerie Kratina, trained them in exquisitely controlled barefoot dancing, with a choreography that came somewhere between ballet and mime, and every term a public performance was staged in the theatre. That theatre was in itself remarkable, for it was the first to use light and shadow as the sole means of creating scenic effects. A permanent set at the back of the stage consisted of steps rising to various levels but it was the strong light and shadow projected on the stage that defined the actions presented. Because it was a pioneer in this method the theatre had a needlessly cumbrous electrical installation, according to Basil Dean, who came from London to study it; he thought the same effects could be produced more economically.

We all enjoyed these performances and became knowledge-able about dancing techniques. After watching a near-perfect production of Glück's 'Dance of the Blessed Spirits' we would troop into Dresden to pick to pieces the performance of some rival school such as Mary Wigman's. There was a vogue for dancing of this kind in Germany at that time. Neill advertised himself as preferring jazz to classical music and modern ballroom dancing to Kratina's, but he was rather inclined to sport chips on his shoulder and no one paid much attention, except that Edwin told me privately he thought Neill was being silly about Bach. I said it didn't really matter, because whatever theories Neill might air, his practice with children was almost infallible. He suffered a good deal from the conferences he had to attend with the headmaster and staff of the German school who, being inclined to the authoritarian, were suspicious of self-government and psycho-analysis. One of Neill's most successful 'turns' of an evening was an imitation of Herr Doktor Harless making a speech, which always began with: 'Die Psÿcho-analÿse, zwar, . . .'

What with dancing and music and poetry and psychology we were living in a bright little world of our own, quite unaware that the climate outside was darkening. Our visitors brought us no awareness of that. The Holmses came out several times and then went off to Italy. We made friends with many Hellerau residents, among them a Regierungsrat who took Edwin and me to visit a rich margarine manufacturer's wife in Dresden so that we could see her modern pictures; but the Regierungsrat gave us no hint that there was trouble brewing in the outside world. The Wandervögel who came into the woods at weekends with rucksacks and guitars looked like simple Saxons, apparently as carefree as we felt. The terrible inflation of the German mark was not so far away, Hitler and the Nazis were already stirring in Munich, yet we had no premonitions at all.

Matthew Josephson, on the staff of an American magazine, came from Berlin to see us and on his invitation Edwin and I spent two weekends in Berlin, the second time to see Čapek's *Insect Play* very well produced in German. None of the Americans we met there was expecting catastrophe. The cabarets to which they took us seemed brittle, smart and strikingly immoral to our unsophisticated minds, but we put down to the aftermath of the war whatever we did not like; we supposed that the old standards of German life had been corrupted in Berlin though not in Dresden, and no wonder, we thought, looking with distaste at the pretentious architecture. Only one group of people did we take to, the Constructivists, and that was mainly because we were both drawn to Lissitsky, a small dark appealing man who was, I believe, already consumptive. The bits and pieces of their collages, tram tickets and match-box tops and rusty wire springs, spoke to us of past stringencies rather than of the future. Moholy-Nagy was there too, and we discovered at last how his name should be pronounced. What we brought back from Berlin were personal impressions of likes and dislikes but no understanding of that feverish city.

Germany did not mean Berlin to Edwin and me; it meant Dresden, and Hellerau where by this time we knew every man, woman, child, cat and dog in the village. It meant Emma, Frau Doktor's dependable maid, who went as a matter of course to the opera in Dresden on her weekly day off. It meant Otto, Frau Doktor's likeable husband, who had to have his bowl of thick sour milk, *Töpfen*, waiting for him in the evening when he came home from his office, or else! It meant the genial editor of the *Dresdener Neueste Nachrichten*, Theodor Schulze from Bautzen, which, he assured us, was a comic place in the minds of all Germans because it lay in Wendish country. It meant Oberammergau, where we went to see the Passion Play, and the country round it we tramped through. How could we have had forebodings?

We were not so naive as to think that Germany harboured no unpleasant types. And in railway trains we noticed that many Germans became nervy and uneasy once their feet were on the floor of a moving compartment instead of on familiar, stable ground; they tended to be suspicious, irritable and quarrelsome on a train journey.

Had we been granted a vision of what was to come, how could we have believed it? Edwin and I went for a week's walking tour at Easter along the Bohemian frontier to Bad Elster and back, together with Frau Doktor and two Eurhythmic students, special favourites of hers, little Nushi from Budapest, who was a general pet, and Gerda, a South German, with dark bobbed hair framing a thin face and large, expressive dark eyes. Had we been told that the road we followed, among all the great trees and the ferns underfoot, was going to be sealed off in the forties behind barbed wire and armed sentries while captives were driven like serfs to work the uranium mines opened up there, would we have believed it? Had we been told that Nushi, whose happy antics delighted everyone, so that in a wayside inn the local miller came to Frau Doktor and said: 'Mutti, die Kleene heerat' ich!' (Mum, I want to marry the little 'un!), was going to be thrown into a gas chamber at Auschwitz could we have believed it? Nushi, for all her brief saucy nose and light brown hair, was a Jewess, a fact nobody in Hellerau bothered to remember. How could we have believed the unimaginable?

The first symptoms of public uneasiness that we noticed came when the French occupied the Rühr. Our friends in Hellerau were forlorn and cast down, disproportionately so, it seemed to us, since they felt it as a deliberately-planned humiliation that the occupying troops were Algerians—black men, they said bitterly. Then in a trickle that eventually became a landslide the mark began to drop in value. The French were our allies and we ourselves were living on dollars and pounds, so that we felt doubly guilty. The dearer everything became for our friends, the cheaper it was for us. We began taking people into Dresden by the half-dozen, to the best restaurant, the Königsdiele, knowing that whatever they ordered, let them begin with champagne cocktails and finish with *omelette surprise*, the bill would not amount to more than ninepence a head. Our usual cigarettes from the village shop, Avramikos, excellent Virginia cigarettes from Hamburg, came down to seventeen a penny while friends of ours were buying them by twos and threes. We could get a bottle of fine hock for four-pence. And still the landslide worsened. In the Dresden marketplace prices were changed every hour, then every half-hour, then every ten minutes. A man would cram his week's wages into a suitcase and run full tilt to the marketplace, hoping that he might still have enough to buy a dinner for his family. Elderly people stood there holding out for sale bits and bobs of family possessions, since even old junk was becoming more valuable than paper money.

I do not doubt that Edwin and I could have bought up house property had we wished to, although we were no capitalists. We did buy an Erika portable typewriter, but by that time, after seeing what was happening in the marketplace, we felt we could not bear it any longer. Our sense of guilt was suffocating us. Neill had put all his savings into the Hellerau venture, changing his money into marks, and every pound he had put in was now worth about a halfpenny. Whatever we did, handing out cigarettes, wine, food, amounted to very little compared with the flood of catastrophe that was coming from outside and overwhelming everyone; its consequences we could neither control nor check nor even effectively palliate. Feeling like cowards we decided to run away.

The Holmses were in Italy and hard up. Holms had been begging Edwin to come and share the expenses of a small lodge they had taken for the summer by the sea, in a place called Forte dei Marmi: it was the lodge of a Florentine professor's villa and they could not afford to pay for it unless we came. Friendship demanded that we should answer this call, and so, with some inward grudging, I agreed to go there.

We were well escorted to the station. Gerda was hanging on to Edwin's arm, Nushi to mine, while Jeju from Helsinki on my other side was explaining that she was not going to give me her address, which I should certainly lose or forget, but was going to tell me how to find her in a way I would not forget. 'You come to Helsinki,' said Jeju, 'and you say: Sugar factory. Everyone knows it, and it belongs to my father. Then at the Sugar factory you say: Jeju. Everyone there knows me. So you find me.'

We were in a highly emotional state when we got into that South Express.

Chapter Eight

ITALY

May – October 1923

The train was hot and Edwin complained of a headache, which was not surprising. We were both exhausted, although I was partly sustained by a shamefaced sense of relief at having got away. I confessed this to Edwin, but he would not admit to sharing it. All day his headache became more and more blinding until when the train halted at Riva, the first station we stopped at in Italy, he did not want to travel further and we got out.

There was a pleasant-looking yellow-fronted hotel near the station, only a few steps away from Lake Garda. Here we decided to stay until Edwin felt better. Just above the hotel the main road led through great cliffs of, I think, sandstone; an inscription marked the place where Italians and Austrians had last faced each other in the war, a melancholy reminder. These cliffs continued down the right bank of the lake from the hotel, towering over small villages near the water, where orderly ranks of lemon trees were growing, not very inviting country for an invalid to walk through, even an invalid who insisted that he was not really ill but suffering only from headache. He had no fever, yet he was irritable and rebutted any attempt I made to comfort him.

Since walking seemed to depress Edwin, I suggested driving out in a carrozza down the left bank of Garda; the road was white with dust but the air was fresh and the mountain background lovely. We tried that, but to my surprise and dismay I found that I too was growing depressed. Sitting beside Edwin I felt miserable, without knowing why, except that I was aware he had withdrawn himself from me, into what I supposed was Muir-family remoteness. It was a desolating experience to sit beside him with my sleeve touching his sleeve and to feel that there was no communication at all between us, as if we were strangers.

In the hotel he was even more irritable and refused aspirins. Next day we went out again in a carrozza, this time down the right bank between the cliffs, and here my depression turned into something like fear, for Edwin cried that the cliffs were going to fall on him and we had to turn back. There seemed to be nothing I could do to help him. That was what dismayed me most. When he first came to London and felt the houses were going to fall on him he looked to me then for comfort, but now he would hardly speak to me, refusing even aspirins, let alone caresses. Yet, although we were travelling into an unknown country we were going towards his friend, Holms, towards what should appear an inviting milieu. I could not at all account for the nervous state he was in.

After three days of inexplicable misery which I tried in vain to dispel and which was growing worse rather than better, I wondered if an excursion by water down the lake might help. A paddle steamer went to Sirmione at the other end, and I very much wished to visit Sirmione for Catullus' sake. Edwin agreed to go, but it was a day of more acute misery, since I felt not only the absence of loving vibrations from Edwin but waves of silent hostility. I saw the drifts of poppies among the olive trees on Sirmione through a haze of unhappiness which the thought of unhappy Catullus did not alleviate, and by the time we came back to our room in the hotel I was desperate and asked Edwin, urgently: Peerie B, my lamb, *what is it?*'

He told me. On the way to the station Gerda had confessed that she loved him and he wanted to go back to Hellerau, to Gerda. A man couldn't just abruptly go away and leave a woman who said she loved him; it wasn't a thing anyone should do. He must go back to Gerda.

When he said that a storm of rage and grief rose up in me and I knew I was going to howl, so I snatched the door open and ran down to the shore of the lake, where I did howl and roar over the unheeding waters of Garda. Edwin couldn't leave Gerda, but he could leave *me*. I had not roared like that since I was fourteen.

In time, my storm of resentment was roared away; I had no feeling left but a heavy grief, a cold grey stone in my breast that no roaring could get rid of. I did not stride by the sea till dawn like my old heroine Dagmar, but I did wander to and fro by Garda until darkness fell and I became aware that I was sopping wet from the knees down. By the time I turned back to the hotel I had lost all confidence in myself, in Edwin, and in the Universe, but I knew what had to be done. If Edwin wanted to go back to Gerda, he must go, by tomorrow morning's express.

This acceptance may look like magnanimity, but I think it was a compound of self-respect and desperation. To me, love that was not spontaneous and voluntary was no love: there could be no love where there was constraint. And how could I live beside Edwin if I constrained him? Four days of misery with a barrier between us had shown me how unbearable that would be. But he had already cut himself off from me, and I thought that this was the end.

I plodded up to our room and stood just inside the door, holding on to the handle. Edwin was sitting at the table with his face hidden on his arms. In as level a voice as I could command, speaking in English, not in Orkney, I told him that we had not made our marriage to be a cage for either of us and that if he wanted to go back to Gerda he should go. He could take next morning's train. As he looked up at me I added:

'But I'm afraid you'll have to leave me some money, for I must find a British Consul and get a passport.'

Edwin stretched out his arms towards me and cried: 'Peerie Willa!' Then he began to sob. I flew to him, wet feet and all, and we clung to each other for comfort. There was no barrier. The Edwin I knew had come back. In the middle of it he asked me to forgive him, and I surprised myself by saying that True Love never found any *need* to forgive; forgiveness was irrelevant and superfluous.

My relief and happiness were too great for any questioning, and to this day I do not know how Edwin came to himself while I was out. It may sound incredible but we never referred to Gerda again. Had Edwin brought up the subject, I should have been glad enough, but I would not initiate a discussion. How impressionable he was in moments of heightened feeling, how vulnerable, had become very clear to me and I think I was afraid to stir up once more what had miraculously been dispelled. I was too thankful to find that after all I was not merely one in the succession of his transient love-affairs to investigate farther.

Next day we took the south-bound express on our way to join the Holmses. I remember that I was able to enjoy the loveliness of the blossoming countryside we journeyed through as I had not been able to enjoy the scenery around Lake Garda. I kept looking through the carriage window and then at Edwin to make sure that he was really there, for I was touching my happiness very tentatively.

We never discussed the Gerda incident, but of course we thought about it. Over and over again I thought about it, because it baffled me, and I am fairly sure that Edwin thought about it, since he was deeply dissatisfied with himself. I could almost sense the conviction of Original Sin that was looming in the back of his mind. The kind of emotional turmoil we had been through does not vanish without leaving traces, and as far as our feelings went, we were both in a convalescent state for some time to come, inclined to be diffident with each other.

My confidence in Edwin was partly restored, my confidence in myself not very much, my confidence in the Universe not at all. I could not forget the utter indifference of the lake and the mountains when I was in agony. I had told myself then that I could no longer 'kid' myself about having a special relation to the Universe, and I still held by that. I had discovered that if Edwin and I did not Belong together, I now Belonged nowhere.

Beside Garda I had looked at myself and did not think much of what I saw. My two accomplishments, which I had always thought of as a stand-by, a gift for languages and a gift for teaching, gave me the prospect of paying my way through Italy by teaching English to Italians, and it seemed a bleak prospect, by no means making up for my failure as a wife. Somewhere, I felt, I must have failed Edwin. I came to the conclusion that I had been taking our relationship too much for granted, as if marriage were a static absolute instead of a process changing like life itself from day to day and needing as much attention as any other living process. In Hellerau I had devoted my energies much more to Neil's school and the Eurhythmic community than to Edwin, assuming, as I did, that he was all right with Ivo von Lücken, and with the poems he was trying to make. He must have felt that something he needed was lacking. I thought I knew, at last, what that was: the glow of feeling which had enveloped us both in Dresden, and, as

I now realized, had gradually faded away in Hellerau. I had been too busy, too much occupied with day-to-day school matters, and finally too much concerned with the troubles coming from the outside world. I had almost been treating Edwin as a brother, like Neill. It dawned on me, too, that Edwin had shown a tendency to pick on Neill for one thing or another, which meant that he had felt stirrings of resentment. He had lacked and needed what I thought of as 'the golden glow', which, too late, I understood to be what now mattered most to me. This sense of irreparable loss had made my grief beside Garda so much the heavier.

Sitting in the train, looking every now and then at Edwin and catching a smile from him, I believed that we could begin to generate the golden glow again, only I could not help wishing that we might be left to ourselves in the process. To be sharing each day with the Holmses would not help. And yet, I reminded myself, I must go warily with the suggestible Edwin who could transform himself and vanish so completely in such a baffling manner; the least I could do was to accept the Holmses as best I might. I made many good resolutions on that journey.

The lodge, when we reached it, proved to be a little more than a mile from Forte dei Marmi, but it was quite close to the sea, the bay of Viareggio. One had only five minutes' walk through a small grove of umbrella pines to get to the sandy beach, where a shelter belonged to us, a roof of pine branches laid across four supporting poles, enough to give us shade. The lodge itself was just inside the gate leading into the Proprietá, on the edge of the vineyard surrounding the villa. It had three rooms, a bedroom looking out on the vineyard, a small kitchen in the middle, and a smaller bedroom with a window giving on the road. Edwin and I got the smaller bedroom, as was only to be expected: we spent most of the day outside, except for a siesta, and ate in the shade of a pergola. The Holmses had engaged a girl to come daily from Forte dei Marmi and do the luncheon cooking and washing-up: she was so beautiful that one could not help watching her—like ox-eyed Hera, I thought, with a broad brow, classical features, a golden skin and golden-bronze lights and shadows in the waves of her hair. The only flaw in Teresa's beauty was the thickness of her legs and ankles, which we chose to attribute to Etruscan ancestors. On the charcoal stove in the kitchen, which she controlled by plying a straw fan, she fried us fish, meat or egg dishes, one of which, her great pride, alone was honoured by the name 'frittata', three layers of egg and two of onion sandwiched together into a large cube, which one sliced. For our evening meal we walked into Forte dei Marmi and enjoyed the excellent, full-bodied local wine, called simply *vino nero*; perhaps it was the same kind of Carrara wine Pliny praised so much.

The marbles of Carrara were shipped from Forte dei Marmi, and the whole village seemed ankle-deep in marble dust. We climbed to see some of the quarries and were shown red and purple flowered marbles much in demand for churches and ceremonial pillars: the ordinary grey blue-veined kind on the other hand was held very cheap. All window-frames, including ours, were made of it and so was the seat of our earth closet, admirably cool on hot days.

The professor was not yet in his villa, which was in charge of the Guardiano and the Guardiana, tallish, thin caretakers, kind and helpful. One of the Holmses' cabin trunks needed a new lock and the Guardiano undertook to get it to the village for repair; we supposed he would drive it there in his little cart, but were much astonished to meet it coming home some days later on the Guardiana's head. Like all the women of the neighbourhood she wore heel-less slipper-like footwear, and there she was, walking along the road easily, lithely, knitting as she went, with the trunk balanced on a pad over the crown of her head, not in the least impeded by the slip-slopping mules on her feet. The peasant women who passed our window on their way to market at five in the morning and the country housewives who brought flasks of wine from the village all balanced trays in the same way on their heads instead of carrying baskets. As for balancing a whole trunk on her head, the Guardiana thought nothing of it; she was amused at our surprise; she had carried it to the village and brought it back: come no?

Edwin was on bad terms with himself and so at first could not come to terms with the Italy we saw around us: his tremulous feelings shrank from the strong colours of hills and sky and sea, which seemed garish to his northern eyes. Holms, who had, in so far as he could get beyond his own ego, a genuine affection for Edwin, perceived that he was feeling low, and not knowing why, inferred that I had been neglecting his creature comforts. That, at least, is how I accounted for the curious conversation between Holms and me which happened one morning when Edwin was in another corner of the garden writing a *Freeman* article. I was sitting waiting for a little girl who came daily with a big pitcher to draw water from the well in the vineyard; she always came shouting the same ballad at the top of a raucous voice, very like that in which I had once sung 'Clementine' in Stirling High Street, and I was trying to learn the verses of her song, which began:

O figlia mia, che cos' ha fatto,
Che tutt' il mondo dice mal di te?

I had memorized it as far as a triumphant climax:

Ma la prigione e fond' e oscura.
E fond' e oscura ma non mi fa paura.

Holms came unexpectedly up to me and in his silkiest voice said: 'I hope you don't mind my mentioning it, Willa, but how is it I never see you washing or darning Edwin's socks the way Dorothy does mine?'

I did not let even the flicker of a smile show on my face as I answered, in the patient voice of a governess instructing an inquisitive child: 'Well, you see, Edwin doesn't have horribly sweaty feet like yours and so doesn't need to wear fine woollen socks or have them washed every day.' (I knew about the sweaty feet because Dorothy had complained to me.) Holms withdrew as noiselessly as he had come. I had already taken myself down so many pegs that this attempt of his to take me down a peg only left me marvelling at the means he thought suitable for achieving it. A saying which I had heard attributed to Sir Richard Burton came unbidden into my mind: 'Servants are rare and costly; it is cheaper and more comfortable to marry them.' At this moment the little girl arrived within earshot, bawling:

Io vogli' amare quel giovinotto
Chi a sofferto la prigione per me.

How much more like True Love that was, I thought, beginning to have a quiet laugh to myself, than the Burton-Holms version.

Amusing as it was, I did not tell Edwin about this conversation until long after we had left Italy. I had no wish to make mischief between him and Holms, not for Holms's sake but for Edwin's. Remembering his yearning for serenity and an unfurrowed brow, I thought that Edwin needed serenity if he were to become what he wanted to become and write the poetry he wanted to write, and he needed it now above all if he were to get back his trust in himself. I rather needed it too, if I were to trust myself more and mistrust the Universe less, which I supposed might happen in its own good time. We both needed a relatively placid life, until our nerves and feelings were steadier.

The remarkable thing was that in these exotic surroundings we did lead a placid day-to-day life. Exotic, to us, the setting was: blue sky without a cloud, warm sea, hot sand, umbrella pines, and the choice of what grapes we preferred for breakfast from among the vine-rows: colombano, fragola, or muscatello. Yet we soon took it all for granted. We domesticated even the handsome stray cat we had befriended, who lived in a hole on the edge of a nearby wood. She came so often into the Proprieta, always leaving at a run with a live lizard hanging helplessly between her jaws, that I surmised a litter of kittens and followed her one day. There was one kitten, the most beautiful I have ever seen, a grey Persian like the mother, bright, fierce and untouchable. I bought sardines for Micino the cat after that, to save some lizards' lives, and persuaded Teresa to buy inferior bits of beef for her. Teresa was surprised but intelligent: ah yes, she said, meat 'un po piu andante'. Edwin and I came upon Micino and her kitten killing a big grass-snake one morning: Micino's teeth were fixed in the back of its head and the kitten's in its tail. When the snake was dead they began to eat it companionably, Micino from the head down, the kitten from the tail up.

Much of our placidity came from the inert hours we spent on the beach, bathing and dreaming by turns. The sand was so hot that salt water dried on one's body in a few minutes, while the water at the edge of the sea was as tepid as new milk. If one stood in that warm water a semicircle of sardines took up station before either leg, noses pointing inwards, tails gently balancing, silver slips of curiosity wondering what these white pillars might be. The water was pellucid even in the deeper reaches and every starfish and shell showed on the bottom. I usually swam out hunting for a cool current, and when I found one, stayed in it.

In this favourable sea I set about teaching Edwin to swim. The first time he trusted himself entirely to the water and lay floating on his back his face looked as illumined as when he had his first visions. That moment gave us both a lift of joy in the heart. He was soon able to turn over and swim breast stroke, but he always returned to floating on his back, paddling gently and gazing into the sky. In the Tyrrhenian sea he began to recover his inner peace.

Mussolini was already in power; we had heard rumours of Fascisti in the north forcibly administering castor-oil to their opponents, but in our neighbourhood there was no sign of them. As the summer wore on, the beach filled up with fashionable holiday-makers and the price of food steadily rose. We found that we were at the socially exclusive end of the beach; the shelter next to ours was now occupied by Queen Elizabeth of the Belgians and her son and daughter, but we did not exploit the chance of splashing sea-water over a Royal Family; we took them for granted too.

Even our meals under the pergola were peaceful. Holms reserved his dissertations and monologues for dinner-time in Forte del Marmi, helped out by *vino nero*. At breakfast or luncheon he rarely uttered more than an affirmative answer to Dorothy's daily queries: 'Yes, darling, I should like another egg.' Towards evening he began to wake up and sometimes ruffled both of us by interposing himself between us and anything we were looking at. He was a monopolist: he could not bear to have other people's sensibilities usurping a landscape already monopolized by his. Yet when we all went on several days' walking excursion among the mountains, I was glad to discover that both he and Dorothy were pleasanter to be with when they were on the move. The inertia of the beach seemed to be as bad for them as it was good for Edwin and me; they needed movement.

F. G. Scott, the Glasgow musician, was going to the Music Festival in Salzburg in August and wrote urging Edwin to join him for that fortnight. Edwin proposed that he and I should first spend a week together in Florence; from there he could go on to Salzburg, which he would very much like to do, he said. I was glad to agree, and we quartered ourselves in a hotel which was very old—I think it was called the Hotel Porta Rossa—an ancient building going back to the fourteenth century. I mention it because there Edwin had another of his extraordinary encounters with unconscious forces, as unexpected as it was alarming. On our first night he had a vivid dream; he was standing outside the palazzo lurking in the shadow of a small archway, dressed in close-fitting black like a page, with a dagger in his hand and hatred in his heart, listening for the footsteps of a man he meant to kill. Taut with suspense, he leapt out when the man came along and drove the dagger into his breast so that blood spurted out over his hand; this woke him up. It was a terrifying dream to Edwin, because of the intensity of hatred in it, and the blood, but it became more terrifying when it recurred on the second night and again on the third night, repeating itself exactly in every particular. We wondered if it could have been an actual occurrence centuries earlier which Edwin had somehow tuned into and could not get away from. We had to get away from that hotel, anyhow, because he felt he could not stand any more of the dream, and as long as he slept there he was apparently doomed to enact it. In fact, once we left the hotel the dream did not trouble him again.

I could not help wondering whether it might not also be a therapeutic dream, a vehicle for ridding Edwin of repressed hatred, but I did not suggest this to him since I could not tell whether it might be hatred of me, or of himself, and had no wish to stir up these possibilities. In any case, although the dream made him feel ill at the time, he was much improved in spirits later and went off to Salzburg quite gaily.

For a week the Holmses had been left to themselves and this was apparently not good for them. The very first night I came back I was roused by screams from their bedroom and, as I started up, Dorothy came rushing in, shaking with sobs and hysteria. She had just thrown a heavy carafe of water at Holms's head and her bed was soaking wet; could she come in beside me? I soothed her as best I could until she stopped shivering and sobbing; then she began recounting her grievances against Holms, the head and front of which was that he had promised her an easy life if she would give up her other admirer and go off with him, and all she had got from it was 'bitter, grinding poverty'. This she repeated again and again, 'bitter, grinding poverty', in a tone of dry ferocity.

I still had much to learn about being a woman, but I did not realize it, and so I despised Dorothy in my heart for expecting nothing else than to be kept in comfort like a pet animal by some partner or other. If you could call such an association a partnership, I said to myself with disdain. Admittedly I was being a kept woman myself at the moment and had no right to despise Dorothy, but I had at least tried to earn some money. (I had written several sketches of our experiences in Prague and Hellerau and sent them to an agent in London; they had all come back; nobody wanted them.) I was sorry for Dorothy, none the less, and patted her silently; if she had no idea what partnership could mean, neither did Holms.

Holms spent the rest of that night lying out in the wood; at least, that was where he was in the morning. He lay about (sulking, said Dorothy) for the fortnight of Edwin's absence while Dorothy kept close to me: the dinners in Forte dei Marmi became ordeals. On Edwin's arrival the atmosphere changed, literally as well as psychologically, for the hot weather broke and we ran out to exclaim in joy at the sight of real puddles of rain. I knew that Edwin was as glad to see me as I was to see him; he seemed very nearly himself again. He had been much taken with Salzburg and said that was where we should go when we left Forte dei Marmi in October. But first, he and I might have a look round Tuscany.

We came to Lucca on the fourteenth of September, the annual fiesta of the Black Christ, a day of comprehensive celebration, including religious processions and services, three equestrian circuses and all the fun of a fair. For us, brought up in the narrowness of Scottish Sabbatarianism, it was a revelation of how the whole fullness of life can be taken as pleasing to God, deep religious devotion being entirely compatible with high enjoyment on swings and roundabouts. Edwin has described the fiesta but I wish to mention something he omitted, the graceful tact he showed, and my lack of it, when we joined the queue forming up to pass before the Black Christ, an ancient wooden statue brought out on this one day in the year and set up at the east end of the church, with a priest standing by. We had gathered that the housewives of Lucca were bringing their keys and jewels to be dipped in holy water by the priest and drawn over the Christ's feet, so that they might be blessed for the coming year, but we had not realized that each applicant for a blessing also kissed the Christ's big toe. As we reached the statue, Edwin bowed as if to kiss, but contented himself with looking keenly at the carving of the feet; it was my turn next and to my own surprise I could not bend my back to do even that: dourly upright I stalked on. I was chagrined at my being so stiff-necked, so ungracious, so unparticipating. On this occasion Edwin's unconscious was clearly in harmony with his conscious intention, and mine was not: my back would not bend even when I told it to. I felt that my unconscious had behaved badly.

At luncheon after this we drank an amber-coloured wine, Orvieto, the first time we had met it, and did not realize until we got up how potent it was. It made us very happy and, despite my *gaffe* in the church, I enjoyed the rest of that day in Lucca.

Early in October we went into Austria, to Salzburg, without the Holmses.

Chapter Nine

AUSTRIA

October 1923 - May /June 1924

In Salzburg we had an immediate sense of freedom. From our very first evening, strolling by the Salzach, I was aware of complete harmony between us. If I felt free, so did Edwin. This may have come partly from our no longer being hemmed in by Holms's monopolizing personality, but its more profound cause was Edwin's being at ease with himself at last. Whatever he had done with the Gerda incident he had now got the better of it. So had I. The thought of Gerda herself had not troubled me; I did not even resent her, for I believed she was just a sentimental goose indulging a 'hopeless passion' for Edwin. What had baffled and worried me was Edwin's transformation into another kind of person, even though I kept telling myself that it must be a flash-back to an earlier Glasgow phase. But I had stopped turning it over in my mind since I had convinced myself that for Edwin I was not after all a transient love, that the bond between us looked like lasting. I felt, too, that he had become aware that I would never encroach upon his inner freedom; his deep dread of that encroachment I believed had been exorcized, once for all. The Gerda incident was important in our marriage, helping it to become a more conscious partnership; it had in a way wakened us up, so that we were now looking at each other with the opened eye of the mind. Fortunately, we each liked what we saw.

Perhaps Hugo von Hofmannsthal, whom we were reading at the time, was responsible for our feeling that the countryside and its traditionally devout peasantry came as close to Salzburg as the little tree-clad hills in and around it, the Mönchsberg, the Kapuzinerberg and the Gaisberg. I still have the impression that for all its formal baroque grace Salzburg appeared to us then as a country town. All the more appropriate seemed the big turnip carved on so many wall-spaces in the castle that commanded the town from its high rock beside the river, a healthy country turnip with fine shaws and a long root, the coat-of-arms adopted by a Prince-Bishop of peasant origin who flaunted it wherever he could to annoy other members of the snobbish hierarchy.

The same hierarchy, we knew, had treated Mozart as a lackey, so that he was unhappy in Salzburg, and yet we could think of Mozart as 'belonging' to this graceful town. Here I first realized how many buildings in Prague were Austrian in style, both inside and out, and that the jostling pavement crowds in Prague had been a little at odds with much of their city, since they had rustic un-Austrian manners. For although Salzburg struck us as a country town its manners were by no means rustic; one did not expect to be elbowed off the pavement in its streets, as sometimes happened in Prague, or to be startled in a tram by the head of a live goose peering over one's shoulder.

The Austrian atmosphere was more amusing and permissive than that of Dresden. The modest lodgings we found provided no bath and so we went, as recommended, to the municipal baths, which surprised us. Any of Schnitzler's amorous couples would have found them an ideal rendezvous. No one asked us to prove that we were married; we were passed at once into a large room in which a spacious bath was sunk, a warm little swimming-pool edged with marble; beside it a sofa and two armchairs stood waiting round a coffee table. We had only to ring for coffee or beer or cigarettes, wrapped in huge towels as we lounged, a most comfortable arrangement which we naturally decided was 'very Austrian'.

Again, in the pretty municipal theatre we enjoyed an experience we never had in a Dresden theatre. I remember in Dresden one character in a play saying in sad, earnest tones to another—Melancthon, I think: 'Sei tiefer, Philipp, sei tiefer!' (Be more profound, Philip!), at which no one else was moved to laughter while Edwin and I were hard put to it to repress ours. In Salzburg we had the pleasure of sharing in the reactions of an audience wholly abandoned to laughing at solemn nonsense presented on the stage. The occasion was a show given by the Rudolf Steiner dancers, produced by Steiner's widow and lavishly billed beforehand. Believing that we knew something about dancing of this kind, after Hellerau, we went to see it on an afternoon which was the local weekly half-holiday, so that the theatre was full. A troop of barefoot girls filed on to the stage in what looked like white nightgowns while Frau Steiner throned herself in the right-hand stage box. Presently her fruity voice, thrilling with emotion, called on April to laugh her girlish laughter: 'Frühling, Frühling, lach' dein kindisch Lachen.' The girls on the stage ran and leaped in all directions, shrilling their girlish laughter, and, the moment after, wilted into a disconsolate group that reminded me of the Kipling simile, 'a decayed aloe clump'. There was no choreography. Each girl leaped and gestured and mimed as seemed good to her. One ought to have been pleased by so much spontaneity, but the spectacle grew wilder and funnier, and Frau Steiner's voice sounded more and more bogus. Not only Edwin and I but everyone around us began to giggle until uncontrollable laughter rocked the whole house.

So we were receptive and gay in Salzburg. Yet the experiences that sank into us remained unexamined where they did not correspond to our preconceptions—a common human failing. Because we loved Salzburg and idealized the Austrian peasantry, finding wonderfully endearing such names as Hans Gmachl, the cobbler in the nearby village of Gnigl, we did not appreciate that there was a dark side to Austrian traditions. Edwin has mentioned the anti-Semitic newspaper he picked up in a cafe, *The Iron Broom*, filled with crude insults that libelled by name actual Jews living in Salzburg; this gutter rag amazed and shocked us but we did not think of taking it seriously. Yet it represented the kind of poisonous stuff that Hans Gmachl of Gnigl was probably fed on and that Hitler was fed on as he grew up. But we did not look at it with the eye of the mind, not then, not until long afterwards.

In the same way we did not really look at another tradition, the Krampuses who accompany Santa Claus on December Sixth, the day when Austrian children get their Christmas presents. We met the Krampuses in Badgastein, where we paid a visit to a married acquaintance of mine, once German mistress in a school where I was Classical mistress. The atmosphere of Badgastein was pleasing; we liked being greeted with a 'Grüss Gott' by everyone we met outside in the crisp new-fallen snow. Special arrangements were made for us to have radio-active baths, although these were officially closed since it was not 'the season'; Edwin and I wallowed in bubbling, streaky green water and came out feeling exhilarated. On December sixth we went with our host, got up as Santa Claus, on a round of visits among neighbouring families; he was accompanied also by two Krampuses, attendant devils with blackened faces, great antlers on their heads and yards of clanking heavy chains round their middles and in their hands. They were only local young men dressed for the part but they looked sinister enough and sounded more so as they roared and rattled their chains. I asked what the Krampuses were for and was told: 'to frighten naughty children'.

In the first house we visited were two small boys, the younger looking not more than five years old. The Krampuses obviously terrified them although Santa Claus, beneficent in red robe and white beard, waved the creatures back and kept them behind him. School exercise-books and reports were produced by the parents and handed to Santa Claus who studied them gravely, asking: 'And have the children been good all the year and done their lessons well and been obedient?' The two little boys stood there trembling while the Krampuses made snatches at them, ducking under the arms of Santa Claus with much growling and clanking. The parents protested that the children had been good, very good, and Santa Claus shut the exercise-books, saying: 'Yes, I see they have been very good indeed.' With howls of disappointment the Krampuses retreated; the children were then patted on the head and given sweets and presents.

Undoubtedly the Krampuses were interesting survivals from an older tradition. The Catholic Church had turned them into the familiar devils of Christendom, but they belonged to a more ancient order of spirits, very like Herne the Hunter who rattled his chains and his horns round the old oak in *The Merry Wives of Windsor*. Yet Edwin and I were made uneasy by finding demonology of this kind still surviving in practice. Neither of us liked the idea of frightening little children into 'good' behaviour.

'Oh,' said our host later, 'children enjoy being frightened when they're in no real danger. They know quite well that they're going to get their presents.'

'It's a thrill for them,' said one of the Krampuses. 'I remember looking forward to it when I was a kid.'

'Better to have real Krampuses to be frightened of than imaginary bogeys,' insisted the other Krampus.

'I don't know how we'd ever keep our children in order if it wasn't for the Krampuses,' said a parent, laughing.

That seemed to be the last word on the subject, so we bypassed the Krampuses. We did not look at them with understanding until the merging of Austria and Germany in the Anschluss, when we realized that beneath Austrian charm lay a deeply-rooted tradition of authoritarianism backed by terror.

Meanwhile strange things were happening in Saxony, which we thought of as inhabited by a collectively simple race; it had staged a Communist Putsch. We could not reconcile this fact with what we remembered of Dresden. Yet Otto Neustatter had said about Saxon industrial towns like Zwickau and Chemnitz, where he made official visits, that they were horrible places, and the inflation was bound to have made people both desperate and more than gullible if they were indeed collectively simple. Neill had had to transport his school to Austria, since parents would not send their children into a Communist *milieu*. I think he chose Austria because Vienna was the great centre for psycho-analysis and he had friends there. From a Youth Organization he had secured quarters in a building the government had assigned to it, on top of a mountain in Lower Austria, the Sonntagberg or Sunday Mountain, from which a miraculous spring of water was said to have bogged the Turks' horses when they were besieging Vienna, in 1683.

We wanted to be in Vienna for Christmas, so I wrote to Neill asking about a cheap hotel he could recommend; that was how we came to spend a few days in the Viennese Jewish quarter. On our first day there, a Saturday, the street outside was filled with groups of male Jews, mostly in caftans, with ritual curls above their ears, fur hats and fuzzy beards, like figures from the Middle Ages, probably Chassidim from Galicia cast up by the war. We soon realized, as we crossed to and fro over the bridge dividing this quarter, the Fourth District, from the centre of Vienna that these outlandish figures were segregated in a kind of ghetto, that they did not 'belong'. Yet we did not then understand that to be governed by an authoritarian hierarchy is desperately oppressive if one does not 'belong'. The Austrian children who were terrified by the Krampuses at least had a sense of being protected because they 'belonged' to their families; these Jews segregated in Vienna could not have been sustained by any sense of 'belonging' to the Austrian family.

Among our Viennese acquaintances, intelligent professional people, we then met some with an obsession against Jews. This seemed more shocking than the gutter insults of the Salzburg *Iron Broom* because it was fully conscious, buttressed by would-be intellectual arguments. Something as absurd as the Russian Protocols of Zion must have made the basis of their insane logic. They proved to us that all subversive minds were Jewish, therefore Bernard Shaw was of course a Jew and, equally of course, Ramsay MacDonald. Bernard Shaw was a red-head as well, clearly a Judas type. Goebbels later provided another clinching argument against Highlanders like Ramsay Mac-Donald: they came from the Hebrides, the Hebrew islands.

We by-passed this nonsense, as we had by-passed the Krampuses, because we were busy discovering Vienna and, despite noticing some obvious signs of misery here and there, appreciating what we discovered. There was still some gaiety in central Vienna then, and enough glitter to impress unsophisticated people like us. At the Volks-Oper we heard for the first time in our lives the whole of *The Ring*. Our hearts being already given to Mozart and Schubert, we went to *The Ring* out of plain curiosity and found that we were not destined to become Wagner addicts. Once our curiosity was satisfied, anyhow, *The Ring* faded from our minds like an evanescent dream, leaving only a blur of melodic themes. At the main opera we enjoyed our Mozart, and on two occasions went to gala evenings there when impressively grand personages filled the house. A ball in the Redouten-Saale provided an evening of sheer delight; waltzing through the rococo suites under crystal chandeliers we decided that Vienna was more civilized than Berlin, where we had seen people dancing the Black Bottom in cellar night-clubs. ('Haben Sie je ge-BlackBottomed, gnädige Frau?' I was asked in Berlin—surely a remarkable word coinage.) But the most entrancing show in Vienna was a performance of *Cosi fan Tutte* given in the small theatre of the Hofburg, an ideal setting for it.

I mention these diversions to account for the spell Vienna cast upon us. We did not feel like tourists. We had our regular table at a restaurant in the Alser-Strasse where we lunched every day with a group of American writers we had come to know, a married couple, an unmarried couple and two bachelors. One of the bachelors was constructing a symbolic novel around the theme of a great, circular staircase, but was himself twisted round the little finger of a Hungarian cabaret star, a dark-eyed, vivid beauty, much oftener than he twisted his story round the staircase. The other bachelor, a man who walked at a backward slant on his heels, studied matrimonial advertisements in the Viennese newspapers and sometimes, after much consultation over the luncheon table, risked answering them, only to recoil in panic when a personal meeting became imminent. The restaurant proprietor had good American apple-pie on the menu every day for the benefit of the many young American doctors attending the clinics in the big hospitals across the way, clinics then famous for the diagnostic skill of the physicians who ran them.

Some of these young American doctors were lodging in our boarding-house, which was convenient for them, being in a small street off the Alser-Strasse, and Fraülein Haüser, the landlady, confided to us that they were Schablone-Menschen, stencil-patterns, stereotypes. They all wore the same suspenders, the same underclothing—B.V.D., what could that mean?— and all asked the same silly questions about Vienna, questions no sensible person would expect to be asked, such as: How fast does the Danube flow past Vienna? How many churches are there in Vienna? How many cafés? How many horses did your Emperor keep in his stables?

We joined Fraulein Hauser in scorning such questions, for we did not understand that these young doctors were harbingers of a new way of thinking in which knowledge was equated with measurement and answers could be given only in numbers. The Viennese did not think in these terms and neither did we.

In what terms did the Viennese then think? Not in a stream-lined way, certainly. The top-heavy ornamentation imposed on the Austrian structure by the Imperial and Royal Court seemed to have been loyally copied through all levels, down to styles in furniture and daily shopping. All the big pieces of furniture we saw, wardrobes and such-like, were heavily encrusted on top with baroque curlicues, and all social relations were loaded with verbal curlicues.

After getting to know our literary American friends, who were quite unlike the stereotyped young doctors, and a delightful woman from Seattle next door to us in the boarding-house, who was unlike anyone we had ever met, we did manage to understand that 'American', a descriptive term unthinkingly applied only to citizens of the United States, was merely a blanket word covering a complex variety of human beings. Sarah from Seattle, for instance, was in her sixties, but had the fresh emotions of a sixteen-year-old. A recent widow, she had made a sentimental journey to Vienna where forty years earlier she and her husband spent part of an idyllic honeymoon. To give herself an occupation she was taking singing lessons, although, as she said, she would do better as a foghorn than as a singer. A young American diplomat of her acquaintance was squiring her round; he was young enough to be her son but she blushed like a girl as she told us he wanted her to go mountain-climbing with him, and would it be O.K. for her to spend a night with him in a mountain hut?

Sarah's turns of speech were novel to us and we relished them. One day she picked up a book lying on our table, an advance copy of Edwin's prose pieces, mostly from *The Freeman*, which were just being published under the title Latitudes. 'My,' said Sarah, 'did Mr Muir write all this out of his own haid?' Then she told us that though she herself was a pin-head she had a very, very clever friend at home who was the Governor of a State and that this book would be raw meat to him. On another day when she was in bed with a cold and I took in a cup of tea for her, she asked me: 'Why doesn't Mr Muir come in to see me?' I suggested that he might be shy of coming into her bedroom, 'Tell Mr Muir,' said Sarah, looking again as if she were about sixteen despite a plait of grey hair over each shoulder, 'that if he comes into my bedroom he'll be as safe as if he were in God's pocket.'

In Vienna we tried to do as the Viennese did. While the snow was still on the ground we went to Baden for a week to practice ski-ing and progressed as far as being able to avoid a tree without falling down. One midnight we went to see a performance of *Miss Julie*, where the name-part was taken by a slinky serpent in clinging black velvet—a slimy, horrible play, we thought it—and one afternoon we attended a performance of Toller's *Der Deutsche Hinkemann*, where the whole theatre, not only the stage, provided the melodrama, since the audience was tense with apprehensive expectation that some German Nationalist would loose off a revolver at the actors, as duly happened. There was full 'audience participation' according to Marinetti's doctrine, and the result was the most exciting theatrical experience I have ever known, although the play was not very good and I had never seen actors so anxious to avoid the limelight.

In the middle of these activities, about Easter, a letter arrived from *The Freeman* to say that it was going to suspend publication, since its three-year guarantee was not to be renewed. No more *Freeman* meant no more dollars. This was an unexpected blow. We had a little money in hand but not enough to take us back to England, not enough to go on living in Vienna, not even enough to keep us going for a while in some provincial town. Almost at once my thoughts turned to Neill's school on the Sunday Mountain; perhaps I could help there again, and Neill might let us stay until we found a way of earning money? Only Neill's school had survived from Hellerau: the Eurhythmic students had been dispersed. Frau Doktor was with Neill, and there would be one or two other familiar faces.

Edwin and I were now on such confident, open-hearted terms that I had no hesitation in putting the question to him: 'would you mind?' Instead of simply not minding he was eager to go, and so I wrote to Neill begging him to take us in, which he agreed to do. Following his instructions we took a train to Rosenau, a small town at the foot of the mountain, on its north side. A drizzle of fine rain met us which had changed to a blizzard of fine snow by the time we reached the top of the Sonntagberg, a climb of about two and a half hours up a gently winding road made for ox-wagons. An enormous church loomed at the far end of the summit, looking big enough for a cathedral; on the near side of it, following the ridge, was a long yellow-stuccoed building that had once been a monastery. In this ex-monastery Neill and his school were housed on the top floor: the ground floor was occupied by the Youth Organization and a caretaker.

A less suitable place for a 'free' school could not have been chosen, as we were to discover, but our first impressions delighted us. The style of the rooms pleased us, old thick bare walls cut here and there into arches, alcoves, vaulting; and in the morning when we looked south from our windows we were enchanted to find ourselves above a sea of cloud rippled like a mackerel sky, curling and fuming in the rays of the sun. The Sonntagberg was the last small summit in a range of mountains which curved round to the right of us, enclosing the Danube basin. Peaks in a wide semi-circle rose out of the thick white vapours, and later on, when the mists had smoked away, we could see clear for ninety miles across country.

A sea of cloud beneath eye-level has become a commonplace for air travellers, but neither Edwin nor I had ever been so high up before and this was our first gods'-eye view of the earth. I feel that it helped to liberate from Edwin's unconscious a gods'-eye view of humanity. He now continued, with excitement and pleasure, a series of poems, begun much earlier, which he called: *Chorus of the Newly Dead*. An Idiot, a Beggar, a Harlot, a Poet, a Hero and a Mystic severally looked back over their lives on earth; a Chorus commented upon each and questioned Those who had sent them there about the meaning of 'the earth, her multitudes and all her dead'. Edwin says in his Autobiography that it was a theme far too great for his powers. I suspect that it was an almost impossible theme even for a mature poet, which Edwin was not. But he was very happy composing it.

* * *

Here I should like to say something about the relation of Edwin's Fable to his Story at this time. I have emphasized the variety and gaiety of our life in Salzburg and in Vienna because the contrast is great between the Story of these days and the Fable, that is to say, the poems Edwin wrote in Salzburg and on the Sonntagberg.

Among his *First Poems*, 'On the Mediterranean,' is a melancholy poem, but it was written when he was on bad terms with himself in Italy and therefore at odds with his surroundings. Yet in Salzburg, where he was cheerful, he composed 'October at Hellbrünn' and 'Salzburg—November' which have an undertone of gentle sadness; they read like notes made by a child-like, melancholy observer. And after all the fun we had in Vienna why should he turn with such excitement to a poem about the Newly Dead?

I thought at the time that he had returned to this tremendous theme because he had been so gay and forthcoming that he had at last acquired the strength and courage to tackle it. In all our journeyings since leaving London he had been coming more and more out of himself, except for his relapse in Riva, and especially in Vienna had been more continuously present, less absent, than I had yet known him. Metaphors are misleading when one tries to describe the mystery of the human personality, but I should like to say that in Vienna Edwin's conscious self struck me as becoming more luminous, as if it were being strengthened by energies formerly repressed which were now finding their way into the open, after having made a turmoil within him for many years.

The material, if I may call it that, which he was now shaping on the Sonntagberg was made up of painful emotions which had been working like yeast inside him ever since those first five years in Glasgow when his father, his two brothers, his mother had died one after the other. The deaths of his brothers in especial seemed so arbitrary, so meaningless, that he could not 'get over' them. In the last years of his life he wrote a beautiful poem about them, which was the final expression of that painful complex, but it took a lifetime to achieve. In the *Chorus of the Newly Dead* he was making his first poetic attempt to come to terms with Death by looking for a transcendental meaning in Life.

The gentle sadness in the little Salzburg poems, as in the Prague poems, when he was really beginning to look with new eyes at the outside world and at himself, was, so to speak, the first trickling-out of past unhappiness. At this stage, then, the Fable reached into bygone experiences which did not spring from the immediate Story. The Fable, if I may put it like that, was still too strong for the

Story. In later life they caught up with each other and there was a better balance in his make-up, to the benefit of his poetry.

Indeed, his attitude to this earliest work of his became sternly disapproving. I have his own copy of *First Poems*—by the way, the P.W. to whom they were dedicated was Peerie Willa—and it is filled with comments and revisions he made years later when he was deciding which of them, if any, deserved inclusion in his Collected Poems. Most of the poems are stigmatized as 'Bad', or 'Very bad', while 'On the Mediterranean' is simply written off as 'Awful!'

Up on the Sonntagberg I had more leisure than in Hellerau, since Neill had already procured an assistant teacher, a Welsh-woman always referred to as 'Jonesie', and there was less need of my help. Edwin and I were able to go exploring our surroundings together. We discovered that the great Church of the Holy Trinity had an array of statues behind it, nearly all of the Holy Trinity, blistered, lichened, weather-beaten statues disposed outside in the open, showing God the Father holding up the Son by both arms in front of Him, while the Dove in front of the Son represented the Holy Ghost, its wings spread out where the Son's phallus should have been. Below these statues stretched wide slopes of short sweet turf on which as the spring advanced battalions of flowers suddenly appeared. To see innumerable flowers growing wild has always given me a sense of glory. In the Italian mountains there had been a field of dark-blue columbines, swathes of sweet williams and a whole hillside covered with orange lilies; here, on the Sonntagberg, there came now a glory of spring blossoms, multitudinous ranks of primulas, deep blue pools of gentians.

At the end of the summit, beyond the church, were pine-woods gently descending; in front of the church, which had a stately approach of nearly a hundred steps, lay the few cottages of the village, including one small shop which sold only cheap ecclesiastical souvenirs and rosaries. But we saw no less than three enormous inns. Not until the first batch of pilgrims arrived sometime in April did we understand why they should be there. Past the village, towards the Rosenau road, there was a pond. Among the cottages before reaching the pond a footpath began which went down the south side of the mountain to Waidhofen-an-der-Ybbs, which was in Rothschild country, a well-tended and pretty little town. The descent to Rosenau was easier and we went that way for a hair-cut, stamps or cigarettes, but often enough, impelled by sheer greed, scrambled down the rocky footpath to Waidhofen for the pleasure of eating fresh trout with melted butter and great bowls of wild strawberries. Rosenau, for all its railway station and post office, was a less civilized place than Waidhofen.

The pilgrims came up the Rosenau road, but their bands did not begin to play until they reached the village pond. Their reception by the officiating priest varied according to the fee paid, so the caretaker told us. For the larger fee priest and acolytes went as far as the pond to meet the pilgrims; for the smaller fee they merely stood waiting at the head of the church flight of steps, which the more pious pilgrims ascended on their knees. Neill is my authority for stating that the whole pilgrimage knocked four hundred days off Purgatory. I cannot help feeling that this may be an over-estimate.

It was usually about five in the morning when the pilgrims arrived, singing to a slow, dolorous tune:

Heil dem Vater und dem Sohn,
Und dem heiligen Dritte Person,
Hei-ei-ei-ei-lig.

The chanting and the band playing—often brass bands— woke us up and we hung out of our windows to watch and listen. After a ceremony in the church there was great feasting and drinking in the inns. Pilgrims who could not afford inn beds spread mattresses behind hedges, and a good time was had by all.

Neill and Frau Doktor fed, warmed and housed Edwin and me, but what I did to help in the school was no sufficient return for their kindness. Providentially, we were soon delivered from our penniless state and could pay our debts to them. Out of the blue a cable arrived from Ben Huebsch, the publisher in New York, asking if we would translate three of Gerhart Hauptmann's plays into English blank verse at a hundred dollars a play. We returned an answer of two words, all we could afford: Yes, Muir.

Only a year earlier I should have put down this miracle to the credit of the Universe. Now I wondered if Louis Untermeyer, whom I had chanced to meet in Kärntner-Strasse the day the bad news came about *The Freeman* and to whom I had confided it, had stirred up Huebsch to this good deed. Ben Huebsch knew about Edwin, for he had just been getting ready to publish *Latitudes*, and it was not unlikely that someone should prod him into doing something for us now that *The Freeman* was dead. We were profoundly grateful. Yet it did not occur to me that in thanking Louis Untermeyer in my heart I was still giving the credit to Providence although at one or two removes. The miracle remained a miracle, none the less.

The three plays arrived and we started gaily on *Der Weisse Heiland*. I was pleased because this was something I felt I could do; I did not know why I had not thought of it before as a possible means of earning money. The many years I had spent translating Greek and Latin into English gave me a sense of competence; I was well trained in accuracy, at least, and that was all to the good, for Edwin's interpretations tended to be wild and gay. We hammered out our blank verse and it was rhythmical enough, but I should not care today to be faced with these translations. When we had finished all three plays and got three hundred dollars we were Rich, with a capital R.

An urgent message now came from the U.S.A. begging Edwin to provide information about himself for a publicity campaign to launch his book *Latitudes*. The mere thought of advertising himself embarrassed Edwin; he disdained to do anything of the kind and was going to refuse altogether when I chipped in, saying: what a lark to provide one's own publicity, and why not? I did not disdain it, although not going so far as to take it seriously, and suggested that if he were to wash his hands of it why shouldn't I send some information? Edwin laughed and bade me do my worst. Which I did, in a letter. Neither of us expected to see my concoction in cold print, just as it was.

Now, forty-two years later, a researcher in America has sent me a copy of that letter, which appeared in *The Bookman* in July 1924, asking if I really did write it? The description of Edwin was accurate within its limits, although flippant, naughty, and fairly useless as publicity, so here it is:

Edwin Muir lived on a small island containing one tree (known as The Tree) until he was fourteen, avoiding school, ostensibly herding his father's cows (i.e., dreaming in the pasture while they ravaged the corn and turnips), and being spoiled by his mother because he was the youngest.

At the age of fourteen he went to Glasgow: saw trains and street cars for the first time in his life, learned to use a knife and fork and to wash daily. Attended church and was twice 'saved' before he struck Pascal and Nietzsche. Acquired a minute knowledge of the seamy side of Glasgow life, and a remarkable vocabulary. Developed a natural gift for 'contradictiousness'.

Wrote his first book *We Moderns* in the office (during office hours) without being discovered by his employers. Notoriously unpunctual, but seldom brought to book, because his fellow clerks spoiled him a little, just as his mother did. Received brilliant testimonials when he left to go to London, certifying that he could above all things be trusted with cash.

Went to London with sixty dollars, abetted by his wife, a reckless woman from the Shetland Islands, with whom he speaks in the barbarous dialect of these regions. In London learned to choose wines and order dinners in Soho: escaped whenever possible to the country for weekends.

Went to Prague because it was in the middle of Europe and he knew nothing about it. Perhaps also because he could speak neither German nor Czech. After eight months of Prague, he went to Germany, and succumbed to its influence completely. Stayed there for a year, began to write poetry, take sun baths, and wear sandals. Tried Italy next, and learned to swim: but driven by a longing for the north (disguised Mother complex) returned to Salzburg and to Vienna. Can't live in a city in springtime: and so is at present marooned on a mountain in lower Austria. Future movements completely uncertain.

Personal Characteristics. Gives a general impression of quietness, gentle kindliness, and a little reserve. Black hair, blue eyes. Very slim, small hands and feet, looks ridiculously young and won't say how old he is. Has an enormous forehead, like a sperm whale's: a fastidious, fleering and critical nose: an impish and sensuous mouth, a detached, aloof, cold eye. Witty when at his ease: elegant when he can afford it: sensitive and considerate: horribly shy and silent before strangers, and positively scared by social functions. Among friends, however, becomes completely daft, and dances Scottish reels with fervor. Smokes cigarettes continually: likes to lie in the sun by the hour; enjoys being petted: and is loved by cats, dogs, small children, and nearly all women. (Women always want to mother him when they see him: but he has a horror of having his independence encroached upon.)

Passionately devoted to football, although now too short-sighted to play. Watches football matches happily for hours.

An unusual combination of clear thinking and passionate intuition.

Has a very Scottish look about him (!) but has been mistaken for Irish and Russian.

This is a true and (I believe) unprejudiced portrait.

Meanwhile we were at last becoming aware that there was a dark side to the Austrian peasantry and that whatever came out of the unconscious was not necessarily good. The Sonntagberg was a holy mountain and the village people, being Catholics who made a living from that holiness, looked on us all with great suspicion, since we were foreigners, aliens who never went to church and were certainly heretics if not altogether godless. Our friendly manners did not disarm them and their suspicions deepened into hostility. The first overt act of hostility was the filling of the village pond with broken glass and crockery, so that our pupils had to go all the way down to the river Ybbs for a swim. From the caretaker Neill then learned that the village accused us of indulging in illicit sexual relations between pupils and teachers; pupils had been seen, they said, climbing naked over the balconies into staff bedrooms. The next stage must have been a complaint lodged in some local office of the Education Ministry, for one day a gendarme arrived with a fixed bayonet and a questionnaire for Neill to answer, a comprehensive document based on the official regulations for village schools enshrined in a Schul-gesetz dating back to the middle of the nineteenth century.

All male pupils had to have so-and-so many hours of physical instruction weekly: the gendarme wanted to know what Heir Neill was doing about that? All female pupils had to have so-and-so many hours of domestic instruction weekly: was Heir Neill complying with that regulation? And so on. Neill refused to provide any answers or to accept the document, which was infuriating enough without the fixed bayonet attending it. He and Frau Doktor began to make up their minds to shift the school to England.

Edwin and I, who now had money enough to travel, decided to go with them. We felt it was time to look at the English scene again. At the end of June the school was dismantled and removed, even the cat, which I carried across Europe wrapped in a woollen scarf and delivered safely to Emma in Hellerau. The Communists had been turned out in Saxony and Otto, like the Vicar of Bray, remained in possession, in his own old house. Frau Doktor and he were on good enough terms with each other but, as she said, the link between them had been broken during her long wartime absence in England and she was now more interested in Neill's school than in Otto. A house was ultimately found for the school in Lyme Regis, a pleasant house called Summerhill, and in 1925 Edwin and I got installed in a flint-knapped cottage in Penn, Buckinghamshire, after a sojourn in Scotland.

Our first European adventure had come to an end.

Chapter Ten

MONTROSE, PENN, MONTROSE

1924, 1925, 1926

Even on our remote Sunday Mountain Edwin had never quite lost touch with London and New York; literary articles and reviews of his were welcomed in the States and he was getting novels to review from London, mostly from The Nation and Athenaeum. One novel, Prince Hempseed, by Stephen Hudson, of whom he knew nothing, he had already reviewed favourably in Vienna, hailing it as the work of a promising young writer, and Sydney Schiff, a man of fifty-four who used Stephen Hudson as a pen-name,was so pleased and tickled by the innocent tribute that he began a friendly correspondence with Edwin which opened a new line of communication with England. Sydney kept the letters Edwin wrote to him between 1924 and 1939, a collection which his nephew has now very kindly let me read, so that I do not depend on memory alone for a record of these years and have had some erroneous dating of mine corrected. Edwin was not infallible in his dating—he told Sydney that we had first gone abroad in 1919—but he was better at calculations and at dating than I was. I used to be amazed at his always knowing how many thousand words he had written in any piece of work, and still more amazed at the certainty with which he estimated the thousands still to write, although I might have had the sense to realize that his years of being a costing-clerk had made him an efficient calculator.

In response to Sydney's friendly probing about what he had done and what he was proposing to do, Edwin confessed to *We Moderns*, which he said was 'in the last degree raw, immature and an expression of a lamentable bad taste'. Then he added that 'in the English edition you will find an appendix of ill-natured couplets full of bumptious conceit'. He mentioned *Latitudes* as being better written and more coherent, and said he was now beginning to compile a volume of critical essays which he thought better than anything he had yet done. This interested Sydney, as it was bound to do, since he was a novelist on the look-out for good literary criticism. I think he was not so interested in Edwin's admission that he had been writing poetry which he had been trying, vainly, to find a publisher for. At this time, especially in the States, Edwin, was gaining some reputation as a critic and literary essayist: he was nowhere known to be a poet, although one or two of his poems had appeared in *The Dial* and *The Nation*.

It had not occurred to Edwin that the demand for his critical work in America should draw him over there; what he wanted was to get a footing, some kind of recognition, in London. But he had no intention of settling in London. He told Sydney that he disliked London and that we were both thirsting for Scotland. This was not owing to a dislike for urban life; after all, we had been living in foreign cities and had been happy in them; but none of these cities was so overwhelmingly large as London, nor had Edwin felt lost in any of them as once in London. It had been easier abroad to get to the opera, theatres or concerts than while we were competing with London crowds, and we did not realize how much it would mean to us to be altogether deprived of them. Meanwhile, we were yearning, each of us, to go on enjoying wide spaces of sky and country, and we still believed whole-heartedly in the legend of Antaeus. So in July 1924 we were headed for Scotland, towards my mother's house in Montrose, although we paused in London to stay with Edwin's old Glasgow friend, Denis Saurat, then the head of the French Institute.

From the moment we set foot on the boat until we came to London we were increasingly surprised by our sense of relief at understanding without effort whatever anyone said or even looked like saying, as if a burden were now lifted. The living bond of a common language, which we had missed in Prague, and to a lesser extent in Dresden, which we had forgotten the lack of in Hellerau, Salzburg and Vienna, now became actual; it was all around us, it was in the air, and its immediate effect was exhilarating. I began to think that the Collective Unconscious was not merely a convenient hypothesis, and we told each other that it was good to come home.

We had not been cutting London down in our minds, yet it loomed larger than we had remembered. Everything in it seemed to be outsize: the hearse-like black taxis, the double-decker buses, the crowds of people, even the neuter cats in shop windows and doorways. We were not quite the same two people who had left it but we might never have been away, everything looked so familiar although large; we almost expected our taxi to turn into Guilford Street instead of the Cromwell Road. The thought crossed my mind fleetingly that Edwin might now feel London to be a safer city than before.

In the French Institute we found waiting for us a pressing invitation from the Schiffs to spend a couple of days with them in Chesham before going north, an invitation we accepted with excited pleasure. That evening Edwin enjoyed meeting his old friend Denis in the familiar Saurat tilting-yard, where we were at once assailed with reproaches for having gone to Europe without visiting France. Denis had a habit of standing on the hearthrug defending his territory like a belligerent robin; I have an affectionate memory of his denouncing the English from that position for being stupidly sentimental about those horrible birds, the cuckoo and the lark. From old habit Edwin returned the attack with spirit, asking why one should go to France at all? Germany, being more undeveloped, had more potentiality in it and was more interesting, even though French literature was the superior.

At that time he did have a bias in favour of the north rather than the south of Europe, and these thrusts of his were not made merely to tease Denis Saurat. In June 1926 he was putting much the same arguments to Sydney Schiff in a letter, although he was then in France, and enjoying it. But when we first went to France he was actually preparing to find that he might want to get out of it again and go farther north.

Our visit to the Schiffs, whom we had never met except on paper, was more than pleasant. My first impression of them was how highly finished they were, compared to us, in dress, manner, sophistication and experience; we must seem very unfinished to them, I thought; but the warmth, the glow of kindness they met us with, brought us out of ourselves to an uncommon degree. Edwin's conscious personality which had seemed luminous in Vienna was now more than luminous; it coruscated. He and Sydney lit each other up. I marvelled at the passion driving each of them as they discussed the making of works of art, the transmutation of experience into structures which they saw as crystalline and immortal. They were both agreed on the need to detach oneself from emotion, and here I could not follow them, for I could never detach myself from my emotions and rise into their immortal world of art. But I was exhilarated by the invisible fireworks they were setting off and at the same time calmed and steadied by Violet, a poised and beautiful woman with far-seeing eyes. Later on I told Edwin that Sydney's eyes, when he took off his spectacles, looked as if they feared to be hurt, so that I felt I had to be kind to him, but Violet's eyes made me nurse the hope that she would be kind to me.

We had here our first glimpse of a world we had never entered. The Schiffs, it appeared, knew all the literary figures of our age, *tout Londres* as well as *tout Paris*. Writers and editors ceased to be merely names and put on flesh and blood, turning into living contemporaries that one might actually meet. This was a quickening experience for Edwin. When we left Chesham he was full of what he called 'a surge of ideas', about the volume of literary essays he was compiling: it was to become a study of contemporary writers seen in relation to the spirit of the age— an age of transition; and the stimulus for this he owed partly to these conversations with Sydney.

The Schiffs said they wanted to see more of us and made the sensible suggestion that we should take a cottage somewhere within reach of London. Our determination to go to Scotland, which had been formed on the Sonntagberg, was still unshaken but we temporized by saying: perhaps we shall, later, take a cottage in the English countryside. Sydney and Violet offered to find one for us when that time came, and so we went off to Scotland feeling that a door had been opened rather than closed.

The eagerness with which we headed for Montrose did not long survive. On the second of August Edwin was already telling Sydney that 'Scotland has been a sad disappointment to us after all the longing we had for it.' What did we expect of Montrose, a dwindling fishing-port with only one mill left of its jute and linen manufactories, though still a market town for the farms around it and a growing holiday centre for summer visitors? The great round of sky, the wide links with their stretches of thyme and eyebright, the wild North Sea beating on sand dunes held together by tough pink liquorice and marram grass, were still as I remembered them; was it not a setting where the wind of the spirit had freedom to blow? I was not flatly disappointed, as Edwin was, and his depression surprised me at first, for I had forgotten that these childhood ways of mine were not his, and I did not yet understand that the secret compass pointing north in his breast really pointed to Orkney. We had room and space enough to work in and we did work; living was cheap since what we paid my mother for our keep did not amount to much; what, then, was lacking?

We lacked a human ambience, vibrations of understanding from the people around us, the responses of a cultivated environment. Edwin and I did not Belong, except to each other. It might be said that in our foreign travels the same held true, but in Europe there had been concerts, theatres, operas, poetry and people interested in the arts. None of my mother's friends in Montrose was interested in the arts. Edwin's conscious intellectual life at this time was strengthening and reaching out, so that he was very aware of his need for stimulation, and after the soaring discourses he had enjoyed with Sydney Schiff the flatness of people's minds in Montrose depressed him. He felt he had been pot-bound in Glasgow and was now afraid of becoming pot-bound again. His comments became barbed and his judgments sharper; he was no longer scrupulous in refraining from attack; he told Sydney that Scotland was 'shut in, unresponsive, acridly resolved not to open out and live'.

This first burst of defensive petulance faded away, since we were ourselves kept busy trying to open out and live. Edwin was tackling the literary essays which appeared later as Transition, and I was thinking out the implications of my inability to detach myself from emotions, which I suspected might be not only a peculiarity of mine but a characteristic of most women. My reasonings on the subject became an essay published in 1925 by the Hogarth Press, called *Women: An Inquiry*.

Besides thinking about Women, I was revising the translation of a Hauptmann play, and later translating a fantastic novel of his: *The*

Island of the Great Mother. From now on, it can be taken for granted that I was always translating something and any other work I did was sandwiched between translations. In the same way Edwin was always writing reviews: all his own work was sandwiched between reviews. If there were a troublesome dead-line for a translation, and if he had time, he helped with it. This was the pattern of our working life until I had our baby. It was rather like subsistence farming, although we did earn ourselves intervals of freedom.

In these intervals the joyous excitement in which the unconscious thrives was plentifully supplied. Edwin, himself in a state of transition, was kept happy in Montrose working out his essays on contemporary literature in an age of transition, and I was following up my inquiry into the nature of Women. I also began teaching him to golf and reverted to old habits of leaping over clumps of gorse on the links and running races along the sands with my mother's collie.

In Montrose, of all places, some time later we first encountered Christopher Grieve, perhaps better known by his pen-name, Hugh MacDiarmid, who had been appointed editor of a local weekly, the *Montrose Review*. He and his fellow-Borderer, F. G. Scott, had already started the ferment of poetry and music with which they meant to regenerate Scotland, then slipping, they felt, into a moribund provincialism. Christopher wrote good modern lyrics in Scots which F. G. set to modern music; then Christopher set himself to getting out, by hook or by crook, magazines which would publicize the new works. Prodded by F. G. Scott, whose enthusiasms were ebullient, Edwin had sent three Scottish Ballads to the first number of *The Scottish Chapbook*, in 1923, and later, for another number, an early, fragmentary version of his *Chorus of the Newly Dead*: but although the two Borderers had generated between them a heat of enthusiasm for Scotland and what they called the 'Scottish Renaissance', Edwin's interest in it was tepid, except that he was fond of F. G. Scott. The Lowland Scottish vernacular was not his vernacular. It was Orkney he spoke, not Lowland Scots or Lallans. In any case, he had already adopted English as his language and preferred to graft his poetry on to the great tree of English literature. Grieve and Scott were involved in a bold but desperate effort to make the Scottish vernacular central for Scotsmen, he felt, although it could not now be anything but marginal. And when Christopher, true to Border feeling, blamed the 'Eng-glish' for the whole of Scotland's backwardness in the arts, Edwin only smiled kindly as if at a little boy squaring up to a bogey.

Christopher and his wife Peggy were living in a council house on the fringe of the town, where Peggy cooked the meals and washed and ironed Christopher's shirts. I noted her efficient ironing with some ruefulness, for I was the world's worst ironer. She was then pregnant with their second child; we thought her most attractive as she stood clinging to Christopher's arm, the day we first met her, looking up shyly through dark eyelashes, with a daisy-like white collarette round her neck, apparently an embodiment of the 'wee wifie' loved by Scotsmen. We noted that she did not care for the housing estate in which they lived: she complained that she had to put extra net curtains across her windows to keep neighbours from peering in. Nor did she like Christopher's susceptibility to whisky.

It was not that Christopher drank a lot of whisky, a very small amount being enough to over-set him, but as the local editor he had to attend farmers' dinners where whisky was the only drink. This inconvenient fact set off domestic crises, one of which we helped to cope with. Calling by chance one evening we found Peggy at her wits' end, Christopher having come home from some farmers' junketing and locked himself into the bathroom, since when there had been neither sound nor movement from him. Peggy was sure he had passed out. Edwin managed to scramble from outside through the high, narrow bathroom window, found Christopher lying mother-naked, cold, insensible but alive in a completely dry bath, and unlocked the door at once. We lugged the poet into the living-room where we laid him on the hearthrug by the fire, covered him with blankets and left him to Peggy's ministrations in that respectable council house.

This respectable background of Christopher's was something we took for granted, but it represents a strand in the lives of each of these wild Borderers, Scott and Grieve, in strong contrast to the rest of the pattern. Scott, belonging to an older generation—he had been Christopher's school-teacher in Langholm—was the more firmly attached to an ideal of respectability, and it was a Victorian ideal. Whenever he had to make an appearance in society he put on a mask of formal Olympian gravity which sometimes did not survive an outburst of his demoniac temperament but often completely disguised him before people who would have better loved the temperament. At home he was a bit of a tyrant, especially to his wife and daughters whom he expected to be conventionally respectable, more so than his sons. He did not approve of 'his' women drinking beer in public, for instance. When Edwin and I lunched with the Scotts in a restaurant Mrs Scott did not dare to have a lager like the rest of us. F. G. wanted a platform of conventional respectability on which to dance his wild fandangos—and wild enough they were. For years he carried on a one-man fight with the Music Department of the Scottish B.B.C., much as an eagle might attack an aeroplane. Again, when he wanted once to try out on the piano a Dance of Pride, one of the Seven Deadly Sins, he was composing, he did so at three in the morning, and to hell with the neighbours. When they retaliated by beating pots and pans outside his house he staged a rival, superior performance, uproariously. He much enjoyed being an *enfant terrible*. Yet he was also a man of most delicate sensibility as appeared in the settings he made to Christopher's lyrics and in his response to all nuances in music and poetry.

Christopher was nearly as pugnacious on paper, and had as delicate a sensibility for poetry, but although still influenced by Scott was not so much swayed by the illusion of respectability. He and Peggy had both been conditioned by serving in the armed forces towards the end of the 1914 war, and had shed a good many conventional inhibitions. Yet at this time Christopher was holding down a respectable steady job and Peggy seemed to be doing all that could be asked of a respectable steady wife. The shock of yellow hair standing on end above Christopher's impressive brow, the restlessness of his eyes, suggested that he might be somewhat unpredictable, but not more so than could be looked for in a poet. Peggy was more completely camouflaged; despite her intelligent-looking forehead one would never have guessed at her future career. No one could have predicted that her 'wee wifie' charm would be so effective as to secure for her a coal business in London, after divorcing Christopher, so that in time she became an authority in the next wartime Ministry of Fuel and Power. Neither Edwin nor I had any inkling of what was to happen to this young Scottish couple, or of the influence Christopher was to wield as political agitator and poet of Scottish Nationalism. And certainly it never dawned on any of us that Scott and Grieve and Muir were all going to become honorary doctors in the course of their lives.

These two Borderers, Scott and Grieve, had a make-up quite unlike Edwin's. He had no wish to fight or 'show off' or score over other people: he had passion, but in him passion aspired towards ecstasy rather than domination; he preferred simplicity in his conduct as well as in his writings, and could never have become a publicist. This difference in temperament separated him from Scotland Grieve's campaign as much as his difference in attitude towards the English language.

Leonard Woolf had made Edwin very happy in September by accepting his *First Poems* for the Hogarth Press, and also by telling him that his book reviews were the best *The Nation* had ever had. The deep satisfaction this gave Edwin increased his desire to get out of Scotland into the more congenial atmosphere of a London neighbourhood. Yet we did not go to Penn, to the cottage the Schiffs had found for us, until January 1925. We were probably short of money for the move, but we were also one after the other struck down by a horrible influenza, which afflicted the back of one's neck like a mild attack of meningitis and left its victims not very able for work.

The cottage was on the outskirts of Penn, at the end of a by-lane that petered out beyond it into a field-path. Penn had an enormous hoarding near its station which said in capital letters 'God First', and yet ours was rather a pagan end of the village, as we learned from the salty gossip of the man who removed our night-soil. Few of the labourers in our lane were living with lawful wives; they meddled neither with Church nor Chapel nor did they expect Church or Chapel to meddle with them. We had fetched up, it appeared, in Darkest England, and our surroundings were primitive as well as pagan. There was no sewage down our way, nor any gas or electricity. Ours was the only dwelling to have piped water laid on; even the public-house opposite drew its water from a well. The village smith, the last of his kind, who had lived and died in our flint-knapped cottage, had not troubled to get a damp-course laid in it, but he left a large, empty smithy close by which made a good enough study to work in once we managed to heat it, although draughts coming through the split door blew smuts all over us at first. In the living-room the old open fireplace gave out smoke rather than heat, until we got a tin hood fitted, and the 'blue flame' paraffin cooker needed constant watching. I hired a daughter of the public-house to carry on the war against smuts while I got ahead with translating work.

None the less, living in Penn, Bucks, suited us better than living in Montrose, because we were in immediate touch with friends in London, old friends like the Saurats and new friends like the Schiffs, who had a house in London as well as Chesham. Edwin even went to a reception given by *The Nation and Athenaeum*, stayed overnight in London with artist friends and to his own surprise enjoyed it all. We felt that we Belonged somewhere again. In fact as spring and summer advanced, we seemed to have the best of both worlds, the city and the country, for the lovely beech woods of Bucks, with their bluebells and rare clusters of white violets, were within reach on foot, and that summer proved to be hot, sunny and dry well into autumn. We were able to work in the smithy with the door wide open, letting in shafts of sunlight.

The improvement in the weather made us feel at home among our own furniture, less like caravanners settled among other gipsies, and we did some landscaping on our estate. A dreary potato-patch stretched from our front door to the by-lane with an elm tree right in the middle of it, and it seemed to us that grass would be an improvement. There was no lack of grass in front of the Baptist chapel next door, far more than was ever attended to, since there was only a meagre congregation of seven or eight, none of whom lived in the lane. Openly, by daylight, a spadeful at a time, we removed Baptist grass to our own frontage until we had a kind of lawn all round the tree; no one said anything and no one interfered.

Our Baptist lawn came in handy for tea-parties. In the brilliant sunshine of that summer many people arrived by car to visit us of an afternoon, and we used to have tea beneath the shady tree with a field-mouse for extra company. Hugh Kingsmill mobilized his friends' cars so that he could be brought to see us, and whole coveys of their friends came too. I began to like Hugh very much, though he was still wary of me; at least, he used to say: 'Willa, I'm sure you are malicious', an uncalled-for aspersion, I thought, although he may have meant it for encouragement, being himself chock-full of highly exaggerated, comic malice.

In June Edwin finished the *Chorus of the Newly Dead* and sent it to Leonard Woolf who accepted it for publication by the Hogarth Press. He was also writing more *Transition* essays, and Sydney was helpful in trying to get these placed in London, putting Edwin in touch with Edgell Rickword, for instance, so that the essay on the Zeit-Geist appeared in *The Calendar of Modern Letters*. Our first meeting with Edgell Rickword was a little disconcerting for some moments, since we did not know that he had a glass eye, and whenever one looked at him the cold, fishy stare from the glass eye was discouraging. But the other eye, mild and beaming with friendliness, soon made its effect: he proved to be someone we liked and were glad to know. Edgell told us that whenever Wyndham Lewis came to the *Calendar* office he would not sit down inside it but had to have a chair set for him outside the door, at the top of the stairs, with its back to the wall, so that he could watch for enemies coming up. Sydney engineered a meeting between us and Wyndham Lewis, for at that time Sydney was a partisan of Lewis's, recommending his work to Edwin, who was reluctant to second what he felt to be Sydney's excessive praise and did not want to include Lewis in his volume of essays. An appointment was made for us to meet for tea in an A.B.C. shop. It was not a successful meeting. Lewis watched us both suspiciously, but on catching my eye or Edwin's slid his eyes sideways at once. He hardly spoke to me, being, apparently, one of those Englishmen who do not have the habit of talking to women. My invisible antennae conveyed to me that he resented my being there at all, that in his opinion a wife was out of place and that Edwin was a coward for having brought me as protective cover, the only motive he could imagine. We parted with relief on both sides. Later, when staying at the French Institute, we went to examine his drawings in the Victoria and Albert Museum: they looked to us like drawings of big-gun barrels, or bowels, just what one might expect from someone who belonged to a group called 'Blast'.

All that summer the strong hot sunshine helped to make a climate of happiness in which we were both continuously busy, yet the moments in it are not sharply etched on my memory as moments are in a foreign place. None of them was shrunken or empty; they brimmed with vitality; yet they are blurred into a timeless here and now as I try to remember them.

One incident caused by an outside agency does stand out. By the month of August the countryside was parched with drought and the wells in our by-lane were down to red mud, hopping with frogs. When my neighbours begged water of me I handed out full buckets as a matter of course and to my dismay was severely reprimanded by an agent of the Water Company, who was far from seeing eye to eye with me. The needs of the many children in the lane counted for nothing against his policy of forcing waterless houses to get piped water laid on. I did not see why children should go thirsty because landlords were unwilling to pay for plumbing and was told that such an attitude was utterly unbusiness-like.

When the dank, blustery autumn set in and the flagstones in our living-room grew black again with damp, I was stricken by what seemed to be lumbago as I was vaulting over a field-gate, and it occurred to us at last that the colds and indispositions which had plagued us in the early spring might have some connection with the lack of a damp-course in the cottage. By November we had had enough of the damp and the smuts and were thinking about a cheap fishing-village our artist friends had praised, in the south of France, an unspoilt village called St Tropez. But Edwin wanted to finish *Transition* first, so we succumbed to my mother's solicitations and went again into Scotland, to her dry, warm house in Montrose.

Unexpected troubles kept us there until February. I had a miscarriage, which left me feeling forlorn and empty, reduced in spirit as well as weak; because of our close companionship this lapse of mine made Edwin low-spirited too and hampered his essay-writing. He still thought he could finish the series by the New Year, having only two essays to write, but when he was ready to put the finishing touches on the book and send it off he fell ill with what the local doctor at first said was threatened appendicitis. An immediate operation was supposed to be necessary, but on the previous night I managed to get him into a deep sleep, the doctor decided next day that it was not appendicitis after all, and he began to recover.

My ability to ensure a good sleep for Edwin was one of the mysteries of our relationship. It was simply done; he laid his head on my right shoulder with my right arm around him and his right arm laid over me; that was all. Whatever nervous tensions were in him relaxed and he sank easily into healing sleep. I had of course to lie very still, but I was able to do that for hours, if need be, until many years later when arthritis hindered me. This lulling of Edwin to sleep was one of the easiest things I did for him; my conscious self had little to do with it; what happened was a secret between his unconscious and mine.

In December, shortly after my miscarriage, Edwin had gone to London for the weekend to see Huebsch and Seeker about, among other business, a novel called *Jew Süss* which we had read and recommended for publication, and which we then contracted to translate. While Edwin was finishing *Transition* I was getting on as fast as I could with this translation, which was wanted by the month of May. As soon as the last essay was finished we set off for St Tropez in late February 1926, taking *Jew Süss* with us, and also, although only in Edwin's head, an idea for a novel and a conviction that he was going to write more poetry. Before we left, Edwin told Sydney: 'It will be lovely to be in Europe again.' We were, it seems, turning into Europeans, after all. So our second European adventure began.

Chapter Eleven

ST TROPEZ, MENTONE

1926-1927

A run of bad luck does not always mean that one has been frustrating the unconscious, but strokes of good luck, which look like the interposition of a guardian angel or of Providence, tend to happen only when one is fulfilling its intentions, whether blindly or not. We were in luck when we went to St Tropez in 1926 before it had been transformed into a fashionable resort, and we were again in luck because we arrived there in time to take over a pleasant villa from an elderly English couple who had to go back to England for a while. They were grateful to us for undertaking to pay thirteen shillings and fourpence a week for the use of their villa, La Vétille, with four rooms and a kitchen fully furnished, a wide stretch of *maquis* outside, including a private path to a rocky beach, eight almond trees, a rosemary hedge and a green bank covered with bright mesembryanthemums.

The Syndicat d'Initiative of St Tropez, then newly formed, put us on to this charming retreat. The Syndicat was still tentative and humble; its sole visible agent was one brown-eyed and very bored mademoiselle caged in a small office on the steep street that straggled up from the harbour. She took it as an act of simple charity when we dropped in to see her for a chat and gave her sweets to while the time away. We did this often enough, since we had to pass her office on our way down to the grocer's shop, and I can swear that the Syndicat did nothing to rouse St Tropez from its age-long sleep until shortly before we left.

There was no bus or coach to bring tourists. One arrived by way of a branch railway from Toulon, in wide carriages perched on a narrow rail-gauge, so that the train looked like a fat woman precariously balanced on tiny feet and was often blown over on its side by the mistral. There were no bungalows.

There was only a *Place*, a square fort bowered in trees, and, facing the small harbour among tall flat-faced pastel-coloured houses, a hotel claiming a connection with the Universe; beyond the harbour, along the beach, there were a few dwellings, at least one of which was ancient, having a couple of *tourelles*. The village was a favourite haunt of artists needing a north light, for it lay on a spur of land that hooked up to face north, unlike the rest of the Mediterranean coast, and in consequence, as we discovered, was pleasantly cooled by cross-breezes during the hot months.

On our first evening there we sat tranced in warm scented air listening to an anonymous bird in the trees overhead gently beating a musical gong, a sound that wafted us into a new, unknown world. Presently a burly, red-haired man in paint-streaked pyjamas passed us hugging a giant shell-fish of a kind we had never seen with an enormous whorled carapace that was quite green—a poisonous green, we thought. Next day this noble delicacy was being eaten for luncheon at the next table in the restaurant of the *Place* by the same man, still in his pyjamas, who showed no sign of bloating or dying. Many other things were as strange and even startling, such as the rainbow-hued oddly-shaped fish in the market by the harbour, or the annual procession of the local Saint, St Tropez himself, along the harbour-side, which woke us very early one morning with loud bangs from small fat mortars and bell-mouthed blunderbusses. As once in Italy, we absorbed all the strangeness and presently took it for granted. By the time we were established in La Vétille we had only one hurdle to surmount, finding drinkable milk for our coffee. In the grocer's shop all the milk that came in, cows' milk, goats' milk, ewes' milk, was emptied into one big wooden tub and sold as '*mélange*', which we did not care for. Then we noticed a cow grazing in the field on the farther side of our villa, and discovered that her milk was carried daily to the village, right past our front gate, to be mixed in the common tub. We soon came to an understanding with her proprietor, and two empty Vichy bottles at our gate were filled with what we thought of as 'real milk' every morning.

La Vétille was a quarter of a mile from the village, on the road that ran along the little peninsula, an extension of the steep street rising from the harbour, but between us and the road was a small-holding belonging to a retired sea-captain, M. Cocoz, who reared chickens on it. We had a narrow footpath leading past his chicken-coops to our front gate, so that Edwin had a longish way to go for the Vichy bottles, and that was perhaps why he never went for them without taking his walking-stick. I have a clear picture in my mind of Edwin blithely twirling the walking-stick on his way to fetch the breakfast milk, walking like a free man with uncramped limbs, straight shoulders and a step that almost danced as he went.

Novel-writing seemed to be in the air, for I was also thinking of writing a novel, to be set in Montrose. Edwin's novel had been germinating for some time inside him, ever since he first met Sydney. On the Sonntagberg he had already begun a story which was to convey the pathos of the temporary freedom an office-worker enjoys on his release at Saturday midday, but since our Chesham visit no more had been heard of that; perhaps Edwin felt he could not sufficiently detach himself from the Saturday emotions he remembered too well. This new novel was to be a different kind of work and he did not talk about it, except to tell me that it was going to be very queer. I did not know what mine was to be like. I thought that even if I could not detach myself from my emotions, I could perhaps use them to present a story in a Montrose setting, imagining what might have happened had I married my Rugby champion and gone to live there, and, I suppose, assuring myself what a nightmare that wrong marriage would have turned out to be.

Meanwhile, if we were to get to our novels, we had to polish off *Jew Süss*. That seems an apt phrase, for I cannot say that we translated *Jew Süss*; what we produced was a polished rendering of it. In Montrose I had already begun to tailor the style to what I felt would better suit an English public, and in St Tropez we went on doing that, cutting out adjectives and shortening sentences. The ultimate result was a popular success which gave us a lot of annoyance because such piles of Press cuttings arrived that our subscription to Durrant's Agency was exhausted nearly every week. We had no royalty on the book's sales; we got only our translation fee of £250, and seemed always to be paying out another three guineas for Press clippings. It was the publishers who raked in the thousands. Then when we went back to England in May 1927 Edwin was hailed everywhere as 'the translator of *Jew Süss*', which amused me but irritated him.

We polished it off, anyhow, by the end of May, and after lazing for a few days began on our novel-writing. Edwin loosened up sufficiently to admit that his story was about an idiot boy falling in love with a wooden marionette and that he was setting it in Salzburg. He suggested that we might run up to Salzburg in August, partly to hear the music festival and partly to refresh his memory of the town. I was interested to note that in a way we were both treating the same theme; that is to say, having found the right kind of love we were now both writing about the wrong kind; but Edwin's handling of it was more detached than mine, for he had transmuted it into symbols while I was relying on the empathy of personal feelings and memories. His novel, I thought (and still think), came right out of the image-making unconscious, just as his waking visions had done; that was why he felt it to be 'queer'. It was queer; it came out of a very queer part of himself.

Sometime in June the Holmses inevitably turned up in St Tropez and found a lodging in one of the houses past the harbour. Then began what became a purgatory for me; we dined with them every night, not in the *Place* but in the much cheaper *Café du Commerce* on the harbour-front, at a rough table set outside its door which we could depend on securing if we came early enough. The Holmses, living nearer, usually got there first and bagged the bench facing the harbour. Edwin then sat opposite Holms and I sat opposite Dorothy, an arrangement that became habitual. Holms talked across the table exclusively to Edwin while Dorothy and I were left, as usual, to each other. I had known Dorothy Jennings slightly in London for a couple of years before I met Edwin; she was then a pretty girl, like a Botticelli angel, with a pale, pointed face and a cloud of red-gold hair. She was now looking the worse for wear; her face was both peaked and flabby, her ankles had swollen and her hair had lost its radiance. Trailing up and down the Riviera with Holms was apparently taking the heart out of her; she was very sorry for herself.

Holms had written nothing since we last met him. All I ever saw of his work was one rather Wordsworthian poem which would have been good had he been able to fill the hollow gap in the middle of it, where several lines were missing. In Dresden there was talk of a poem he had in mind to write, about the emergence of animals into the world, but now he seemed to be providing Edwin with evidence, in half-sentences mostly, about how cruel and meaningless the world of Nature was, so that it was too horrifying to write about at all.

Every evening he fixed his eyes on Edwin, using him, I thought, as others use drugs or incantations, to induce a state of self-hypnosis or trance, in which he delivered himself of interminable monologues. He was in a worse state than I had yet seen him, as he kept fingering at his childhood memories of 'thick horror' when not wallowing in the horrors of the animal world.

Could it be his vanity, I wondered, that impelled him continuously to finger his own feelings, because he wanted to make sure that they would make great poems? For he wished to be not merely a poet, his will was set on being a Great Poet. The more despairing he felt within, the thicker the armour his vanity provided without, so that his airs of superiority became more than irksome. I decided, unkindly enough, that he would never now be able to shape poems, because he could not let go of any feeling he had once found significant.

One evening it occurred to me that he could never let them go because he was afraid to let go. That theory fitted his monopolizing habits too, his insistence on another bottle and yet another when he found a wine he liked, his unwillingness to put an end to any occasion that gave him pleasure. I knew he was much troubled by nightmares, for Dorothy had told me so. To let go probably meant abandoning himself helplessly to fears and nightmares. Besides, in a funereal voice he kept on reciting every now and then favourite lines from Wordsworth:

> Huge and mighty forms that do not live
> Like living men, moved slowly through my mind
> By day and were a trouble to my dreams.

I began at last to feel a little compassionate towards him, yet at the same time afraid that he would never let go of Edwin. I did not believe he would ever write anything worth while for good poems are not made by determination to write them, and I thought, too, that it was bad for Edwin to be used as a hypnagogic medium, evening after evening.

Edwin felt that he owed a debt of gratitude to Holms. On one long afternoon early in the summer of our marriage they had rambled together through the countryside near Glasgow and Holms, reciting poem after poem, had conveyed by direct transmission a whole world of poetic feeling to Edwin from which he had been excluded by the habits of Scottish intellectualism, an experience that amounted to a liberation which he thought he could never be too thankful for. And he had dedicated his *Chorus of the Newly Dead* to Holms. All this I knew and tried not to forget. That was why I put up with these monologues, even although they were beginning to revolt me.

At the beginning of August I was rescued from them when F. G. Scott arrived on a fortnight's holiday before attending the Salzburg festival, closely followed by Mary Robertson, now Mary Litchfield, for whom we found a room in the village. These two visitors, whose Scottish temperaments got free rein on holiday, led us a gay dance. More and more St Tropez was filling up with artists from every quarter, including some from Scotland, and we found ourselves caught up in what Edwin denounced as 'the excessive gregariousness of artists'. I was both startled and amused to discover that Mary's seven years in London had turned her into a siren capable of annexing at once any man she wanted, and still more startled to observe her effect upon Scott. One evening, when Mary had vanished with a new man, Scott raged up and down our sitting-room shouting: 'Such a damned tangential bitch I never did meet!' Edwin was quite immune to her magnetic power, and I realized that she actually respected me for having succeeded in marrying him.

We had given up the idea of going to Salzburg; it would be a needless expense, since Edwin was getting on well with his novel and St Tropez in August was cool and fresh. After our visitors departed, the dreary evenings with the Holmses set in again, and now seemed a waste of the whole Mediterranean ambience, which was made for ease and light-hearted gaiety, not for the solemn self-obsession of Holms and the pale self-pity of Dorothy. I began to resent, more and more, the insulting way Holms parked Dorothy as if she were an inconvenient umbrella and expected Edwin to do the same by me.

The force of my rancour made it impossible for me to discuss the situation with Edwin in a civilized manner. All I could say was that I had got a 'scunner' at Holms, using an expressive Scottish word, that I could not stand any more of him, that I would die if I had to sit at the same table with him again. Edwin, reluctant to admit my unreasonable complaints, said that Holms was in great difficulties and needed him. I denied that he was ever going to solve his difficulties or that Edwin could do it for him. In short, driven to desperation by fears coming up from my unconscious, I was tactless and childish. Edwin felt my desperation although he disapproved it, and as I cooled down a little pointed out that he did not know how to tell Holms about my attitude: what was he to say? 'Tell him what thu likes,' said I, bursting into tears, 'tell him thu has a difficult and unreasonable wife.'

Later that evening, when I had got back some modicum of sense, I remembered having heard Holms say that Mentone was the last place on earth he would ever be found in, so I suggested that if we two went to live in Mentone that would provide a solution. We were now in September and had to leave La Vétille at the end of the month. Why not Mentone? We needn't tell Holms that we were going there to avoid him.

Next day we set off to have a look at Mentone and see how we liked it. The Victorian charm of its New Town, the mediaeval look of its Old Town, took us by surprise and we stayed for two or three days, during which I was at last able to explain myself a little. What most outraged me about Holms, I said, was his attitude to Dorothy and me. Where women were concerned, Holms was living entirely within the conventions of his upbringing; women were sock-darners, yes, bedfellows, yes, intelligent companions, no. Simply lizard tails, I said, to be shed when inconvenient. Edwin and I, making our marriage day by day without any of the usual *a priori* conventions, taking each other as we were, as I was, as Edwin was, the good and the bad together (I admitted that I had been behaving badly), might find out by experience what was true and lasting in such a relationship, but not if Holms kept interfering. And he did interfere, I insisted. He might even infect Edwin with his devaluation of me.

We never had so painful a disagreement again. During these days in Mentone the black smoke I had been emitting vanished at last into thin air. Luck was again with us; avoiding the expensive sea-front hotels we found in an interior street the hotel with the best cooking in Mentone, done with loving care by the patron himself, and we also engaged a lodging for October which we thought enchanting, near the top of a hill called 'Les Ciappes'. The hillside belonged to a M.Ribaud, whom our hotel sent us to see, and he looked as ribald as his name, a large man with a sardonic red face who might have come out of an Irish story by Ross and Somerville. He took us himself to survey his property. The first house, on street level, was a grand Palladian mansion, but just as we were ready to protest he said casually that he let it every year to an English nobleman, and opened a small garden gate through which we passed into a pleasance of trees and shrubs where after climbing a little we came upon a Victorian-looking villa, less grand than the other but equally unsuitable for us. 'Let to a Vicomtesse', said M. Ribaud, leading the way past it and farther uphill. Now we were among vines and could see the last house, which had a saucy turret on it, clipped to a point in the French manner.

'It's the top half of that villa,' said M. Ribaud. 'There's a Dutch journalist and his family in the lower half.' So we reached by a side path the topmost and least regarded dwelling, which we fell in love with at once, partly because of the turret, in which Edwin fancied himself installed, while I was fascinated by the views from either end, one towards the sea, there a thicker blue than at St Tropez, a deep turquoise into which one felt a brush could well be dipped for instant painting, and the other up the valley towards Mont Agel, a rampart that helped to keep the north winds from Mentone. The front door faced the hill, with a marble table beside it, a lemon tree and a mimosa tree. We scarcely bothered to look inside, although we did climb a corkscrew iron staircase into the turret. It was ours, at about twenty-five shillings a week.

I do not know what Edwin told Holms when we got back to St Tropez, but until the end of the month we dined with the Holmses only now and then and I found that he had ceased to be a bogey to me. About this time there began to appear the first portents heralding the later fate of St Tropez. The Prince de Ligne's yacht dropped anchor in the harbour and one met exotic fashionable creatures sauntering about. A café opened up at the lighthouse end of the quay, and a bunch of barefoot sailors in blue berets with red pom-poms danced in front of it singing 'Valencia'. One of the Scottish artists took to sunbathing on the flat rocks with an alleged Russian princess, while by the harbour his home-bred wife drooped alone over cups of coffee. Across the bay a new resort called Ste Maxima was being rapidly completed. 'The Twenties' were catching up with this part of the Mediterranean coast.

The Twenties never caught up with us, because they ignored Mentone, as Holms professed to do. They caught up with the Holmses in the end, I do not remember exactly when. In the early spring of 1927 Holms and Dorothy turned up in Mentone after all, but we were already buttressed by other friends and they did not stay for long, but went back to St Tropez again. From there he suddenly eloped to Paris with Peggy Guggenheim.

He died in 1934; we were living in Hampstead at the time and had been seeing him quite often; the news of his death was a shock. Edwin was still dreaming of him in 1943, and wrote a poem about his dream ('To J. F. H.').

We loved Mentone. Our turreted half-villa was as if made for us to be happy in. Not that we lived in conventional luxury: the furniture was sparse, formal in the French style, conceding nothing to comfort, and our diet was frugal; yet even frugal living in Mentone was good. By running down to the garden gate at street level with a tin plate I could get from a barrow-boy excellent Portuguese oysters at sixpence a dozen, and I never picked a fresh lemon from the tree at our door without feeling as if I were in the Garden of Eden; the fragrance of the lemon-blossom, the savour of the fruit, were paradisal. Nearly every day through the winter months we were able to have breakfast and luncheon in the open; we allowed ourselves a more adequate indoor meal at night in the hotel we had discovered, where we presently made friends with a young French bank clerk who brought Norman Douglas in one evening to dine with us. No, the sense of luxury came from the magical quality of our surroundings. The marble table at our door was set between spectacular mountains and sea that were like some dream landscape of the imagination. The mimosa tree, richly blooming, belonged to that dream, and when a bank of unregarded green shoots behind it suddenly flowered into countless freesias, merely breathing the air became sheer luxury. Nor was animal life lacking from our Eden. In the vineyard lived seven stray cats, of all colours and shapes, whom I fed on the doorstep and whose wounds I healed at need. All seven of them frisked round us and accompanied us, in a casual, independent way, whenever we strolled to the hill-top instead of climbing the higher ridges that ran down from the mountains to the sea.

We had been warned against walking on the high ground towards the Italian side, since the frontier there was an unmarked line, a mere abstraction, which one could overstep without knowing it, and the outcome might be a Fascist jail and much unpleasantness. There was no love lost between Italian and French officials, although, perhaps because, that whole countryside still spoke an Italian-flavoured *patois*. While we were in Mentone a bunch of Fascist police one day chased some criminals of their own on to the international express at Ventimiglia without asking leave from the French, and there was a first-class brawl when the express reached Mentone. With yells of abuse and revolver shots the French police hauled their Fascist colleagues on to the platform while the criminals, not a finger being laid upon them, went on comfortably to Nice. So Edwin and I noted the warning and headed away from Italy along stepped mule tracks leading up to one or other of the sand and gravel ridges where heather and silver birches grew, a complete change from the cypresses, olives, and cascades of pelargoniums along the coast. These varied levels of climate suited us well; we were in better general health in Mentone than in any other place we ever lived at.

Whether because of the climate, or because we were at peace with each other, we were indeed vigorous and gay. We had not been long in Mentone before Edwin admitted that he was finding it a relief to have got away from Holms; a pressure was removed, a burden eased; we had room to breathe and grow. In general, the lack of external pressures is a main reason, I think, why visiting transients like ourselves can have a strong sense of well-being in a foreign country. By instinct we avoided resident compatriots and made friends with various Americans who were also transients, thus avoiding the possible constrictions of the English way of life, which, we suspected, was still bound to wear a Victorian mask in Mentone. There was a band-stand which could have been a social focus for any Victorian resort, as well as an English church, English tea-rooms and a very Victorian English library. On the other hand, it was wonderfully easy to get seats in the Casino to hear Cortot play or Paul Robeson sing, or to slip into a front row in the Monte Carlo tennis grounds to watch Mr G., King Gustav of Sweden, playing singles with Big Bill Tilden. Monte Carlo was only a short tramride away, and although we did not do any gambling we went as a matter of course to see the Monte Carlo ballet companies on many an evening. It was all very unlike the home life of Montrose.

This kind of transient sojourning in a foreign country has been stigmatized as escapism. We certainly escaped a great deal of *malaise* in Britain, including the General Strike, although we knew much about what was happening there, since Edwin's sister Lizzie kept us informed, her husband being an out-of-work victim of the crisis. But if it was an escape, Edwin needed it as much as any invalid needs the peace and quiet of a convalescent home. In our sojourns abroad, which were adventures rather than escapes, Edwin, little by little, was shaking himself free from the pressures which had distorted his life in Glasgow.

Yet though changes in environment had given him room to grow straight, what made him flower was the practice of writing out of his imagination. Already in Penn he had told Sydney Schiff: 'art is for me the only way of growing, of becoming myself. ... I know it is my *good*, the only real good for me, and the personal feeling, the personal integration seems to me more and more the thing that really matters.'

In Mentone he finished the first draft of *The Marionette*, which he sent to Holms for inspection. Holms criticized the second half of it as being imperfectly objectified, so Edwin set about rewriting that and produced the final version in January. My novel was far from being finished, since I had been translating three more Hauptmann plays, but I got back to it again until it was interrupted by the Mentone Carnival. After finishing *The Marionette* Edwin was ready for that carnival; he had the same feeling of release that he had after recounting his visions to me in London, and we both delighted in taking a holiday and having fun. We danced in the streets, dressed up as Pierrots in yellow suits with black ruffs and buttons, pelted our friends with flowers and sang the absurd little carnival song:

> *Coucou, coucou,*
> *Coucou, soulève ton loup. . . .*

Our son Gavin was begotten and conceived during that Carnival interlude; he could not have had a more carefree origin.

In April we were commissioned to translate another book by Feuchtwanger, *The Ugly Duchess*, and this time we asked for and got a small royalty. Since we were going to have a baby, we thought it just as well to do what we could for our financial prospects. But it never occurred to me that I could ever become unable to earn money for the baby's keep: I had no such fears for the future. Yet neither Edwin nor I had very much business sense. For instance, instead of exploiting the technique which had helped to make *Jew Süss* so popular, polishing up Feuchtwanger's style, we set ourselves this time to produce a faithful translation of *The Ugly Duchess*. In one sense it was a good translation, but it was not destined to be a popular success. The British public, presented with authentic Feuchtwanger, did not take to him.

Everyone told us that during the summer months Mentone became unbearably muggy, so we meant to go up to the Tyrol and return in the autumn. Then a prescient friend warned us that if the baby were born in France and turned out to be a boy, he might find himself liable to military service in the French Army when he grew up. 'Supposing you were to die, and supposing the boy did not know about his liability, what then?' We took fright a little at this prospect and at the end of May 1927, left for England instead of the Tyrol.

The heats of summer had already begun as we bade farewell from the train to the places whose very names we had come to love, Cap Martin, Roquebrune, Villefranche. Two years later I made a song out of that journey to please my baby, but it was a sad progress and I found relief in napping a straw fan most of the way to Marseilles. I know now, although neither of us realized it, that it was better for us to go back then among our own people. We might have settled in Mentone into what could have become a frustrating life, for although we felt that we belonged to Mentone, our Mentone did not belong to anything but a dream-world. We had been living our own inward life, outside all social pressures, and in time that lack of pressure, which so far had been good for us, might have made us eat each other's hearts out. Edwin, after all, could not help being a literary man, and there was no literary ambience for him in Mentone. One Norman Douglas does not make a literary summer.

The unconscious (whatever it is) having jockeyed us into Mentone at the right time got us out of it again at the right time. We were ready and braced for the discipline of living under the pressure of public opinion and public feeling in our own country.

Chapter Twelve

BASIC UNDERLAY

We were neither of us likely to be conformists in Britain. In Mentone we had been living on our own level hand in hand, as it were, and seeing eye to eye; though we had come to that level separately, by different roads, in our meeting-place we shared the same belief: that one should try to live through the imagination in a climate of loving understanding. Yet in Britain we should have to cope with a more or less unconscious inheritance of militant patriarchal feeling, not so aggressive or publicly acknowledged as in the nineteenth century, not so stark and arrogant as in the Middle East, and the Far East, but pervasive enough to raise in British boys and men the expectation and desire of becoming dominant males and as a corollary to depress girls and women into being subservient females. But earlier, in London, after experiencing his visions, Edwin had decided that he could not be and was not going to become a dominant male, let alone a Superman. The desire for domineering self-assertion confined a man within what Edwin saw as the False Dilemma of being always top dog or bottom dog, master or servant, on the aggressive or on the defensive, and that was a constriction he felt his true self could not bear.

Edwin's true self was a rare phenomenon, a wonder to me, and a mystery. Born the youngest child of a poor but respected Orkney farmer, he was less like a farmer's son than anyone I had ever met. His small, finely shaped hands had what are called 'tied thumbs'; that is, he could not stretch his thumbs away from the palms for even half the distance that I could stretch mine. His were no hands for grasping a spade or a pitchfork; they were as if made for holding a pen. As a small child he was cherished and petted by the whole family, but neither then nor later could he be trusted to carry out the simplest tasks about the farm. His attention was always elsewhere. His imagination had free play and seems to have been the strongest element in his life at that time. He took for granted the atmosphere of kindly interest and helpfulness that was all around him, but he could never have become a farmer.

Thrown into Glasgow at the age of fourteen, into a whirlpool of struggling competition, he became an office-boy, all day at someone's beck and call for the doing of trivial jobs. His elder brothers and sisters were not so disabled by the shock of this changed life as he was, though his parents suffered. In Orkney they had been known and respected; in Glasgow they were of no account. Edwin found that he was on the lowest rung of a ladder up which he had to climb or perish. His two brothers died; his parents died; the home broke up, and he was left to struggle alone, at the age of eighteen, on his earnings as a clerk. He read books; he haunted Literary Societies; he sought for enlightenment on every side of him; but he became increasingly absent-minded and miserable. It was no wonder that Nietzsche, in Oscar Levy's translations, came to him as a great light in his darkness: the poetic imagination in *Thus Spake Zarathustra* encouraged his inner self to go on, although in the wrong directions. The Will to Power strengthened but imprisoned him. The Superman nickered brightly on his horizon for a while, yet his true self finally recognized that the Superman was a mirage.

Where did his true self come from? That is the mystery. How did it happen that he had such a deep-ranging imagination and so much more of it than the people he was born from or lived among? That is the wonder. 'Good God, Ned,' his fellow clerks used to say, 'do you *read* those books?' He did read them, and with an increasingly lucid mind even though his true self was being given little to feed on. But he was inured to living on little nourishment. I suspect that there were deficiencies of diet in Orkney while he was a small boy, for his long bones, his upper-arm and thigh-bones, were proportionately shorter than they should have been, and he once told me that the only kind of cooking his mother knew was boiling everything. And yet, with the odds so heavily stacked against him, his true self still lit up his eyes when I first met him.

This true self of Edwin's was now the mainspring of his life. Having very human limitations, I used to think of it as reaching *down* into his feelings and imagination, and reaching *up* into conscious lucid thinking. The 'down' and 'up' notion is rather absurd, and yet human feelings do seem to come up from the midriff and human thoughts to take shape higher up behind the eyes, so that one is easily misled into believing the administrative centre in one's head to be more important than the feelings moving down below. But in my thoughts I did not cut off Edwin's true self at either end, since for me the air around him seemed always quivering with something like electricity. I thought his true self, that elusive mystery, reached down beyond him into that other mystery, the unconscious, out of which we all arise, and that it reached up beyond him into the air; how far, I could not tell, but far enough to catch invisible and inaudible radiation from goodness knew where. His true self, I was well aware, was a very sensitive and delicate instrument both for receiving and giving out radiations.

So he was bound to feel acutely the pressures of public opinion in England. I was no more of a conformist than he was, but the pressures were to reach me from a different angle. He refused to boost himself up the ladder into becoming a dominant male, and I refused to be pushed down it into female subserviency. Both of us ignored the ladder as if it were not there, which was bound to annoy people struggling upon it. Edwin should have expected to be sometimes decried as a weakling, with his gentle voice and gentle ways, although no weakling could have withstood the stresses he had withstood, and I should have expected to be sometimes decried as a virago, since I did not have the deprecating voice and manner of a background Englishwoman. Yet because the climate we made for ourselves seemed natural and right for us, we did not look for these snubs and misunderstandings and were surprised, even a little hurt, if we met them.

Edwin's was to be the harder task; the patriarchal framework of our society laid all legal responsibility for the family, which meant financial responsibility, on his shoulders alone, and whether he liked it or not expected him to act as Head of the Family, signing all contracts and paying all taxes. Yet this formal responsibility daunted him less than the widespread acceptance of domineering self-assertion as a masculine attribute, an end in itself needing no justification or questioning, even though it led to violence, fighting and warfare. Not many people in England at that time, in 1927, shared this attitude of his. Even those who were alarmed by industrial violence and had had enough of warfare between nations, where the lust for dominance was, as it were, written large, looked elsewhere for remedies and did not see that the desire for dominance could also be overbearing and destructive when written small in civilian life. Many felt that male arrogance was a built-in component of human nature, to be kept in check by deterrents but hardly to be eradicated. You couldn't change human nature, they said, could you, now? Men would always exploit weaker creatures if they could, beat down opponents and triumph over rivals.

To Edwin this was a very primitive attitude, an anachronism which had long outlived any one-time social purpose. Besides, he thought that in his visions he had had a revelation from some outside Source that the world need not be run to suit the egos of domineering males, that the development of Man was meant to take a different direction, away from fragmentation. In the core of his own nature he knew he himself could not live in that way. He was, in fact, a very small David facing a very large Goliath, with nothing in his sling save some as yet unwritten poems.

Instead of bossing other people and animals Edwin believed that one should respect the grain of their natures; if one could not cherish them one should at least try to understand them. This understanding, he was sure, came through the imagination and was implicit in great imaginative literature, especially poetry. He was also sure that what he called the 'true imagination' could not engender hatred. Years later he crystallized this belief of his in a sentence I find unforgettable, occurring on page 235 of his Autobiography: 'It is easy for the false imagination to hate a whole class; it is hard for the true imagination to hate a single human being.'

Because he shrank from the rhetoric of self-assertion and propaganda, he did not set out to convert other people to his personal way of life. What he felt he had to do was to embody his own insights in poems, and to recognize insights in the imaginative work of others. But he could not write in one way and live in another: from day to day he disciplined himself to live according to his own gospel, sustained by his belief that he was in the front line of advance for the making of a new, unwarlike order of society

I was not caught, any more than Edwin was, in the pincers of the false dilemma, of being top dog or bottom dog, in which so many lovers let themselves be confined. A belief in True Love was my brand of non-conformism, and it matched Edwin's in many ways. True Love, I felt, never seeks to exert power, especially over the beloved. If he is kind, one does not conclude that he is under one's thumb: if he is unkind, one does not retaliate. Punishment and forgiveness seemed to me equally irrelevant to True Love, which had no need of either. I did not assume that Edwin and I had invented marriage based on True Love, or even marriage comprising intimate partnership, but I did think that we were in the front line of advance for such marriages, and therefore very much in the front line of advance for the making of a new unwarlike order of society. Here Edwin's gospel and mine coincided.

Yet although we were at one, we were separate human beings, and another aspect of my non-conformism was a streak of irreverence which Edwin had little of, although he found mine amusing. Male dominance had been my mother's creed and as a child I met it like a toad meeting the teeth of a harrow. 'Why should I brush the boys' boots? Why can't they do it themselves?' 'Because you're a girl and they're boys.' My early reaction was simple defiance. Later, by the time I was twelve, I was beginning to recognize most of the boy-and-girl stuff as nonsense, though why people should believe it baffled my young comprehension. 'I do want to learn to play the fiddle.' 'Certainly not; the fiddle is for boys, it's the piano girls learn to play.' As a schoolgirl I shrugged my shoulders at the gap between the self I knew and the female stereotyping expected of me, but when I moved to the university I began to find the discrepancy comic. There was no lack of discrepancies affecting all the women students, not merely myself; the arbitrary conventions made eccentrics of us all. The patriarchal Law rated us as second-class citizens (we could not vote) and the patriarchal Church assumed that we were second-class souls (being suspect daughters of that Original Sinner, Eve, we had to cover our heads in church and could not hold ecclesiastical office). There was now no 'parity of esteem' as between male and female in patriarchal structures, whatever values they may have started with. And yet we females were strong natural forces deserving a status of our own as free citizens. The theory of female inferiority did not square with the actual strength and courage of women, and probably never had done so, I decided; as a theory it was flying in the face of common sense and experience. By the time I went to teach in England I was already alert to the comedy of my position as a woman in a patriarchally-minded country.

Then I attended a friend's wedding in an English church, my first acquaintance with Anglican marriage ritual, and was startled to hear the question: 'Who giveth this woman to be married to this man?' On the face of it, in this ritual the bride was taken to be a chattel, a possession handed from one man to another, not at all a self-respecting individual who, as I knew, had chosen her own husband. Yet she ranked as the most important individual in the ceremony; not even the bridegroom, nor her father who had 'given her away', had a look-in beside her. I observed too that the veto on bare heads for women in church had been turned by women themselves into a triumphant parade of fashionable hats. It appeared that women simply flowed over, under and round the artificial barriers hedging them in, and this intransigence enchanted me.

After the 1914 war was over, I noted that the increase of violence in the air was paralleled by an increase of female intransigence, and that the gap between the fiction of women's inferiority and their actual strength was widening fast. Well before I met Edwin I believed that sooner or later the formal disabilities imposed on women would have to be thrown into discard to avoid becoming utterly ridiculous, and at that time a good many women in England felt as I did. So my status as a woman did not trouble me acutely, as Edwin's problems troubled him.

I was lucky, and I knew it, in having married a man who was not striving for dominance, either in-fighting at home or out-fighting in the world. The climate we made for each other and carried with us was to be one of freedom. I could not dare to assert that we achieved it, since one can never rightly see oneself from outside, were it not for testimony given me by someone else. Dr Drury Oeser, who met us first in St Andrews in the middle thirties, has told me that she and her husband, on entering our house, felt that they were entering into a climate of freedom, where they could be themselves, as in no other St Andrews house. In our marriage there was at least no social pretence of being better than our neighbours, no conceit of dominance, no *hubris*. It was a climate that suited Edwin as it suited me.

Chapter Thirteen

DORMANSLAND, CROWBOROUGH

1927 – 1932

In Dormansland, Surrey, we found a pleasant cottage, ready furnished and inexpensive, near the Lingfield race-course, and settled down to finishing *The Ugly Duchess*. By September, when the translation was done, I was learning what it meant to be a heavily pregnant woman. I could not run or even walk fast, but had to progress across fields with a slow, majestic gait. I looked like a bulging fruit and my head, when I caught sight of myself in a long glass, seemed small and unimportant on top. No wonder, I thought, that women are often supposed to be mindless. 'But I am still me,' I said aloud, more than once, as I stared at the figure in the glass.

Yet with this affirmation of myself beside the visibly encroaching mystery of the processes going on in my body, I began unwittingly to go wrong. Since quitting St Tropez I had been trusting to the winds and currents of True Love, mostly coasting alongside events as they happened without plotting a navigable course. It now seemed reasonable that I should think the time had come to use my mind like a civilized woman. But the time had not come. I should have done better to be less reasonable and to go on trusting in the unconscious till my baby was born.

Neil's assistant, Jonesie, had recommended an inexpensive nursing home in London, and in my new, reasonable frame of mind I went to see the two doctors there. In a matter-of-fact and utterly reasonable manner they frightened me. The baby's head was already so big, they said, it would be dangerous for me to let the pregnancy go on until full term. Thirty-seven was too old an age to take such a risk with a first baby. I must have the birth 'induced' some weeks beforehand. I had no counter-arguments, for the doctors appeared rationally certain and I knew myself ignorant. Convinced that I must be 'reasonable', I agreed. The result was an unnaturally prolonged labour, since my baby did not want to be born before his time and my body did not want to bear him before his time. I did not know, and the doctors apparently did not realize, that I was unusually susceptible to drugs, and I got chloroform poisoning. Despite everything, the baby and I both took our time. In the end I was badly torn at the birth and in the flurry the doctors forgot to stitch me up. They did not tell me that I was torn open, a defect which was the basic cause of the troubles that began to bedevil me in about three years and later brought me to hospitals time and again.

The baby throve. I had milk enough for two babies, and he kept us awake only one night during his whole infancy—and that was when a tooth was coming through. Edwin and I were awed and happy at finding ourselves turned into these traditional figures, a father and a mother, all the more as the baby was a credit to us both. We now felt more deeply that we belonged to the human race, not only to each other: his presence made an extra resonance in the chord of daily life. In a contemplative way Edwin once said: 'It's quite remarkable how unlike the human young is to the young of the chimpanzee,' a remark I should never have thought of making as I looked at our son.

We called him Gavin. There was something odd about our giving him that name, which became evident only years later. When the question of naming him first came up Edwin declared that he did not want two Edwin Muirs in the world, so we spent much time deliberating what name to choose which would be something like Edwin, but not Edwin; a name of two syllables ending with -in would be suitable, Robin or Colin, or Martin, or something like that. We finally hit on Gavin, a purely literary name to us, suggested by the existence of the old poet Gavin Douglas, or the Gavin Henderson known to Burns, a good old Scottish name now fallen into oblivion, we supposed, a unique find, a private discovery of our own. We had never met anyone or heard of anyone called Gavin. Yet by the time our son was growing up countless other Gavins began coming into sight, more and more of them. One could hardly pick up a Sunday newspaper without meeting a Gavin somewhere.

As householders we were not taking things seriously, rather

playing about. The cottage we lived in was furnished in pretty-pretty style; among its gimcrack trimmings we felt like characters in someone else's story. We did not trouble about our future, in so far as we ever looked at it, being both in a state of heightened tenderness, so that our hearts swelled with loving emotion until there was no room left for getting outside our feelings and looking at them. The future, in any case, seemed an endless vista of possible achievement. Edwin's novel, *The Marionette*, published in May when we came back to London, had got some good reviews and he was now acting as a reader for Cape, with the offer of writing a book on John Knox. He had a second novel in the back of his mind. We did not think that we could ever be bankrupt of ideas or resources; as a stand-by there was always translation, there was always reviewing; something was bound to turn up to keep us going. So we played with our lives and, in between, with our baby.

Our cottage backed on to a lane on one side and on the other adjoined various small houses, whose tenants made friendly neighbours. Here we became aware how widespread the bossy false dilemma was in English minds and how unthinkingly accepted. People used its *clichés* freely. 'You're making yourself a slave to that baby,' said one neighbour to me, quite fondly. I could not help smiling but did not point out how irrelevant the master-slave dilemma was to a nursing mother with her baby. 'Well, I don't blame you,' was another frequent remark of hers, which I took as kindly as was intended.

My whole life, it was true, was governed by the baby's needs, for I was the milk, and the milk couldn't walk away in search of other amusement. I was following the regimen prescribed by a New Zealander, Dr Truby King, who was then regarded as the best authority on baby-rearing. I doubt now whether I ought to have stuck so rigidly to his time-table, feeding my baby exactly every four hours on the tick. I used to wonder whether this insistence on mathematical pattern helped to influence Gavin's mind, for by the time he was rising three he was fascinated by number and number systems. The sense of glory I got at his age from seeing a wealth of growing flowers he got from grand totals of telegraph wires, and would shriek in ecstasy: 'Mama, the seventeens are going here on to the twenty-ones!' Yet I was comforted because he was musical as well as mathematical: he sat singing to himself long before he made any attempt to speak.

After he was weaned at nine months he became more mobile and so did I. In April I had already done a little light translation of two plays by Feuchtwanger, while Edwin was finishing a small book, *The Structure of the Novel*. But Feuchtwanger, as Edwin said, seemed unending: we were threatened in the not so distant future by another novel of his, a long one, to be called *Success*. Meanwhile Secker wanted us to translate a couple of other novels and Edwin had undertaken to produce a Life of John Knox. We were going to be up to our ears in work, if we were to earn ourselves the needful leisure for our own writings. So I began, little by little, to do translation again. 1928 was a hot, dry summer and we parked Gavin in a play-pen on the lawn while I got down to work.

In the middle of all this Edwin produced some queer poems: 'The Trance', in which an armoured warrior lies stricken in a field, able to hear and see but not able to move, 'Tristram Crazed', a ballad of madness finally healed, 'The Stationary Journey', an indulgence in one of the occupations dear to Edwin, going back against the flow of Time in defiance of the 'astronomic world', to see

the dead world grow green within
Imagination's one long day,

'The Fall', an attempt to express what he had experienced in one of his visions, and 'Transmutation', in which there sounded clearly a new and living hope of fruition and peace. One and the same autumn field shows, first, mailed heroes walking in it; they vanish like leaves, and on their helms and armour sweet birds then make nests and sing; finally, ripe grain

stands up like armies drest.
So my deep dread is lightly taken away. . . .

I think I should mention here the tentative relationship now beginning between Edwin and T. S. Eliot. About the end of 1927 Edwin had sent 'After the Fall' to the *Criterion*; Eliot accepted the poem but it had not yet appeared and Edwin began to think it never would. (It did appear in 1931.) Edwin was critical about Eliot's poetry, and, likely enough Eliot did not care for his.

In *Transition*, published in 1926, Edwin had praised Eliot's criticism almost unreservedly for being in reality concerned with organic structure although at times apparently concerned with craftsmanship alone; he presses a small lever, Edwin says, and releases an unsuspectedly heavy weight. But—and here comes the reservation—his sense of tradition often makes him too cautious; he 'draws back where a genuinely classical writer . . . would have gone on'. None the less 'Mr Eliot deserves to be ranked with the chief English critics.' Eliot's poetry on the other hand, has not 'the fullness and suppleness, the mixture of extreme refinement and natural coarseness of Elizabethan poetry' which Edwin assumes he is trying to restore; although these elements are present, 'they are set down side by side in contrast, not in combination.. . . There is no intermediate world of life connecting and modifying them.. . . The raw fact and the remembered vision, the banal and the rare, the crude and the exquisite, reality and art, are set down side by side,' in simple or violent contrast. The mood, which is more than despair or mere depression, is not 'pulled into the light frankly and cleanly as one of Mr Eliot's Elizabethans . . . would have pulled it out... he does not express it fully enough.' It rarely brings release. 'It is not false or shallow, but it is inconclusive.' Consequently 'as a poet Mr Eliot lacks seriousness. He is bitter, melancholy, despairing, but he is not serious. There are moments when seriousness is given him. It is his in the two beautiful and terrible verses which conclude *Sweeney Among the Nightingales.*'

Eliot might well have retorted that the poet's own consciousness was a medium combining the disparate elements in his poems, or he might have ignored Edwin's analysis; instead, he wrote a letter which Edwin told Sydney Schiff was 'a very nice letter ... he mentioned my essay on him, thought it very good, disagreed with it but said it had been useful to him. An astonishingly nice letter and very honourable to Eliot.' One can assume, therefore, that Eliot and Edwin respected each other at this time, although they disagreed. They were both still in the making—Eliot had not yet produced the *Four Quartets*— but Edwin was penetrated by German thinking while Eliot was more influenced by French. A year or two earlier Edwin had said that he would not give one page of Lessing for the whole of Sainte Beuve, and that he distrusted the exquisite Valéry simply because his chief virtue was exquisiteness, as if the poet were living in an impossible world which one good breath of life would blow away, although within these limits he could not help admiring him. He was captious, too, about Gide, from whom, he said, he got no valuable stimulation. He was more interested in the underdeveloped, the potential, which he felt in the German spirit; he did not mind being labelled a romantic although he did not care for labels, but he would have refused to be called classical. To Sydney Schiff he said that 'classical literature is a very good thing if we could be classical; it is like asking a man to be calm when his house is burning'. In preferring German to French sources he was going against the fashion among English literary men of his day, even though he felt that he was influenced far too much by the time he lived in and was more and more 'beginning to think of independence as the greatest virtue, or at any rate as the beginning of all the other virtues'. The standpoint from which he judged Eliot as lacking seriousness came from Germany, from the belief that a poet should express a total experience of life as he lives it, with his total personality, not, as Edwin thought Eliot did, from a fragmented personality patterning aspects of experience into a mosaic. It took Edwin about twenty years to come to a liking and understanding of Eliot's poetry: it probably took Eliot even longer to approve Edwin's.

The poem 'Transmutation', in which Edwin says that his 'deep dread is lightly taken away', was not in the prevailing literary mood of his time, either. That mood, in Aldous Huxley as in Eliot, was one of disgust with modern life, and in 1928 Edwin felt that life was very much worth living.

In this state of euphoria we began looking for a house to rent into which we could put our own furniture, for our baby to knock about. Remembering how much we had liked Crowborough and the Ashdown Forest when we were convalescing from the Spanish influenza, we took a semi-detached house on the outskirts of Crowborough, at forty pounds a year. We were attracted to it by the enormous garden, blossoming with huge peonies and flowering shrubs, which stretched down to a vista of fields open all the way to the horizon, with not another building in sight. During the summer that garden enchanted us as much as we had expected. One moonlit night I saw a red fox crossing the bottom fence, a bright image of the wild sense of freedom it gave us. The other half of the house had a similar expanse of garden shut off by a low hedge, but the retired major who occupied it, with his mother, never became friendly after we begged him not to play his gramophone so loudly out-of-doors. (The gramophone had a harsh grating voice, always slightly off-key, which distressed our son and made him scream.) On the other side was another large garden, full of what we thought charming pergolas draped with hops; it took us a long time to discover that the hops were used for making a potent, if illicit, home-brew of ale that was sold at the side-door to furtive customers, including a cook of ours, who baffled us by lying drunk in the kitchen when we could have sworn there was no alcohol within her reach.

Our next-door neighbours, then, were not friendly, and once the winter closed down neither was the house, despite the comfortable armchairs we had bought in Tunbridge Wells, where we used to go to watch Duleepsinhji playing elegant cricket. The whole house was cold and draughty, difficult and expensive to keep warm. We were both working very hard, anyhow, to cover the expenses of moving and furnishing, and Feuchtwanger's long book was exhausting us. Translating it seemed worse than breaking stones. When one is not interested, uplifted, exhilarated by the material one is translating, so that the unconscious delights in doing the work, and the quick of oneself is responsive to the quick of the foreign writing, the labour of digesting sentences can become drearily depressing. A short break in Scotland, where Edwin tracked down sources for his biography of John Knox, was not much of a holiday for him. But by good luck we now struck a book which we thought worth translating, *The Castle*, by Franz Kafka. When Knox was finished in the summer of 1929 Edwin persuaded Secker to publish *The Castle*, and we began the translation. It was the second work in that year which had moved Edwin profoundly, the first being Rilke's *Die Aufzeichnungen des Malte Laurids Brigge*. To Sydney Schiff Edwin wrote: 'Rilke's poetry I don't really much care for, subtle and supremely skilful as it is, but this strange prose work proves him a genius.. . . . Kafka's book is still more strange in its atmosphere ... it appeals particularly to the part of me which wrote *The Marionette*.'

Rilke's book I had a curious hankering to translate, an obsessive hankering. All my resources, I felt, would be needed to cope with the queernesses of *Malte Laurids Brigge* and I longed to try; but the publishers were already bound to accept a translator authorized by Rilke himself and I did not get the chance of trying. *The Castle*, however, excited us both and we busied ourselves with it, Edwin having given up reviewing for the time being.

There was a difference in emphasis between our separate appreciations of *The Castle*, rather like the difference between our appreciations of Edwin's waking visions. As then, Edwin was more excited by the 'whence' and I by the 'how'. That is to say, Edwin tried to divine and follow up the metaphysics of Kafka's vision of the universe, while I stayed lost in admiration of the sureness with which he embodied in concrete situations the emotional predicaments he wanted to convey, situations that seemed to me to come clean out of the unconscious, perhaps directly from actual dreams.

People have often asked me what was our technique in our joint Kafka translations? It was simple enough. We divided the book in two, Edwin translated one half and I the other, then we went over each other's translation as with a fine-tooth comb. By the time we had finished the going-over and put the two halves together the translation was like a seamless garment, for we both loved the sinuous flexibility of Kafka's style—very unlike classical German—and dealt with it in the self-same way.

After that we set to work on our novels, Edwin's second (*The Three Brothers*) and my first (*Imagined Corners*). But when we were about halfway through these we had to rush up to Scotland to see my mother, who was seriously ill with cancer and had had a heart attack. I had been off colour with a bad throat beforehand, and when I got back to Crowborough my health worsened again, with unaccountable aches and pains and an inability to lift and carry heavy weights. Edwin began to fail too, lacking energy, and we put it all down to overwork, especially as Feuchtwanger was occupying us again, so that in the late spring of 1930 we engaged a nurse for Gavin and went down to Mentone without him for a recuperative holiday. On our return home we felt much restored and Edwin's novel was finished, though mine was not, since I was translating books by Hans Carossa. In January 1931 Edwin's *Three Brothers* was published by Heinemann, and we should have felt happy, but there was a kind of fatality about our winters in that Crowborough house. My mother died. Edwin's novel got bad reviews. He told Sydney: 'The book, I should say, has been a pretty complete failure publicly ... so I have started on another one, which I am writing at odd moments ... and which already seems to me to be much better.'

Since writing *The Marionette* Edwin had apparently decided that prose novels had better not come out of the 'queer part' of himself which produced his poems, and that he could distance his personal emotions sufficiently by setting his scene in the sixteenth century, as in *The Three Brothers*. The result was not quite convincing nor was there enough romantic glamour in it to draw public interest. Undaunted, Edwin then wrote *Poor Tom* as a purely contemporary study of life in Glasgow, again using his own family experiences, but again in this book, which contained much that was finely imagined and moving, he failed to attract a public.

The time was hardly propitious for novels that harrowed one's feelings. The American slump in 1929 and the consequent Great Depression had caused bank failures and unemployment throughout Europe, and Britain was of course involved. Pessimism and turbulence were spreading, and Edwin's optimism also began to fade; an undertone of dejection, even of misery, crept into the poems he was writing. He was not helped this year by the fact that a competent Crowborough doctor had discovered what was amiss with me and put me into the local Cottage Hospital to be stitched up, assuring me (and I believed him) that now my troubles would be over; but my absence had distressed Edwin meanwhile. Nor was he helped by the book we then began to translate, intelligent and perceptive though it was, a trilogy by an Austrian, Hermann Broch, called *The Sleepwalkers*, which had as its real theme the inevitable break-up of civilization in contemporary Europe—towards which, according to Broch, we were all sleep-walking.

We spent nearly a whole year of our lives translating this trilogy, and so were bound to be influenced by its pessimism. Broch, who admired Joyce's experiments with form and language (especially *Finnegans Wake*) had experimented with the form of his own narrative in the third novel, breaking it up into disconnected pieces, set down side by side, much as Eliot in his poetry had set side by side disparate aspects of experience; perhaps Eliot, too, had fragmented his observations as an image of disintegration.

Into his third novel Broch inserted an abstractly intellectual essay on the Disintegration of Values, an almost diagrammatic logical version of all that he had been treating imaginatively throughout the trilogy.

We refused to be bludgeoned by Broch's logic, we did not admit the supremacy of abstract philosophizing, we set up a stout inner resistance to his arguments. We felt that Broch, in his attempt to be rigorously logical, had merely rationalized his deeper fears. In any case, we did not agree that the unconscious should be despised as Broch despised 'the irrational', and the notion that it could and would overwhelm European civilization in a cataclysm like the break-up of an ice-floe gone rotten was entirely repugnant to us, even unthinkable. None the less, Broch's ambience of bleak despair affected us deeply enough during 1931, and set the tone for Edwin's next book of poems: *Variations on a Time Theme*.

In the very next year we were to learn by personal experience that Broch had come nearer the truth than we thought and that Europe was indeed getting ready to break up. This revelation came as a shock to us in Budapest, at the 1932 International Congress of the P.E.N., an organization of Poets, Essayists and Novelists. The Scottish branch of P.E.N. had begged us to represent them as official delegates to the Congress, and the prospect of meeting imaginative writers from all over Europe allured us, so that we agreed to go.

Our instructions enjoined us to prevent the English P.E.N. from claiming the Scottish P.E.N. as one of their regional offshoots; we had to insist on the separate national identity of the Scottish P.E.N. This part of our official duty we faithfully performed. I do not know the Hungarian language, but I have never forgotten the sentence drilled into me: *Nem Angol vodyok, Skōt vodyok*; I am not English, I am Scottish. When all the delegations were presented to Admiral Horthy, the Scottish delegation of two was presented separately, quite independently of the much larger English delegation.

As official delegates with all expenses paid, we set off for Budapest in happy expectancy, never having attended a P.E.N. Congress before. We got there late on a Saturday afternoon and were surprised to find in our luxury hotel, the St Gellert, an enormous pile of glossy brochures, pamphlets and notices waiting for our perusal. We did not read them, since the welcoming reception was to be held that very evening and we were barely in time for it. Off we rushed, pleased with the St Gellert which looked down on the Danube from the Buda side, pleased with the prospect of meeting so many writers, and pleased too, with the prospect of junketing in a wine-growing country.

The reception was packed, and we had to get official tickets for this and that; it was a good while later in the evening that we discovered the first little rift in the lute, a split in the Hungarian P.E.N. itself, which was agitating the young members who told us about it. The Hungarian P.E.N. had allotted a money prize to a novelist for an excellent book he had published, but only a fortnight before the Congress the government had intervened, forbidding them to choose that work and ordering them to give the prize to another. 'A Blubo book!' chorused the young rebels indignantly. (Blubo was the current term for the kind of books the Nazis were sponsoring, 'Blut und Boden' literature, Blood and Soil.) 'And when our secretary refused to do it, they said they wouldn't give us a single pengo for the Congress. So he had to knuckle under. But we're not going to put up with it.'

We glowed with sympathy for the young idealists, and they made us promise to attend a rebel meeting next day, Sunday, at the country house of a Baron Hatvany, which we did, escorted there by our new friends. We did not follow the windings of the intrigues that were discussed or the Nazi conspiracies hinted at, but found the excursion interesting, even although there was a stronger whiff of politics in it than of literature, so far as we could make out in the medley of German, English and Hungarian speech.

We were escorted back to the swimming-pool behind the St Gellert, where every fifteen minutes great billows were impelled through the sulphurous water by machinery from behind a grille at the deep end, breaking in refreshing surf over us at the shallow end. Then we sat on the surrounding terrace under a gay umbrella and discussed Hungarian poetry with our young friends, one of whom, the others assured us, was a first-rate poet.

So far, although we thought it odd to be welcomed by a fractional split in the Hungarian P.E.N., we had no misgivings. But as the Congress went on, the whiff of politics became a miasma. The pile of glossy literature in our room, which advertised the beauty spots of Hungary, advertised also Hungarian resentment of the Versailles Treaty, or the Treaty of Trianon, and this was again emphasized on an afternoon when delegates were invited by twos and threes to take afternoon tea in Budapest with private citizens. Our host and hostess spoke of nothing but the unfairness of the Treaty, except when they praised the embroideries and other home crafts of Hungary. That was when we first learned the phrase: *Nem, nem, shoha!* (No, no, never!) which we understood the whole nation to be repeating; it was even prominently displayed on every tram in the city. Never would they put up with the Treaty of Trianon and they choked with wrath whenever Roumanians or Slovaks were mentioned.

This attitude explained the malice shown at the Congress whenever Roumanians and Hungarians met in a discussion. Since we resented political propaganda, we had refused to take sides. Much worse, because more widespread and difficult to explain, was the general *malaise* among the various delegations. The French were detested because, it was said, they took for granted that they alone were capable of providing leaders in discussion or settling details of procedure. The Austrian delegation, a large one, included men whose work we liked, such as Felix Salten, but he was going about with a worried face, and Roda Roda, the Viennese columnist, was also unhappy-looking despite his cheerful red waistcoat. Of the others the most ubiquitous was a stocky, tweed-clad Lesbian, with a *von* in her name, said to be an agent of Prince Starhemberg's, who was constantly engaged in excited conference with some of the Germans. The Germans had brought as a respectable 'front' old Theodor Daübler, looking with his curling white beard like Olympian Jove, but the rest were Nazi supporters to a man, on the telephone to Berlin at all hours receiving instructions and transmitting information. The atmosphere of Nazi intrigue and political conspiracy between Austrians and Germans was so thick that no one could miss it, and the smaller countries' delegations were resentful and apprehensive.

Edwin and I mostly took refuge with two Yugoslavs, who pointedly kept aloof from the turmoil, Stefanović, a Serb, who had translated nearly all Shakespeare, and Ćurćin, a Croat, who had accompanied Dr Elsie Inglis's Scottish hospital unit through Serbia in the 1914 war. These two were more interested in literature than in politics, but they knew more than we did about the tensions in that Congress, and we learned a good deal from them.

Every day Hermon Ould, the General Secretary of the P.E.N., joined Edwin and me for luncheon at a restaurant in a quiet square, where wine and food were excellent and not too dear and where we could escape from the Congress ill-will. Then Ernst Toller, whom we knew quite well and personally liked, although we did not care for his plays, discovered our retreat and begged to join us. In a way, that was the last straw for us both, since Toller daily brought with him some new story of oppression in Hungary itself. One day it was a man who was hanged on a tree at his own front door, where his wife found him when she came home from an errand. Another day, we were told a man had been bound upside down between two chairs and bastinadoed on his feet so agonizingly that his pregnant wife, who was in the same room, died of shock when he leaped out of a window and broke both legs on the stones of the courtyard below. Whether these stories were true or not we had no means of knowing but we could not believe Toller to be altogether a liar. He warned us, too, that the government certainly had sent a spy to the rebel meeting at Hatvany's house, and that our names would be noted down in some dossier or other.

The P.E.N. International Congress, in short, was being used as a cover for political intrigues. Hermon Ould could not dissipate the political ill-will, devoutly though he tried. And so, on an afternoon when I could not do any swimming in the pool, leaving Edwin to go by himself I lay down on my bed and sobbed my heart out over the state of Europe. I could not stop the sobbing until startled by the arrival of Edwin, white as a sheet and dripping wet, almost unable to speak. When the bell was rung in the pool as a signal that the machinery was going to be turned on behind the grille, he had been at the deep end of the bath, and, a slow swimmer, could not get away from it in time; besides, a woman in a hurry gave him a push that sent him below the surface. The engines started and he could not get up again; he was sucked down in a vortex whenever he tried to rise. Finally an attendant hooked him out with a long pole. I had a moment of near terror on learning this: it seemed as if the whole occurrence had been evoked like a dream from Edwin's underworld, so perfectly did it find a shape for his own situation in the Congress, plunged in deep misery before the power-machinery at work there. And he might have been drowned. But he was only half-drowned, shocked, distressed and reeking of sulphur. My moment of terror passed, though I was thankful to remember that the Congress was nearing its end.

The final banquet, given by the City of Budapest, was also symbolic enough. It was supposed to start at half-past eight in the evening, but when we reached the hall we were informed that half-past nine or ten was a more likely hour, since admission tickets were being separately checked and verified. All the grandest prostitutes in Budapest had somehow got hold of admission tickets, and sorting them out was bound to take a long time. By ten o'clock the scrutineers simply gave up and let in the rest of the crowd; famished as we were, we did at last get something to eat and were able to admire the invaders' jewels and furs.

We were never so glad to cross a frontier as on our departure: the train seemed to flee with us as hares flee before hounds. This was the first time in our lives we experienced political fear, which is more faceless and more like a chill, penetrating fog than any other fear in the world.

Once over the border into Austria, we felt, irrationally, safe, and at Vienna went to see Broch in the flat where he lived with his mother away from wheeled traffic in the Inner City. But there we were not comforted. From his tall height Broch looked down on us compassionately as on a pair of children who had just been learning the facts of European Life.

Chapter Fourteen

HAMPSTEAD

What we had seen and felt in Budapest, what Broch had told us in Vienna, left us convinced that things might go very far wrong in Europe and that Hitler with his Nazi gangsters was by no means harmless. As a result we became not more politically-minded but less so, being revolted by the lust for dominance with its political fevers and intrigues. Ironically, we found, when we got back, that a small sample of the general disease had even invaded our home: the cook and the Nanny left in charge of Gavin had spent the whole fortnight loudly bickering about which of them was the more important member of the household, entitled to give orders to the other, and Gavin, unused to bickering, was wheezing a little nervously. We cured our son's nervous wheezing but it would not be so easy, we thought, to cure Europe of its apprehensions.

In troubled England, as in troubled Europe, the economic hardships of the Great Depression were still increasing. It looked as if London were the only possible location for us, since commissions for work could now be got only by practically sitting on publishers' doorsteps. As we were determined not to spend another winter in the Crowborough house and could now afford the shift to London, because my mother had left me some money, we began hunting for a house in Hampstead, at that time a focus for literary people. By great good luck we eventually found a delightful one at 7 Downshire Hill, with a rent of £120 a year.

Before that we had bought a second-hand car, a blunt-nosed Morris Cowley, and each learned to drive it. For the rest of that summer we comforted ourselves by exploring Sussex most afternoons. Gavin usually sat in my lap and Edwin did the driving. Sticking to minor roads he got us to the places we aimed for, at his favourite speed of twenty-five miles an hour; he had no affinity with machinery but I learned to be a calm passenger, whatever happened to the gears. Sussex, unlike Budapest, roused no fears in me that dangerous situations might be evoked from Edwin's unconscious. Nor were they. We had no accidents.

Our house in Hampstead faced the top of Keats Grove where the Carswells, Donald and Catherine, were living. They had helped us to find it, and we loved it dearly, as we had loved our half-villa in Mentone. Affection sometimes makes one foolish, and I remember saying to Cathy Carswell: 'Just look at the lovely lino we've got for the hall', to which she replied with the same foolish fondness: 'Lawrence was so good at laying lino.'

D. H. Lawrence was not long dead; we regretted never having chanced to meet him. But as it would have been barely possible at that time to throw a stone in Hampstead without hitting a literary man, we now met many young poets and other writers. This made a wonderful ambience for us and was part of Hampstead's magic. Our street itself was charming, as were our front and back garden and, of course, the house, with its Gothic windows and absurd battlements. The Heath was only at the end of Downshire Hill, although one had first to cross a traffic-laden downhill road.

These young poets—all of them, I think, except David Gascoyne who had been among the surrealists in Paris—were committed to what was called 'engaged' poetry, dealing with the contemporary social *malaise*. Edwin, who felt that the narrowness of topical outlooks distorted one's true imagination, which had a deeper and wider insight into life, shrank from this kind of poetry, but found the young men themselves very attractive. What they thought of Edwin it never occurred to us to wonder, although he was forty-five and they were anything from nineteen to twenty-five, David Gascoyne, with a still schoolboyish face above his long stilts of legs, being indeed only seventeen. They may have seen Edwin as an elderly romantic steeped in bygone sentiment, but I did not get that impression. Edwin was gentle and ageless; he still looked young and appeared quite at home among the youngsters.

Other writers dropped in and became friends; in London fashion they often brought strangers with them. If there were too many strangers in our sitting-room Edwin and I at first tended to lose our poise; he retreated into Muir-family remoteness and I covered up by becoming too voluble. Our idea of good company was a quiet meeting of friends, preferably not more than two or three, rather than a scramble of casual acquaintances.

154

In his Autobiography Edwin says he does not know why we were so happy in Hampstead, and puts it down partly to our having had so many congenial friends near us. The background of serious political trouble in Europe and at home, the serious work we were doing, did not make us solemn or gloomy in our daily life; we had many pleasant hours. One afternoon in especial stays in my mind, the day we acquired our golden cocker spaniel, Matthew, whom we had no intention of owning; he was simply wished on us.

Matthew was bred by two friends of ours, Flora Grierson and Joan Shelmerdine, who combined the breeding of cockers with running a hand-printing Press, the Samson Press, then at Warlingham, Surrey. In April 1932 they had already printed *Six Poems* of Edwin's, the queer ones he wrote in Dormansland, in a beautiful numbered edition now very rare since much of their stock was destroyed by a fire. Joan is a first-rate printer who outwitted the trade union ban on female apprentice printers by shifts which I am not going to betray. Flora kept the books, attended to the packaging and organized the other doings needed for a Press. Her father, Sir Herbert, belonged to Sumburgh on the mainland of the Shetland Isles, so that she was half a Shetlander; I should be happy to think that it was the Shetland heritage which made her direct, outspoken, warm and intelligent. Whenever these two came to Town we were more than pleased to see them.

On this afternoon, then, I was unexpectedly rung up by Flora. She and Joan had just been to see Matthew, and were heartbroken. They had sold him to a girl who proceeded to take a job that kept her at work all day, and Matthew had been left miserably alone for weeks from morning till evening in a small paved back-yard with nothing in it but dustbins, where he howled continuously when he wasn't upsetting the dustbins. Poor Matthew was in such a state! Would I take Matthew? They were *not* going to leave him where he was. In any case, his present owner was threatened with eviction from her flat because he was being a nuisance. Wouldn't I be an angel and take him in? They could bring him along in a little over half an hour.

I had already seen Matthew and his three brothers, Mark, Luke and John, when they were very small, and I agreed to be an angel.

Matthew arrived in a taxi, a wildly lolloping puppy, tangling Joan in his lead and leaping all over her, trying to snuggle his nose under her chin. The yelping and the laughter brought Edwin down from his study, and this is the picture that stays in my mind: Edwin in an open-necked shirt and grey flannels coming across our back lawn looking gay and beaming a welcome, Joan and Matthew inextricably mixed up with the lead and a deckchair, Flora helpless with mirth and the sun shining brightly over all. While Edwin righted the chair I got biscuits and a basin of water for Matthew. 'He's the biggest and the greediest of that litter,' said Flora. (He was a noble-looking creature, altogether a pedigreed aristocrat, but we never could cure him of an interest in dustbins.) He added to that afternoon's delight by clearly conveying to us that he had been translated from hell into heaven.

An afternoon of very simple happiness; why should it stay in my mind? To begin with: we were three intimate friends, liking, trusting and respecting each other. Then something personal to myself comes in: my flash of perception as I watched Edwin crossing the lawn, when I saw that he could now come out of his secret inner self without having to shut any doors behind him, letting the whole Edwin Muir flow out naturally to meet an occasion.

Yet there were limits to Edwin's out-flowing. When we were able to hear ourselves speak and there was some mention of Nippies, Edwin asked innocently: 'But what *is* a Nippy?' Cartoons of Nippies were then on all the buses and most of the hoardings in Town, yet Edwin literally never saw advertisements. As long as he lived he was as unaware of popular images and slogans as any judge on the Bench.

We felt that we belonged to Hampstead, even although there was a kind of marital General Post going on around us and some people thought us antediluvian for sticking to each other. I remember saying to a pretty, honey-coloured girl who was getting ready to leave her husband that there was no virtue in my being so 'faithful' to Edwin, for when one lived with one's True Love falling in love with another man was sheerly impossible. Her husband, she said, was not her True Love and never had been. I was sorry for her. I could not think of a worse nightmare for any woman than being married to the wrong man.

For us, living in Hampstead was like living with one's True Love; there was no possibility of ever preferring another part of London. In the mode proper to True Love I embraced it all, including the shops and the woman who sold flowers halfway up the Hill. The tradesmen and the flower-seller were like friends rather than acquaintances. I did not stop to wonder if these feelings of mine were one-sided but perhaps my simple friendliness gave pleasure too.

More happened in Hampstead, of course, than our basking in loving feelings. We did a lot of work. These were stringent times, when Welsh miners on the dole were singing with heart-rending sweetness through the London streets. Yet we managed to keep going. Janet Adam Smith, then the new Literary Editor of *The Listener*, commissioned Edwin to write the novel reviews for it every two weeks, a task he carried on until 1945. Secker provided some novels for translation, including one by Sholem Asch which was the precursor of several Asch books, and there was another Kafka to get out: *The Great Wall of China*, and another Broch. Translation went on busily. After some argument we had jacked up our fee for translation to two guineas a thousand, which was supposed to be very good pay, but many hours of hard work were needed to earn a sizeable sum. In his study at the top of the house which contained only a table, a chair, an ink-pot and a fine view over roofs and tree-tops, Edwin now and then produced a poem. The bareness of his study was how he liked it; my memory may have exaggerated that, but slightly. Ten poems, some composed in Crowborough and some in Hampstead, were published in 1934 by Dent, with the title: *Variations on a Time Theme*.

My study on the ground floor was neither so bare nor so secluded. Here I was intruded upon at all hours by household staff, the weekly washerwoman, any casual caller ready for a gossip, and Gavin whenever he came home from school. Gavin's Nanny had become redundant as soon as we found a pleasant little school for him round the corner from Keats Grove, not more than five minutes away, where he was learning among other things to play the piano. Toys, picture-books and hoards of Gavin's were in my study, an upright piano, a wicker wash-basket for laundry, a sewing-machine, a small sofa for visitors and goodness knows what else. I envied Edwin's power of sitting down immediately after breakfast to concentrate in solitude on what he wanted to do.

Yet there was always a press of work, and so I reverted to a student habit of mine, working at furious speed late at night into the small hours, after the vibrations of the day had died down. During the summers I sat up all night once in a while, hearing the birds sing at dawn and tumbling into bed for a few hours' sleep after breakfast, but I did this only when a translation had to be finished in a hurry or proofs corrected against a deadline. I cannot now tell how I managed to finish a second novel, but it does not surprise me that I lost control of it in the second half, although the first half is quite good. My first novel had come out in 1931; it had enough material in it for two novels, which I was too amateurish to realize at the time.

Among our visitors we saw Hugh Kingsmill frequently. He was on bad terms with his father, Sir Henry Lunn, and had cut 'Lunn' out of his name. Being now an outcast from the family business, he was harassed by the need to earn a living, which was for him an apparently insoluble problem. He covered up his anxieties with a kind of fooling, novel to us, that we appreciated; we thought it peculiar to Hugh yet presently discovered that others were also skilled in it, notably Hesketh Pearson. When Hugh and Hesketh were in conjunction we could not help laughing until our ribs ached. It was literate, defensive, throw-away fooling, a type of fun-making belonging to the upper middle-classes of English life whom Hugh called 'the mupples'. Years later we found it also in the works of P. G. Wodehouse. 'She looked like something that might have occurred to Ibsen in one of his less frivolous moments.' That is Wodehouse, but it might have been Hugh, said with a blink of the eye and a twitch of the mouth; he could never quite keep a poker face.

By the time we were in Newbattle Abbey, in the fifties, P. G. Wodehouse had become Edwin's favourite reading when he needed light relief. In his own way he purged Edwin's soul of petty troubles again and again. Hugh, unfortunately, did not have Wodehouse's knack of making money out of his fun. He was permanently baffled by the fact that even younger writers were able to earn themselves a living as he could not, and was given to totting up the age of any young man supposed to be 'making good' and comparing it ruefully with his own. When his pockets were too light as they often were and his heart too heavy, his fun could become embarrassingly forced.

One evening he turned up in Hampstead as someone else brought in William Empson, newly back from Japan, I think; we had not met Empson before but he had a growing reputation for his poems, and his prose book *Seven Types of Ambiguity* was causing a stir. Hugh, large and florid as usual—one felt he should be wearing a driving-coat with at least six capes over the shoulders—must have been in deep waters that evening. 'You're looking well, Hugh,' said I, and he returned: 'Willa! If you had met Christ staggering to Calvary under the weight of His cross, you would have cried: How well you look, old man!' After that, he smote Empson on the back and said: 'What about the eighth type of ambiguity, Emp, old man?' Empson winced and went on wincing as Hugh persisted in goading him and calling him 'Emp'. Edwin and I both suffered; Empson, naturally, never came to our house again; yet we realized that Hugh himself was suffering more than anyone.

Christopher Grieve surprised us on another evening by turning up in high feather, a gay Borderer carrying out a raid on the English. He was staying with the Carswells, having come to London with enough money in his pocket (so he said) bestowed upon him by some trusting Scot, to engineer the removal of the Coronation Stone from Westminster Abbey and its return to Scotland. The removal of the Stone of Scone was a pet scheme of Christopher's and he had been advertising it up north for some time. His enterprise was supposed to be a Top Secret, but he had already told the Carswells about it, confidentially, and he told us about it, confidentially. During the next few days we discovered that he was telling various other London Scots about it, confidentially. He was so exhilarated by the ingenious devices he had thought up that he could not keep them to himself. In his mind's eye he saw the whole ploy brought to a triumphant conclusion. I think he did not bother about the mere technical problem of prising the Stone loose; he was gloriously racing north with it in A Fast Car—he kept repeating these magic words, A Fast Car—and was going to drop it in some

Border stream where it would look like any other boulder until the time came to escort it through Scotland after the hue and cry had been baffled. The brilliance of this idea illumined Christopher. His yellow hair fizzed up; he was radiant with sheer daftness.

In Westminster Abbey he had several good looks at the Stone, yet spent much more time in his favourite pub, The Plough, in Soho, where he stood drinks all round most generously. What else he was doing I cannot vouch for; two or three times he turned up on our doorstep early in the morning needing breakfast and a shave before he could face Cathy Carswell. Many rumours of what he was up to came to our ears, some of them probably untrue. He enjoined us all to watch for Headlines in the papers 'on Wednesday of next week'. Wednesday duly came, but not the Headlines.

What had happened? The story that reached us was that two Rugby forwards came from Edinburgh by train to help Christopher in lugging out the Stone, and he met them with the information that there was a 'technical hitch'; the job could not be done; the Stone would have to stay where it was. He had enjoyed himself too much to have any money left for A Fast Car to take them north again. But the idea had been let loose into the air of Scotland, with all the panache of Christopher's personality, and the queer thing was that it stayed alive there until the fifties, when it inspired some students to accomplish what Christopher had failed to do. We were in Scotland at the time, in Newbattle Abbey, and I well remember the incredulous delight with which the news was generally received that the Stone of Scone had actually been looted from Westminster.

Edwin and I were never members of the Scottish Nationalist Party. Where political organizations came in question we were now non-joiners. In Hampstead we non-joined Communism, as we would have non-joined Fascism had it come our way. We distrusted systems ending in -ism, especially political systems, abstractions one and all, we thought. Yet Edwin still called himself a Socialist because his old-fashioned Socialism was anything but abstract, being rooted in love and hope, words which he was always able to use naturally, without self-consciousness. Abstract systems, in his opinion, were attempts made by the intellect to short-cut human feelings. Give an intellectual a dogma, said Edwin, and he would set up a system of political machinery that was inhuman, since in the interests of achieving power for his dogma he would over-ride the needs, bewilderments and simple affections of ordinary human beings, power politics having no respect for individual lives. In his Autobiography he said that Russian Communism then seemed to him 'very like a huge clock with metal bowels'.

In his own journey through Time he had now reached a stage of personal integration on his way to becoming a whole man, and thought of other people as each making the same kind of journey from a long past, in the same uncertainty about the future, though with the same hopes as himself. He usually thought of life as a journey; this comes out in his poetry, much of which is concerned with travelling on unpredictable roads to reach unlooked-for places. When Communists told him that Communism was 'historically inevitable' he was horrified by their determinism, which he felt to be an arrogant lie, as if human history were not a living, growing process. He objected also to the vaunt of Communists that their system was 'impersonal', in the sense that it disregarded personal values. For Edwin personal feelings were a source of strength and poetry, not an emotional mess as these doctrinaire theorists assumed. Hampstead was then well furnished with Communists and near-Communists, but among their pressures and tensions Edwin took refuge in asserting his independence and his belief in personal values.

So it happened that in moving from the abstract towards the personal he was swimming against the currents that were taking many of his acquaintances in the opposite direction. He was becoming finally certain that imaginative insights were best conveyed through personal, concrete situations like those invented in dreams or visions. (Here he was perhaps reinforced by his admiration for Kafka.) He went on writing his unfashionable poems, drawing largely on his visions, which gave him a sense of continuing tradition, and, as time went on, more and more using ancient myths as a vehicle to convey individual personal experience that yet reached beyond an immediate present into a timeless past.

In this way, weaving together mythical framework and personal experience, he brought the Story and the Fable ultimately into close relationship. Nor did he feel that his Story and his Fable were merely personal and therefore private; he never ceased to believe that his experience resembled the experience of everyone else involved in the process of living on earth.

But the poetry critics among the younger generation did not agree with this assumption. Geoffrey Grigson had started *New Verse*, and in his first review of Edwin's poetry praised it; in a second review he changed his mind and disparaged it; in subsequent reviews he sent Edwin right down the drain. *Variations on a Time Theme* appeared in April 1934, and, in June no. 9 of *New Verse* contained an article by L. M. (Louis MacNeice?) which described the Variations as being like 'a type of Royal Academy picture of a decade or so back—stilted allegorical nudes walking through a grey landscape'. This made Edwin unhappy; he felt very discouraged, and had some nightmares.

We belonged locally to Hampstead, but did not feel cut off from Europe, which had become part of our consciousness; the Channel was no longer a barrier. Not only were we translating European books and writing letters to European friends, we were in touch with Europeans in London itself. Our old friend Janko Lavrin now suggested that a European literary magazine should be started for the English. Edwin agreed willingly and *The European Quarterly*, edited by Janko and Edwin, made its modest appearance in 1934. In its fourth number Edwin was able at last to publish an essay on Hölderlin which had been rejected by Eliot and had aroused no interest in other London editors.

Some of our European encounters in London were very odd. Our Serbian friend, Mitrinović, for instance, was now established in Gower Street as the centre of a cult. He sent a message to Edwin begging him to be the editor of a magazine about to be issued from Gower Street, I think it was to be called *New Britain*, and it was to deal with the function of Albion in Europe and the world. Expecting an amusing reunion as in the old days in Guilford Street, we made an appointment to see Mitrinović and were not merely disappointed but distressed by what we found. We were received by an incisive secretary who said that 'The Master' would appear in a little while; she looked shocked when asked if he could still imitate the Serbian bagpipes. The room was fluttering with devotees also waiting to see The Master, and some of them talked to us. Apparently they were all laying their possessions at Mitrinović's feet. One young man told us happily that he had sold his only pair of gold cuff-links for The Master, and two little old ladies had sold a country cottage, they said, for The Master. When Mitrinović came in, the whole roomful thrilled and moved reverently towards him. I first caught sight of him from behind. There was a gross roll of fat round the back of the neck I saw, and I could hardly believe that it was Mitrinović's. When he turned round I was surprised to see that his mouth looked much the same, but his eyes did not, and his voice was portentous with self-importance. We non-joined his bogus cult. Edwin refused to edit the new magazine, which came out grandiose in size and expensive in makeup. Some part of London, it appeared, was indeed Looney-bin.

On another day we were invited by Denis Saurat to have luncheon at the French Institute and 'assist' at an interview between Middleton Murry and the editor of *Les Nouvelles Littéraires* who had come over from Paris to write a series of articles about English authors, called 'Une heure avec'. He had just had 'une heure avec' M. Arnold Bennett and was now to have another with M. Middleton Murry. It was hard lines on the sensitive Murry to have Denis and Edwin and me all goggling at him as he sat on a sofa while the French editor stood up before him, his pose a little spoilt by the tabs at the back of his boots sticking out below his trouser-ends.

'Qu-est-ce que vous pensez de votre Shackspeare, M. Murry?' he demanded.

Murry, who had been nervously self-conscious all through the luncheon, now began to squirm. To our embarrassment he squirmed more and more, drawing one hand across his brow and the other over the top of his head.

'C'est très difficile,' he got out, C'est trop difficile à expliquer.'

He was agonized, and so were we. The interview looked like petering out altogether. Eventually the Frenchman, in despair and contempt for this English *gaucherie*, thrust one hand into a lapel and treated us to a dissertation on Plato's Republic, on which he claimed to be an authority. Denis intervened and by way of Plato turned the conversation on to Valéry. Here Murry began to get himself more in hand; he brightened visibly; he, too, loved Valéry. Presently the editor and Murry were sitting side by side on the sofa fluently discussing Valéry, and the rest of us breathed more freely.

During these Hampstead years Edwin went as a Scottish delegate to another P.E.N. Congress in Dubrovnik. Remembering what had happened to Gavin while we were in Budapest, I stayed at home this time. I remembered also what had happened to Edwin, but I had now no fears at all for him; I was sure that nothing would disturb his harmony, and nothing in fact did disturb it. Yet I can hardly account for my memory retaining little of what happened officially in that Congress. Yugoslavia could not have been very peaceful just then; the assassination of King Alexander a few months later could not have been an isolated accident, and in Germany Hitler was now on the crest of popular favour, so that the Yugoslavs, like the other new nations, had cause to be nervous. But this Congress must have been more tightly controlled than the Hungarian one, for Edwin came home apparently quite unaffected by political tensions, gaily recounting what fun it had been to breakfast every morning in his hotel with H. G. Wells. The queer thing about Wells's eyes, he said, was that they looked so shallow, without any depth to them, like bright, flat discs of colour. One day as Wells and he were strolling up a steep street after breakfast they met two magnificent Montenegrins, a young man and a young woman in full national rig, each of them about six foot tall and very handsome. 'Wells is a wee man,' said Edwin, 'but he couldn't resist casting his eyes up at the young woman as if wondering whether he might take even that citadel by storm.'

The P.E.N. was already concerning itself about what should be done with the Germans, but Edwin had been more deeply stirred by the sheer beauty of his surroundings than by any political moves. Again and again he returned to describing the serene loveliness of the cruise from Trieste to Dubrovnik, and how impressive were the ruins of Diocletian's palace. I think he had quite withdrawn himself from political awareness and had been simply enjoying the holiday.

We never considered ourselves as belonging to any one social class. We were not Bohemians; we shrank from drunken squalor or drug-induced fantasies. In our house, rooms might be untidy with books and papers but chairs and beds were comfortable, meals reasonably punctual, the ambience tranquil. Yet we did not belong to what is now called The Establishment, nor did we seek to belong to it. Our style of behaviour must have been as un-English as our accents and voices, only we never thought about these at all, until Gavin told us one day that in his school they said he spoke like a little Scotch boy. Living at ease in our own rhythm we were at home with everyone else. We had no sense of being Outsiders; we felt that we belonged to a wide literary culture; our thoughts and feelings reached out into the cosmos and into the unconscious with a sense of natural freedom, and the whole world of books was ours.

Yet a train of events now set itself in motion which brought us ultimately to leave Hampstead. I engaged a new cook and housemaid, Irish Catholics, an aunt and a niece. It was a package deal; they would not be separated; I had to have both or neither. Mary the aunt I loved at sight, and rightly; she proved to be a kindlywoman and a good cook. Julia the niece, a tall gaunt girl who looked rather like De Valera in petticoats and had hard, suspicious eyes behind her spectacles, gave me a sinking feeling which I ignored, for I was busy with a press of work; both reason and expediency told me I should not waste more time in having to hunt for other maids; besides, I believed she was bound to improve, to grow less suspicious under friendly treatment. The press of work continued, and I had to delegate Julia to take Gavin and Matthew for their afternoon canters on the Heath. Presently I became aware that Gavin was obscurely troubled about something, and when I took him out one afternoon I thought I had discovered what it was. He was afraid of the first pond on the Heath, afraid that it could drown him. The pond was reputed to be deep in the middle and people had in fact been drowned there, but who had told Gavin that? We went round it as far as we could, planting my walking-stick every so often in the water, not too far from the edge, to show that it was not very deep and could not come over a little boy's head, until in relief my son told me that Julia had said bad boys were drowned there.

Had I understood then, as I did not, that she had been frightening him with Hell and Sin, I do not know what I should have done to her. As it was, I forbade her to frighten him with bogey stories about drowning. She looked sullen but said nothing. I sang Gavin to sleep as usual that evening and told him again that Julia's talk was nonsense, thinking to myself that he would soon be quite reassured.

In a day or two it happened that I was again tied to my worktable and had to let Julia take out the boy and the dog, and on this afternoon the catastrophe occurred. Gavin, running home across the road that divided our street from the Heath, was knocked down by a petrol tanker; his right leg was broken in two places and his head severely concussed; it was a miracle he was not killed. A breathless small boy beat upon our door to tell us; Edwin and I ran to the place just as the ambulance came to take Gavin to the local hospital.

In the middle of our distress I dealt with Julia, having realized, too late, that I should have heeded the heart-sinking message from my unconscious when I first saw her. How could she have held on to Matthew and let Gavin run in front of the tanker, I demanded, how could she have been so stupid? I could not possibly keep her in my employment, now that I knew she was not to be trusted. She must leave as soon as possible. Julia then told me that ours was a godless house and we were bringing Gavin up to be a little heathen. At last I understood, with certainty, that the boy had run in front of the tanker because he had been running away from Julia. She was sullen, enraged and unrepentant, reiterating that she had only been telling him things every child needed to be told. Mary, her aunt, in tears, said she had always thought Julia and her brother, who was a priest, too hard on people outside the Church, but she could not help it; if Julia went, she would have to go too.

Ultimately, it was my fault, I decided, blaming myself, first for having engaged Julia, and then after I knew she was frightening Gavin for having let her take him out again. 'O, bad bad peerie Willa!' I sobbed, to Edwin's distress. 'If thu keeps on saying that,' he protested, 'thu'll make me believe it.' I knew that this was true, Edwin being supremely suggestible in moments of heightened feeling. I kept my sense of guilt under cover after that, and so began preparing an inward sump of self-accusation and grief.

As soon as Gavin could travel we took him up to a farmhouse in Orkney for a month, to get him away from motor traffic. On our return to London, by great good luck I found Hilde Weissenseel, an 'Aryan' but non-Nazi German, who became our cook and housekeeper, a mainstay of our lives, and Eja Bergmann, a Finnish student learning English, who was the housemaid. Hilde spoke German but little English, Eja spoke some English and very little German; they bought miniature pocket dictionaries of English-German from Woolworth's and tied them to their belts, exchanging words with much laughter as they went about the house. Edwin and I were both hopeful that Gavin would stop twitching and trembling whenever he heard a car engine, and that he would come all right. We became almost a happy household again.

Almost, for the shock to Gavin's system had gone deep and the clear brightness of our little boy was now shadowed by clouds of opaqueness. His confidence in the world and in us had been severely shaken. As Protecting Powers we had failed him and he resented our failure. The hospital doctor had told us to treat him very gently, never to cross him or attempt to 'discipline' him, treatment which was entirely in accord with our own desires and practice, although we sometimes had difficult moments to endure with our resentful child. His leg had been well mended and massaged, but it went to my heart to see that he had lost the thoughtless lightness of his gait and now planted his feet down almost like an infant policeman on a beat. Fortunately, Hilde and Eja, the newcomers, he did not resent; their playful, light-hearted ways with him helped us all. Yet we began to realize that London, with its incessant motor traffic, was not the milieu in which Gavin could quickly recover his confidence. Even our quiet street had its traffic lane at the end of it and was bound to keep him in mind of the accident that had shattered him. These considerations helped us to detach ourselves from the beloved house in Downshire Hill. Also, Edwin's inward unhappiness about the reception of his poems was an extra help to him, although by that time we had already made up our minds to leave London. But for years afterwards, until 1950, whenever we were in London we made a pilgrimage to Hampstead and stood fingering our old garden gate, ostensibly to see if the latch still had the same defect.

Chapter Fifteen

SCOTLAND

1935-1945

We were leaving London, but where were we to go? Edwin had been hankering for Orkney and now Providence took a hand and gave him a leading. He was asked to write a book to be called *Scottish Journey*, in a series already begun by J. B. Priestley with *English Journey* and Philip Gibbs with *European Journey*. To Edwin a journey through Scotland inevitably led north to Orkney, and so, he announced, we were all going up to Orkney. The commission for the book would take care of our expenses. He would borrow Stanley Cursiter's old car, which he had already been offered in case of need (our own car we had given away when we moved to Hampstead), and would make the Journey in that while the rest of us took the steamer from Leith.

Stanley Cursiter, Edwin's one-time class-mate in Kirkwall who had become Director of the Scottish National Gallery in Edinburgh, not only lent but presented him with the old car, a Standard 1921, which was supposed to be run over an Orkney cliff and find an honourable bed in the Atlantic once Edwin had no more use for it. And the most unexpected thing about Edwin's Scottish Journey, I reflected, as Gavin and I waited for him to come off the ferryboat, was that he had accomplished it with the old car still holding together; there sat the Standard among the other cars on the *St Ola's* deck, Edwin at the wheel. But it was the last to come ashore, since something apparently had gone wrong and it would not move. Two members of the crew then suggested, grinning, that the brakes should be taken off. Gently, with dignity, Edwin took them off and successfully ran the car off the boat, drving us afterwards to Isbister House, the front half of a farmhouse which we had rented furnished for three months.

Isbister House faced south on the far side of the Wide Firth, a good way from Kirkwall but only a few miles from Finstown at the head of the bay. The farm fronted the sea, or rather, a small tidal lagoon known as the 'oyce' (pronounced oess) into which a burn partly choked with blossoming yellow flags meandered through the farmyard. A long sandy ridge, smothered in pink thrift, kept the oyce from encroaching on the fields. Isbister was a flowery place, since it got the summer sun all the long day, and the house boasted a fine fuchsia hedge on its west side. One of Edwin's favourite flowers, Queen of the Meadow, the fragrant meadow-sweet, bordered every field and ditch.

Our last visit to Orkney, when we took Gavin there to help his immediate recovery, had brought me under the enchantment of Orkney summer light. On this July day also as we drove to Isbister the sky was cloudless, the surface of the bay glassy; the landscape was tranced in a diffused luminosity shed down from the sky and reflected upward from the sea; the rounded, unspectacular hills of the Islands lay like blue plums on the water. The light was as magical as Italian light, only transmuted from gold into silver under the paler blue of a northern sky. I had thought that it was the great enchantment of Orkney, but now I was to discover another enchantment.

For our previous visit we had no car and were in sole charge of Gavin, so we never went far from our base, spending most of our time by the sea-shore. But now we often left Gavin with Hilde and Eja beside the oyce and in the old Standard visited every haunt of Edwin's boyhood on the main island. There was hardly a field in Orkney without its reminder of legendary past generations, were it only a so-called 'Picts' House', some stone-lined hole half underground or peering from the slope of a hill. There were the brochs, also legendary, many hundreds of years old; another large one was then being excavated at a place called Aikerness. There was the Late Stone Age village dug out of the sand at Skara Brae, how many thousands of years old? We took the whole household to see that and to visit the great tumulus of Maeshowe, entered by a low,wriggling passage but rising inside to cathedral proportions, where chambers of megaliths were hewn as tombs for ancient kings laid in the womb of Mother Earth, possibly with the hope of re-birth, three or perhaps four thousand years ago. Maeshowe was already ancient when some Vikings on their way to Jerusalem left remarks scratched in runic writing on its rock walls. Set up presumably by the same megalith builders the Standing Stones of Stenness, too, still watched the lochs on either side of their circles and registered the journeys of the sun and moon.

It would be difficult for any sensitive child to grow up in Orkney without being aware, not from schooling or other instruction but simply knowing from inside himself, that a long, long line of people had lived there before him. These imagined predecessors had surely enchanted Edwin and made him the kind of poet he was, as the light on rocks and sea had enchanted Stanley Cursiter and made him a painter. Edwin, dreaming in the summer light, with stories and legends filling the air and growing out of the ground at his feet, had used his imagination to people the islands with figures going back to Adam, figures real to him, I thought, however a London critic might dismiss them as 'stilted allegorical nudes walking through a grey landscape'.

On the day we went to Wyre, the little island that was Edwin's earliest remembered home, I was more sure than ever that he had been under the spell of this kind of enchantment. We set off to Wyre in a motor-launch at high tide, between the flow and ebb, the only time at which it is safe to cross that Inner Sound, and made for The Bu, the main or seigneurial farm on the island. Like all old houses in Orkney, The Bu is a long, low, one-storeyed building designed to withstand furious winter winds. It was then little changed inside from what Edwin recollected; he was excited to find the same stone-flagged kitchen with the meal-chest in the same place and the same kind of four-square iron cooking-stove. Yet it was outside the house that his pleasure rose to its highest pitch, when we reached the big grassy mound where he and his sister used to play. The mound was already admitted by scholars to be the remains of a castle built by a Viking free-booter, Kolbein Hruga, and has likely been already excavated and enclosed by the Office of Works, but to Edwin and his sister Clara it had been Cubby Roo's Castle, a witness of ancient adventures, peopled by childish imaginations. From earth to sky the world must have been alive with imagined meaning to the young Edwin. That was an enchantment he carried round with him, I thought, in what he called his true self. Whenever he felt discouraged, if, for instance, the stretch of his imagination back to Adam were mocked in New Verse, he needed only to come to Orkney to be again assured that the extension of the present into the past and the past into the present was no illusion. If his rendering of it were mocked, the fault might lie in his own imperfect rendering, but what he had wished to convey was a reality, the long descent of Man and what he himself hoped for in the continuing destiny of Man.

These enchantments, the luminous veil of summer light and the ubiquitous presence of the past, had not changed in Edwin's lifetime, but the round of seasonal growth on the islands had changed enough to astonish him. As we could all see, Orkney looked very prosperous. The farms Edwin's father had worked with meagre results were now each bringing in about a thousand pounds a year. Acres of waste land, once given over to bracken, had been and were being reclaimed by growing wild white clover or lupins over them, to fix nitrogen in the soil: pastures were lush, cattle abundant, Aberdeen Angus of the glossiest black; waving crops of barley and oats were full and heavy. The people one passed looked as happy as the crops, smiling and friendly, acknowledging one's existence by saying: 'Ay, ay', the general greeting, accompanied by a sideways inclination of the head. Young men and women working in the fields laughed as they worked. How had Orkney escaped the Great Depression?

Eric Linklater, then living in Orkney beside the Harray Loch, told us that the Rowett Research Institute at Aberdeen had done much towards the improvement. Orkney farmers were its best pupils, better than the Highland crofters, who were apparently drained of vitality by their past history and had not the initiative of the Orkney-men. Besides, so many small farms in Orkney belonged to the farmers themselves that labour did not need to be hired. The only financial snag was the cost of shipping animals and cheeses and grain to Aberdeen—sometimes a heavy cost.

Eric was enthusiastic about the intelligence of Orkney farmers and told us this story. Rowett Institute experts had asked one Robertson of Lyness, whose family had owned his farm for three hundred years, to assign them some land for experiments with turnip seed; they were trying to produce a strain of turnip that would resist the saltness and dampness of Orkney winds. After they had sown their drills of seed, Robertson quietly suggested that they might care to add a drill of Lyness seed, of his own growing. When the seeds came up, Robertson's were so much better than the others that he was now paid by the Institute to grow turnip seed for distribution all over the world.

'What a difference between Scotland and Orkney!' said Edwin. In his book, *Scottish Journey* (p. 241), he made the apparently naive statement that Orkney 'represented the only desirable form of life that I found in all my journey through Scotland'. Yet this was not merely wishful thinking, for Orkney was prosperous and happy, and the mainland of Scotland was derelict and depressed, with disused coal-pits, silent shipyards, shut-down factories, and a rate of unemployment twice that of England. The sense of nationhood, Edwin thought, was being quite lost; too many men were idle, on the dole, living in slums, and he was struck by the emptiness of Scottish life. Yet he insisted that the root causes of these evils were economic and that political Nationalism would never cure them. Scotland was suffering from being on the circumference of an economic circle centred on London; it was a victim of the Industrial Age and the banking system and would have suffered as much had it been English. Nationalism would only enable its people to draw a dole from a Scottish instead of a London government; the slums would still exist and most of the people still be poor, since the Scottish National Party was not proposing to revolutionize the economic structure of the country. Only the industrial system itself could modify and ultimately cure the ills it had produced, and that was where lay the main stream of social development for the future, making towards some new kind of Socialism, Edwin thought. And in that main stream Scotland would learn to sweat out the factional intolerance which had begun to ravage it even before the Industrial Age.

As for Orkney, in his book Edwin called the life of Orkney 'an erratic fruition'. Having been isolated for so long from the Industrial Age, it had retained its traditional virtues yet was now able to use and enjoy the discoveries of science which industrialism had made possible. In other words, Orkney had managed to have its cake and eat it. But none the less it lay outside the main stream of future development.

This ruthless setting of Orkney aside as a separate enclave rather surprised me. Looking back now I can see, I think, that it was the beginning of a process in Edwin's mind which separated Orkney from ordinary life and turned it into a kind of Eden, so that the radiance shining over Eden in his later poems was very like the radiance of Orkney summer light.

Meanwhile, enclave or no, Orkney was a holiday gift to us. We did much less work than we had intended and enjoyed a fuller social life than we expected. Another schoolmate of Edwin's, Eunice, the youngest daughter of the one-time parish minister of Kirkwall, the most attractive woman I have ever known, had rented for the summer a house on the other side of the main island and brought her husband, a London stockbroker, and other friends, while Eric Linklater had a cluster of family relations living near him. Among them all we were caught up in a round of gay hospitality. We seemed always to be running the old car across the Lyde Road on our way to a luncheon party or a dinner party or what have you, when we were not giving parties ourselves. Matthew had a delirious time vainly chasing hares up the hillsides; Gavin, daily losing his tensions, played beside the oyce; Hilde and Eja swam in the sea and made excursions all over the island. Edwin, when he felt adventurous, took his walking-stick and hat for a stroll along the ridge beside the oyce. The hat was balanced on the walking-stick handle and held high above his head to ward off fierce dive-bombing attacks from the Arctic terns who were nesting among the papery pink flowers of the sea-thrift, glorious birds with wings like scimitars and beaks that could well have damaged his skull, had they not been surprisingly daunted by the inexplicable hat.

During the third month of our stay we began to think about going to St Andrews. Ever since attending a P.E.N. Congress in Edinburgh, in 1933, the year after Budapest, we had been urged to return to Scotland, on the flattering plea that Scotland needed us. We had certainly proved useful during that Congress; having discovered that 'drinks' at all receptions were hidden in speak-easies tucked away round corners at the end of corridors or at the very top of a building, to be reached only by a lift, we had devoted ourselves to guiding bemused foreigners away from the main display of tea and coffee urns, flanked by mineral waters, towards the beer and whisky so furtively sequestered. Yet we did not think seriously of moving into Scotland until after Gavin's accident. The most persistent urging had come from James Whyte in St Andrews, who said he was building two modern houses in North Street and one of them should be ours. In St Andrews he was doing his best for the Scottish Renaissance by publishing a magazine: *The Modern Scot*, and opening an up-to-date bookshop.

I thought, mistakenly, that I had not much of the nostalgia for which St Andrews graduates were then notorious, but the prospect of a house there attracted me and I believed that it would be a satisfying place for Gavin to grow up in. I had already assured Edwin in London that St Andrews would not be disappointing like Montrose since it had an ancient university and a large girls' public school, St Leonards; there would be intelligent company on the staff of either institution; we should make friends there and feel at home. So it came as a disappointment to me when James Whyte wrote to say he could not keep his new house waiting any longer and had let it to the French lecturer. He offered to find us a furnished house until we could rent one for ourselves, if we were really coming to St Andrews.

Instead of being disappointed, Edwin, it appeared, was nursing the idea of staying permanently in Orkney. The Church of Scotland and the United Free Churches had merged with each other and in each parish there was now a redundant manse for disposal. Edwin suggested that we could at least go and look at one or two of them; perhaps we might rent one, since we could not buy.

My immediate reaction was: why not? Edwin's *Scottish Journey* had roused in him a shrinking from Scotland and a deep attraction towards Orkney, and if he wanted Orkney he should have it. We went to look at various manses, all in country parishes full of light and fresh air. But to my own astonishment, the more manses I saw, the less willing I was to live in any of them. I used not to shrink from new environments, yet now I felt vulnerable, even a little scared at the idea of settling permanently in Orkney, as if it meant our crawling well out on a limb. Commonsense objections began to rise in my mind, and this in itself I thought peculiar. What I most wanted to do was to live with Edwin, and I could not bear the feeling that we were beginning to lean in opposite directions.

This failure of confidence, I supposed, came from the failures of my body, for I was still unable to lift and carry heavy weights, while the manses all needed to have buckets of fuel carried upstairs to bedroom fires, and only one of them had a gas cooker in the kitchen as well as a large coal-fed range. But if Hilde were willing to stay with us we might manage. Eja was due to go back to Finland almost at once, yet surely some stout domestic help could be found? With these considerations I tried to beat down my unwillingness, but in vain, and its persistence made me uneasy. My cowardly lack of enthusiasm surprised Edwin, too: he assumed that I must be afraid of that dark tunnel, the Orkney winter.

So I began to ask questions about winter living conditions. The winter climate, I learned, was not bitterly cold but was harassed by strong winds that were also damp. Any room without a fire lit in it once a week through the winter would have mould and fungus growing over everything. Eric Linklater supplied alarming accounts of hurricane force winds, which, he said, not only whipped the tops off the waves on the Harray Loch but lifted the surface water clean off in one great sheet and crashed it on to his house. He had amused us earlier by boasting that he was building an enormous nursery wing, but I perceived now that he was not so keen on living in Orkney as he had been. In winter the Orkney winds were tyrants; like all tyrants they were the subject of many jokes. (Before the hurricane me auntie had three hen-hooses, and now she's got a dozen.)

Yet winter in Orkney might be possible for us in a town, in Kirkwall or Stromness, where some shelter from the elements could be found, where Gavin could get easily to school and it would not matter so much that darkness closed in before three in the afternoon. My heart was still heavy none the less and I was relieved to discover that no houses to let could be heard of in either of these towns. Then I began to produce financial reasons why staying in Orkney was impracticable. We did not own a house and have successful fiction to our credit as Eric Linklater did, nor did we own a farm or a share of a farm to back us up. We should be freelancing at an end of the earth remote from London publishers; even if publishers were willing to send us work it would be precarious. I did not choose to remember that the Sonntagberg had been even more remote. I argued instead that our funds were running low, and it would be expensive to get our furniture up as far as Orkney.

In short, in the confusion of my self-ignorance I went through all kinds of mental contortions to make staying in Orkney appear unwise. Then the true basic cause of this unwillingness became evident. I was acting as goalkeeper at the bridge over the burn outside Isbister while Gavin and Edwin kicked a tennis-ball about,and my inside suddenly fell out again. Something within me had been aware that my organs were once more displacing themselves. The only doctor we could get from Finstown was elderly, ham-fisted and inexpert for my troubles; I needed more medical skill than he could provide. Edwin wrote to James Whyte at once and we set about preparing to leave by the cattle-boat for Leith.

I had suspected that all my objections were absurd. These arguments I had been trotting out were mere puppets, pulled into action by unguessed-at strings. My unconscious, I felt, had let me down badly, in every sense, and in turn I had let Edwin down.

But the cruise in the cattle-boat, the Amelia, during two days of halcyon weather, was so pleasant that we all enjoyed it. We ate with the friendly crew in the open space below decks amidship, round which our bunks were ranged, and we ate well, mostly herring, washed down by mugs of strong black tea qualified with condensed milk. The whole boat was ours to stroll in, and we all spent time on the bridge chatting to the captain. He told us that no cattle-boat carrying pigs would ever venture into a rough sea, since pigs were bad sailors; if the Amelia found bad weather ahead of her she ran for shelter into the nearest roadstead, so that we need not fear being caught in a storm. As it was, pausing only at Aberdeen, we dreamed our way down the coast on the smoothest of seas, from which Scotland looked lovely.

We had taken passage in the Amelia because she was cheap; the fare was one pound each for an adult all the way from Kirkwall to Leith, ten shillings for Gavin and nothing at all for Matthew the dog. Our travelling expenses were covered by the five pounds the local postman paid us for the old Standard, which we were shameless enough to sell, being hard up. And our combined food-bill for the two days came to ten shillings, including rations for Matthew.

On our cruise we overhauled a graceful tall ship, with *Suomi* painted on her black hull in large white letters, and discovered from Eja that Suomi meant Finland. Eja was leaning over the bulwark, all eyes, murmuring Suomi, Suomi, with long-drawn yearning vowels; this was a Finnish timber-ship perhaps going home, she said, and she might even get aboard that very ship in Leith, as indeed she did.

The peace of these days was tranquillizing; all our problems seemed simplified, and small buds of hope opened in me. Orkney had been Edwin's starting-place, but I could not feel it was meant to be his destination. After all, he had said himself that Orkney lay outside the main stream of future social development. He would be less cut off from the contemporary world in St Andrews. In this way I sought to comfort myself for my dereliction.

At first things looked as if they were going to turn out well for us at St Andrews. We liked the terrace house James Whyte had taken for us, on top of the cliffs beside the Castle, with the North Sea at our front door instead of a garden. Edwin wrote to the manager of our London bank asking for an overdraft and got it. An intelligent and sympathetic woman doctor, Dorothy Douglas, took me in hand and fixed me up so that I could at least carry on. Everything was within easy reach, a school for Gavin, shops, ancient ruins and pleasant walks by the sea. We had only to come to terms with it all, and first with James Whyte, his bookshop and his magazine, *The Modern Scot*.

We went to dine with James in his house, an old one in South Street thoroughly modernized inside. It was padded everywhere with cushions; the sitting-room ceiling had been painted blue to match them and silvered with stars. James was obviously a young man who liked to be in the fashion and could afford it; ceilings like his must have then been 'the fashion', and walls outfacing each other in contrasting colours. After dinner we heard a Sibelius symphony on his gramophone, for Sibelius was in the fashion too; we did not know the symphony and felt, as we told each other later, that we were being ushered into a whole new world, since in James's house the furniture, the pictures, the lighting, as well as the music, were all fashionably avant-garde.

James himself was self-conscious but kindly, and arranged for us to visit his shop and look at his two new houses. The shop had been ingeniously constructed out of a barrel-vaulted room on the ground floor of another old building, a little farther along South Street. Both his house and the shop, seen from outside, were built in a traditional Scottish style with stones somewhat rough and full of character, carefully restored, a credit to their new owner. The barrel-vaulting inside the shop made an attractive setting for books, but its old-world atmosphere was startlingly contradicted by a fresco that faced one on entering; beside the end of the counter there was a large caricature of John Knox astride a beer-cask, raising high a reaming tankard, recognizably John Knox although he had a raddled nose and a wicked leer.

'We thought the young people would like it,' said James, a little peevishly, 'but the St Leonards girls have been forbidden to enter the shop.' The fresco had been suggested by his right-hand satellite, John, whom we had not yet met. So far, James complained, very few students had come in. Perhaps when term began again more of them would venture.

The shelves were impressively well stocked, and on the counter all the most modern magazines from France and the United States were laid out, together with a copy of nearly every book one had seen recently reviewed. Only customers were lacking. The ingratiating young salesman behind the counter was filling in time by embroidering a brown silk counterpane with his own design of autumn leaves.

Edwin said little, except to remark that one would have expected the students to find it an exciting shop. He told me later that he had been struck by its sheer incongruity with the Scotland he had seen on his Journey, and that he was inclined to be sorry for James.

The new houses, which had been designed by James and John between them, had a perverse ingenuity in their lay-out. The main entry was by the back door; one went in off the street into a long hall leading to the front door, which faced a walled-in quadrangle of grass, occupying a site which in my day had held three fishermen's cottages. The fishermen's quarter was gone, said James, for no trawlers went out now from St Andrews.

The house which should have been Edwin's and mine, opening off the right of the hall, was shut, because the lecturer and his wife were not at home, but James showed us through the left-hand house belonging to John. From one side of the reception room on the ground floor a spiral staircase corkscrewed up, leading, James said, to a picture gallery on the roof. Its steps had a new kind of composition laid over them, giving a mosaic effect. James was proud of that staircase; he pointed out the composition, guaranteed non-skidding, and stood gazing affectionately up the spiral. The furnishings of the house were all expensively modern; the large desk in John's study was sumptuous, the lamps grandly angular and the curtains opulent. The other house had no spiral stairway, said James; this house had been specially designed for John, who enjoyed having up-to-date comfort, after working on a newspaper in Dundee all day, and liked going up to the picture gallery.

We met John that evening. He had changed into a becomingly faded kilt and was charming; his fair hair and blue eyes made him look younger than he was. His view of the Scottish Renaissance in St Andrews was brightly hopeful. Only a little more time was needed until the students got over their shyness. Some of them had already been coming to coffee in his house of an evening, and more would yet come.

It seemed an odd set-up. James was an American whose mother had married a Scottish M.P.; he had adopted his stepfather's country as well as his name. John claimed to come from an originally English family and had been boasting that a kinsman of his was an Anglican bishop. Apparently they were both Scots by adoption only. James's love for Scotland was tangled up with his love for John, while John's love for Scotland was largely, we thought, a love for John himself. In London we had observed that such relationships, with some few exceptions, tended to be unstable, and the future of James's magazine and bookshop began to look dubious.

The magazine was better than one might have expected, for its lay-out was harmonious and its contents not too parochial. Christopher Grieve and F. G. Scott and Edwin were all contributing to it from time to time. One felt that it deserved to succeed. The bookshop on the other hand did not thrive at all, not even after the University term had begun. As for the relationship between James and John, that proved to be as unstable as we had feared. Every now and then James had spurts of feeling that he was being exploited, which provoked him to outbursts of masterful bad temper. I suppose that people brought up to great wealth from infancy are given to these suspicions. As a baby, James once told me, he had always had a bodyguard beside his pram in the Central Park of New York, for fear of kidnappers. Influenced by John he had spent a great deal of money in St Andrews, and it was not unreasonable in him to feel that he was reaping a meagre harvest. But any outburst of his drove John into hysterics at once. I never knew of an evening when I would not hear sounds of sobbing from the newel post at the foot of our stairs over which John would be bowed in grief, crying: 'Willa, I must speak to you.' And after hearing from John what James had said, I would receive a more dignified message by James's housekeeper, begging me to call on James, please, at such-and-such an hour next day, in order to hear his side of the story.

After some years of increasing tension, during which James's bookshop went on being shunned by most people in the town and his magazine never achieved a satisfactory circulation, the near approach of the war made his position untenable. In the bar of the Royal and Ancient Golf Club he was denounced as a spy for Hitler. A picture-gallery on the roof of his North Street houses? Nonsense: that was a concrete emplacement for machine-guns, commanding the bay. Innocent excursions into the bay by motor-launch? Obviously the fellow had been nosing out secret rendezvous for submarines. He had written a book about Fife, hadn't he, with special emphasis on its hills? Outlook posts for

Germans, of course. If he wasn't a spy, what was he doing in St Andrews at all? These aspersions spread into the staff rooms of St Leonards and presently the town was buzzing with dark suspicions about James. He gave up the struggle. He left his super-charged car to John and departed to America, on the reasonable plea that he was tired of paying double income-tax, once in America and once in Britain. In Washington he got married and opened another up-to-date bookshop, which was presumably appreciated by that city. Meanwhile, once war had been declared, the St Andrews gossip-mongers accounted for his absence by saying that the government had very properly arrested him and put him in the Tower. I was even told that he had been beheaded. This was one aspect of the town in which I had assured Edwin we should feel at home.

We did not at once discover what St Andrews was like. The people who generated fear and disapproval of James's shop and all his doings were at the upper end of the social scale, Hugh Kingsmills 'mupples', but we began to run up against uncivilized anomalies at all levels of society.

There was the affair of Gavin's schooling. He had been put into the youngest class of the junior school in the town's academy, the Madras College, which I remembered as an excellent school. I had done my training as a teacher of Classics there, and I delivered my son to the headmaster without any special misgivings. But day after day for the next few weeks Gavin became nervier, until he was beginning to jerk and twitch as he had done in London after his accident. The teacher was strapping him, he said, nearly every day.

This startled me. In my school-days every teacher in a Scottish elementary school kept a leather strap, or tawse, in the desk and used it regularly, but I saw no strapping done either in Montrose Academy or in the Senior Madras College. That Gavin should be strapped was something I had not expected. Besides, I had told the headmaster that he was still recovering from the shock of a bad accident.

I let him stay off school that day, and went down to see his teacher at the school break, preparing to reason with her in the manner of one who believed in imaginative understanding. But I had reckoned without the residue of unreconstructed viking in me that rose to the surface when she told me, in a voice as angry as Hitler's, that boys needed to be hardened if they were to grow into Men, not Mollycoddles. She had strapped Gavin because he was very disobedient. He had not folded his arms when she told the class to do so, and when he did at last fold them he drove his elbow into the side of the little girl next to him. I then informed her that I was not going to leave my nervous little boy to be hardened by her drill-sergeant methods, and that he would not be returning to her class.

This unforeseen gesture of mine landed us in a difficulty. If Gavin were not to be safe from strapping in the Junior Madras, he would be even less safe in an elementary school. That left only the preparatory school, New Park, which had just been started at the end of the Lade Braes, a school for small boys only, on the English model. Edwin and I, being accustomed to the traditional pattern of Scottish schooling in which boys and girls were educated together as a matter of course, thought the English model of segregation much less sensible and natural. Yet the New Park school was now being patronized by the same professional classes who in my time had sent their sons and daughters to the Madras College. The daughters were attending St Leonards and the sons went to New Park before going on to boys' public schools. So New Park conferred superior social status and its fees were high. Yet Gavin must be sent there, we decided, and for a long time did not regret the decision. The prep, school teachers used neither strap nor cane and were kind to our nervous little boy.

As a student I had not been aware of social stratification in the town, although the tendency may have existed, and there had been little of it in the University. Nowadays things were different. This I learned from Dr Drury Oeser, whose husband Oscar had just been made head of the new Psychology Department. Drury, herself a doctor of psychology and fresh from Cambridge, passed on to me her astonishment at the rigid protocol observed in the University. When she was out shopping on her bicycle, she said, and saw one of Oscar's research students, of course she waved to him in a friendly manner. But the students had privately begged her not to do so, pleading that they would get into trouble, since staff and students were not supposed to recognize each other in the street. She had also been told, by a professor's wife, that she should not have invited professors' wives and lecturers' wives to the same tea-party. Some of the Top Brass were simply awful, said Drury. One old professor had found a couple of Freud's books in the library, and swore they were covered with 'pornographic thumb-marks'. Oscar had had to fight to keep them from being removed.

Had I not been unsuspicious, I might have guessed from an incident happening to me that the University climate had changed. A fellow-student of mine, who took her Classics degree the year after I did and had inherited my text-books and notebooks, was now a war-widow, with one little girl, and had come to live in St Andrews as junior assistant in the Latin Department, a post I had myself held for a year in 1914. I dressed myself in my best London clothes, took Gavin by the hand and went to call on her, expecting a warm welcome. I did not get it. Apparently I had come to St Andrews to carry on the kind of anarchic life we had been used to in pre-war days, when students lived in town lodgings, and I was likely to undermine the respectable status she had now acquired, married as I was to 'a man who wrote for the papers' while she was sending her daughter to St Leonards. This unexpected rebuff hurt my feelings so much that I had taken it only as a personal matter, not as a symptom of a changed social climate.

But my one-time friend was not the only member of the University staff to high-hat us. The whole English Department, where we might have expected to meet some friendly interest, ignored us, taking its tone from the professor, who refused to admit that any contemporary work could be regarded as literature, or any contemporary writers as literary men. For Yeats he made an exception; he boasted that Yeats had once spent an afternoon on his sofa; but for an upstart like Edwin Muir, who was now labelled in the University as 'a man who wrote for the papers' (so we were told), no exception could be made. Only the Oesers, the Greek Reader and one or two professors from the Divinity College of St Mary's were humanly friendly.

At first we were more amused than resentful. I remember a hilarious Sunday morning Edwin and I spent composing libellous clerihews about all the University high-hatters.

We had also other eccentrics to keep cheerful company with us, a classical scholar and a mathematician, for instance, refugees from Hitler's Germany. The classical scholar, Otto, conveyed the information that Werner Jaeger, the distinguished classicist, was booked to lecture one evening in St Andrews on his pilgrimage from Germany to the States, but that no one had arranged to show him any hospitality. After the lecture he was supposed to go back to his hotel room without even the offer of a drink. This seemed a scandalous let-down on the part of what was, after all, my University, and after consulting Hilde I invited Werner Jaeger to sup with us at the close of his lecture. We had a delightfully uninhibited European evening with plenty of wine. The professor went back to his hotel room warmed and exhilarated, and so the honour of St Andrews University was saved. Again, when the Prager Quartet came to play in St Andrews, we seized the chance of having another unbuttoned European evening and invited them to supper after their performance.

Edwin always enjoyed a social occasion where wine flowed freely. He did not get drunk but rose into a state of benevolence towards the whole company, which sometimes led to his dropping a light butterfly kiss on the cheek of any lady sitting beside him. Drury Oeser was surprised the first time this tribute was paid to her, but, like Drury, people got used to Edwin's pleasant way of expressing affection. As the thirties wore on, each year after 1936 seeming worse than the one before, these occasions became rarer, since we did not have much heart for even small celebrations, but they did not altogether cease. We were never quite in the wilderness, although aware of many blanks in our social life.

Men who 'wrote for the papers'—never mind what papers—had apparently no standing in Scotland. A Scottish publisher proposed to Edwin that he should write a book which would take him about a year to do and offered him an advance of £30. When Edwin rejected the offer, pointing out that it was ludicrous, the publisher was surprised. He did not actually say that writers were lucky to be published at all and that the triumph of being allowed to 'show off ' in print, almost the equivalent of being granted a pulpit, should be largely its own reward, but we sensed that attitude in the back of his mind.

Our own new friends did not despise us for earning a living by writing, but they were interested in too many other things to have time left for modern literature. We found ourselves caught up in discussions on psychology, sociology, politics—most especially politics, since the treachery of London politicians concerning the Spanish Civil War and Hitler's bullying demands in Europe was a never-ending topic for the Oesers. Professionally, Oscar was interested in group-reactions—he was running a team of researchers into group attitudes in Dundee, where more women than men were in employment—and he made us aware how many groups in St Andrews were at loggerheads. Between them, the University and St Leonards Girls' School were buying up or taking over more and more space for new buildings, acquiring more and more old buildings for reconstruction, and the townsfolk objected, complaining that they were being crowded out of their own town. In my time, the students living in town lodgings had formed a link between town and gown; the landladies took money from but also a possessive and maternal interest in their lodgers. Now that the students were confined to residential hostels the town made no direct profit out of them and there was huffy resentment among the townspeople. They were beginning also to dislike the Royal and Ancient Golf Club, since it was filling up with retired proconsuls, mostly from India, who did their own shopping with large marketing bags and were heard in loud voices referring to the townsfolk as 'the natives'. As for the University itself, it was split from top to bottom not only by academic jealousies but by a rift between partisans and opponents of the new Principal. There seemed to be no community to which people felt they all belonged in spite of differences.

This fragmentation bore out Edwin's conclusion that Scotland lacked a unifying centre. Perhaps the Scottish Kirk brought people close together on Sundays, but even on Sundays they were censorious. To make a little focus of our own, we fell in with Oscar's idea of starting a Discussion Club that would counteract this factional exclusiveness. There were thirteen members including the Oesers and ourselves; we met alternately in the Oesers' house and in ours; we talked openly and freely to each other, without condescension from the more educated to the less, and we became warmly friendly. The topics discussed tended to be anything but literary, which was not surprising when one considers the membership: two workmen from a nearby paper mill, a master mason who was a Socialist of Edwin's old-fashioned kind, three junior mistresses from St Leonards, one of the town's scavengers, the Congregational minister (a woman), and a senior master from the Madras College. The Thirteen Club carried on until the war was imminent. We had not thought of it as an experiment in Adult Education, but it was; we all learned something from each other; and it had at least one result we did not expect. With tears in his eyes one of the paper-mill workmen thanked us for helping him to sort out and express his ideas, for he had just been appointed secretary of his local Trade Union, and without the Club, he said, he would never have found the necessary confidence. I suspect that Oscar was taking professional note of our group reactions; had we realized that at the time we might have been self-conscious.

Yet the Club discussions, friendly as they were, did not fill the blank in Edwin's life. He felt about them as a keen air pilot might feel if he had to spend his time tinkering with faulty engines instead of flying gloriously into space. We all knew too little about politics to do more than tinker with ideas about them, and in any case Edwin felt that they were only part of the machinery of living. Translating Kafka, in his opinion, was a more meaningful occupation than political argument. But no one in St Andrews except ourselves had ever heard of or cared to hear of Kafka and no one knew what Edwin was driving at in his way of life, or in his poetry. He began to wonder whether he knew himself what he was driving at, and that made him ultimately start taking notes for an autobiography in 1938.

For some years before then our private life went on well enough. We were merely ignored, not persecuted, and the natural man in Edwin took comfort from the natural woman in me. In a way, I was the more fulfilled of us two, for I could see Gavin growing fast and happily, while poems dawned on Edwin only at rare intervals.

Hugh Kingsmill and Hesketh Pearson came to see us on their way to Skye, following the footsteps of Dr Johnson and Boswell, in order to concoct a book which they called *Skye High*. They hoped to make some money by it, but I fear that was a forlorn hope, although they were overflowing with their usual brand of fun, which refreshed us to such an extent that I still remember my gratitude for their visit.

Before that, another London friend of ours, Leslie Mitchell, had started Edwin on something which had consequences. After writing many varied books, novels of adventure, historical novels, archaeological studies, Leslie had composed a trilogy of Scottish novels under a pseudonym, Lewis Grassic Gibbon, deriving from his mother's name, and had been visiting Aberdeen, one of the possible locations for the third novel, *Grey Granite*. He had put his heart into the first two novels, *Sunset Song* and *Cloud Howe*, which were about Kincardineshire, the rural countryside round the Cairn o' Mounth where he had been born (practically under a stook in a harvest field, he boasted), but he had made his trilogy finish up in a city. Here I think he was following a theory rather than the promptings of his heart, and perhaps that was why on this occasion Aberdeen had put him in a wry mood of indignation; he kept dwelling on the boorishness with which his Aberdeen host had been treating the hostess, his wife, the kind of behaviour that raised all Leslie's hackles. But it did not take long for his natural gaiety to rise above that mood, for he generated an exciting vitality around him when in congenial company. In high spirits he then sketched for us a scheme which he and Christopher Grieve had been planning: a series of small books about Scotland to be called *The Voice of Scotland*; in which Routledge, of London, had already shown an interest. Neil Gunn was to write about Whisky and Scotland, since he knew more about good whisky than anyone else in the country, Eric Linklater was describing the fighting between England and Scotland (*The Lion and the Unicorn*), Compton Mackenzie was to tackle Catholicism, William Power of Glasgow had already been asked to do *Literature and Oatmeal*, but Leslie wanted Edwin to take some specifically literary subject; why not Walter Scott? And he wanted me to write about *Mrs Grundy in Scotland*, while A. S. Neill would be the very man to do *Education in Scotland*. Christopher was to end the series with a volume on *Red Scotland*. It all sounded like great fun to me.

In that spirit I wrote my Grundy book, more or less to entertain Leslie Mitchell, and it was a slap-dash performance. But when Edwin sat down to do *Scott and Scotland* (published in 1936) something of a very different nature emerged, with an undertone of personal exasperation in it, to be found in no other book of Edwin's. The emptiness in Scottish life which he had been aware of during his Journey and was now aware of in St Andrews, a hiatus caused, he felt, by the lack of an organic society with an alive centre, seemed to him to have crippled Walter Scott in spite of his genius and was bound to cripple any writer still trying to produce Scottish literature or any critic trying to assess it. The personal feeling conies through in quietly devastating remarks like this: 'Scott spent most of his days in a hiatus, in a country, that is to say, which was neither a nation nor a province, and had, instead of a centre, a blank, an Edinburgh, in the middle of it.' Or in contemptuous comment like this: 'Such is Scottish criticism; without standards, sensibility, or even common sense; more like a disease of literature than a corrective. I have tried to analyse some of its causes and thus explain it. To justify it would be beyond the skill of any writer.'

Scott's predicament Edwin saw as a conflict of allegiances between Scotland, where tradition was already breaking up— 'the end of an auld sang'—and England, where tradition was still whole and solid behind the Hanoverian government. The breakup of Scotland had been brought about by many causes, by history, geography, economics as well as by the nature of the Scottish people, but, for a literary man, was most acutely felt in the devaluation of the Scottish language itself, which had been impoverished ever since the Reformers set up an English Bible with all the prestige of sacred writing, making it appear that their God understood English rather than Scots. After the Reformation, English became the Sunday language for serious thought and reflection while Scots was the language of everyday domestic sentiment, not a whole language but only part of one. Edwin says succinctly 'the lack of a whole language . . . finally means the lack of a whole mind'. He deduces that 'a Scottish writer who wishes to achieve some approximation to completeness has no choice except to absorb the English tradition', since in Scotland he will find 'neither an organic community to round off his conceptions, nor a major literary tradition to support him, nor even a faith among the people themselves that a Scottish literature is possible or desirable, nor any opportunity, finally, of making a livelihood by his work'. All these provocative statements occur in the Introduction, which finishes by saying that the problem cannot be solved by writing poems in Scots.

Nothing in the rest of the book could make up to Christopher Grieve for this flat denial of the gospel according to Hugh Mac-Diarmid, neither the delicate discrimination with which Edwin compared Scottish poetry before the Reformation with that produced after it, nor the candour of this tribute: 'a really original poet like Hugh MacDiarmid has never received in Scotland any criticism of his more ambitious poems which can be of the slightest use to him'. For Christopher, Edwin now became The Enemy, and his fighting blood, like that of a Border cateran, prompted a literary vendetta against Edwin Muir which went on for years, during which he published many vituperative polemics to which Edwin made no answer of any kind. I think Edwin's indifference to all this invective was genuine, although he regretted the rupture of friendly relations; these attacks on himself seemed a small issue compared to what was happening in the world at large.

Yet I grieved. The uncharacteristic acerbity of Edwin's remarks about Scotland was a measure of the effect living in St Andrews had had on him, and I knew that I was responsible for his being in St Andrews. Neither by look nor word did Edwin blame me, but I blamed myself.

To the eye, St Andrews was as pleasant a small town as it had been in my student days. Besides its natural advantages of sea and sands and links it had an aura of past history that helped one's imagination: the old ruins and half-ruins were integral parts of the town, as St Salvator's Chapel and tower were parts of the University. Past and present belonged to each other, wherever one turned. I knew that Gavin felt he belonged to St Andrews and loved it; as for me, I could not help still loving its old stones, not to mention the clefts and dells to the south of it where I had enjoyed so many student picnics among the kingcups and the little shell-sand beaches. Yet I felt like an embodied ghost in these familiar surroundings—worse than being a disembodied ghost—and the sunlight, the glow had vanished from them; colour and tone were changing to an unending grey. It was as if an invisible storm-cloud were darkening all the air, and for Edwin there was not even the memory of student sunlight.

The storm-cloud was not merely local, not merely produced by the dissensions in the town and Edwin's aversion from Scottish parochialism. It was a storm-cloud that stretched all over Europe, from Spain to Moscow, where Stalin was staging faked political trials. The turbulence around Hitler came most nearly home to us, even more than the Spanish Civil War, since Hermann Broch was projecting directly into our own climate of feeling all that was happening in Austria. With violence and murder crossing the Austrian frontier from Nazi Germany and appearing openly in the streets of Vienna, Broch, a Jewish writer, could not but feel despairing about the future; at the same time, being a philosopher and mathematician, he could not help schematizing his despairs into logical systems over which he brooded incessantly, passing them on to us. What shattered him most, he told us, was to find the prophecies actually coming true which he had been elaborating for the past twenty years, ever since the 1914 war. And since these prophecies included the forecast that Europe's devotion to Art, romantic outlook, way of thinking, basic philosophy, would have no meaning at all in the coming epoch, the great collapse into Nothingness which was beginning in Germany, he was beset by the temptation to cry: What's the use? 'We must march through Nothingness', he said, through the coming war' of which we all speak but which is nearer to us than to you because we are too close to Germany'. It was foolish of Edwin and me to say 'only politics'; for one could no longer apply the word 'only' to politics, which were already emitting a deadly breath that would change all other values into a heap of cold ashes. 'Kunst! Dichtung!! I can almost no longer see them,' wrote Hermann at one point. It might be more sensible, more becoming, to give up trying to write and start instead some textile or grocery business or a shop for selling gas masks.

Yet he had no money to start a business with, and since his father's death, which had left him, he said, poorer than before, he was responsible for an array of people whom he could not leave to starve. The realization of this finally shocked him out of his broodings and he made up his mind to write after all. He was planning three books: one about *The Death of Virgil*, one a philosophical work to be called *A Theory of Humanity*, and one a novel about peasant life.

I was finishing translating a novel of his, *Die Unbekannte Grösse*—'The Unknown Quantity'—but as his personal danger in Austria loomed larger he began sending also, for safe-keeping, great wedges of manuscript from *The Death of Virgil*. Almost gaily he pointed out that in one chapter he had written the longest sentence that had ever been composed in the world, a sentence that would need signposts on its slopes to keep readers from losing the way. It was, indeed, a sentence that stretched over at least six large pages of close typing.

Broch had also written a play that had been produced in Zürich, and already in 1934 his secretary, Anja Herzog, had come to stay with us during a visit to this country to find out if there was any chance of the play's being put on here. (It was not put on.) Anja, who had all the charm of a sensitive Viennese, was born an Austrian, had been transformed by political events into a Hungarian—or was it a Roumanian?—and was now willy-nilly a Czech. That was why Broch had sent her instead of coming himself; he was so sure that war would divide Austria and Britain that he feared he might be regarded as a potential enemy, while Anja was nominally a potential ally and should run no risk of a concentration camp. At the same time as he smelt war coming, even in England, he had an exaggerated notion of the stability of English cultural life. 'In England,' he told us (ignoring Scotland), 'development is going more slowly, I hope so slowly that the new forms of the Zeitgeist will have time to find a shape for themselves, so that one will not abruptly fetch up on that verge of Nothingness which ends in madness.'

'We are here a whole generation ahead of you,' he said again; 'you still have the old values, art is still a reality, you still have something like an eternity before you, perhaps only a small one, but one in which you can live.' Eternity, or Infinity, or Unendingness, 'Ewigkeit', was for Broch the only thing worth devoting oneself to; it was what man lived by, he said, and by that only. In the coming age of Nothingness there would be no Ewigkeit, no lasting devotion, no disinterested loyalty.

This, then, was the general darkening background against which Edwin's poems came into being, one by one. They were published in 1937, entitled *Journeys and Places*. None of the Journeys or the Places was a direct representation of raw personal experience. Feelings of bewilderment, of baffled loss, of mental trouble, of 'conclusion without fulfilment', are transmuted by his imagination into other strange, remote forms. Tristram goes mad and recovers, Hölderlin goes mad and does not recover, Troy appears as a 'sack-end' of history, the Enchanted Knight stricken in a field comes back again, the poet meditates on his life before the Fall and wanders through solitary, private places, which are not at all like St Andrews, 'a lost player upon a hill' which is no hill that could be identified.

Meanwhile we kept urging Broch to come at once to St Andrews and stay with us, to escape from Austria while there was yet time. He seemed surprisingly unable to take the decisive step, as if he had argued himself to a standstill. Yes, of course he would come, very gladly, he said, only not yet: there were money affairs to settle, his mother must be looked after, and then there was his son. This was the first time we had heard of a son, and he had never mentioned a wife, but we asked no questions; we merely kept on pressing him to come, while he went on building up his books and his philosophical systems, heroically striving 'to find some shape for the bestiality of the world'. He told us that perhaps it would come to something, more anyhow than *The Unknown Quantity*, which 'was written in the deepest depression and got by main force on to paper'.

When Hitler took over Austria, in 1938, Broch was cast at once into prison. But there, as he told us later, he had luck, for the prison Commandant was an admirer of his work and let him have writing materials and various other privileges. He was released about a month later and was now ready to come to us if it could be arranged, since a brother of his was to take care of his mother. After some difficulty, with the help of literary friends, including the Schiffs, we got the Home Office persuaded that he was a desirable person to let into Britain, and he arrived in St Andrews.

By this time we had rented the Congregational manse, which the minister could not afford to live in, and had our own furniture again around us. But the spare bedroom at the top of the house— all we could offer Hermann—was spare enough in comfort, like our other bedrooms, and had only a small gas fire to warm it. Yet he confined himself to it day after day, answering letters from desperate people in Vienna who thought he might help them to get out too. I could not persuade him to shift into the much warmer drawing-room to do his writing; he came out of solitary confinement only for meals, for going walks in the afternoon, and in the evenings. He was glad to have escaped from Austria, glad to be with us, but he was profoundly unhappy. He did not believe that for people of the old order, like himself and us, there was any possibility of collaborating with the forces of the new, no chance of modifying their destructive rush into Nothingness, their abandonment of all recognizable ethical motives, without which humanity would become inhuman. Germany, he said, like all paranoiac people, was urged on by a love-hate for Death, which had become the prevalent European disease. Not for nothing had Heidegger, that philosopher of Angst and Death, been accepted as *the* German philosopher. Broch saw only darkness ahead, although he admitted that Ewigkeit might possibly have a temporary break in its continuity every now and then.

For more than a month he stayed with us until he yielded to the solicitations of the Schiifs who wanted to look after him in London. They were better able to surround him with the physical comforts which I was ruefully aware we could not provide— I had moments of remembering the rich luxury of his mother's flat in Vienna, with its finely wrought linen and engraved glasses, all monogrammed—and they were in touch with influential people who could do something for his future. Willing as we were to keep him, we could not guarantee a future for him. From London he went to America, where his son followed him, having got out of a French concentration camp, and eventually he was given a Guggenheim Fellowship; he settled in Princeton, where later he died, still heroically writing books of words to serve as a formulation of the new forces, if not as a bulwark against them.

The letters he wrote from America were more foreboding than ever. He told me that although Edwin and I might refuse to buy tins of minced Jew (hygienically canned, I suppose, and attractively packaged) or Fresh Child's Liver, plenty of other people would accept them in a hungry world. He saw a totalitarian France coming, a totalitarian England, and an America under dictatorship. The bargaining at Munich had shaken his faith in England, and he did not see victory coming: perhaps he believed that the Germans were going to overwhelm everyone in a world tyranny.

One thing we were at variance about: I would not, I could not promise to translate *The Death of Virgil*. I did not care for it, nor did I feel able to cope with it, for I was growing unaccountably tired. Shortly after Hermann left us, we had lost Hilde too, on a plea we could not resist. She had been used to think there was nothing to be said for marriage, she told me, but now she had been watching Mr Muir and myself for four years and had come to the conclusion that there was a great deal to be said for it. So she wanted to marry before she was too old. She had learned some sense, too, and since it now looked as if Hitler were going to last a long time and she wanted to marry a German, one of her own people, not a foreigner, she would probably be able to put up with the regime and hold her foolish tongue. So she would now be going back to Germany. In a thorough, Hilde-like fashion, she had drawn up a list of men who had wanted to marry her, was writing to ask each of them what he looked for in marriage, and was going to choose the one whose answer pleased her best. Neither Edwin nor I felt that we could oppose these sentiments, and in due time Hilde selected a man on the list, a dentist, I think, and sailed to Germany from Dundee. All of us were in tears at this parting, including Hilde. But, besides being troubled by our affection for her, we found it impossible to get even a near replacement for her efficient services. A Berlin refugee who turned up, a Ph.D., was resentful and humiliated because she was expected to do the cooking while I was busy with translations which she was sure she could do better; then we got a local girl, who cooked rather badly. I grew tireder and more tired, until one day I fainted and Dr Douglas had to be brought in.

My heart was missing beats, she said; I had clearly been living for months beyond my strength. It was high time the strain on my system was eased through my being finally and definitely stitched up by a first-rate surgeon. The best gynaecological surgeon in Scotland was Professor Margaret Fairlie in Dundee and she would book her. But first I would need to lie on my back till I was fit for the operation.

So it happened that the year 1939 which ended in war began for me with a spell in hospital. Margaret Fairlie stitched me up thoroughly and her stitches never came undone again. I had known her well when she was a first-year medical student at St Andrews, a plump, rosy, giggling girl with a drawling, humorous voice. She came to see me some little time after the operation and sat on the edge of my bed, a tall, still woman with a pale, unmoving face and icy-cold hands, and what she then told me about herself I shall now tell for the first time. In my feeble state it made a strong impression on me and is relevant to something that happened later. To tell it cannot trouble Margaret now, for she is dead.

The price she had to pay, she said, for being such a skilful surgeon was that she had to repress all human feeling. She could not risk allowing the faintest quiver of emotion to deflect her hand when she had to make incisions and cuts. She could not risk being aware of her cases as human beings; they were merely objects, areas for operating on. The result was that she was turning into ice inside: she could feel the icy coldness growing within her; but she could not risk other people's lives by trying to save her own and allowing her feelings free play.

This was the time when Edwin, going alone to bed one night, surprised himself by reciting the Lord's Prayer aloud, and discovered that he was, after all, a Christian, 'no matter how bad a one'.

Chapter Sixteen

THE WAR

The Professor of Greek, an elderly, thickset man, could be seen digging a trench on the hill above the pier, in shirtsleeves and braces. More than anything else this brought home to one the change in St Andrews, where the menace of war had closed up the cracks in its social structure almost overnight. Edwin joined the Home Guard, one of a miscellaneous awkward squad including men of all classes, put through their drill by a tradesman who had been a sergeant-major in the first war. Shyly, almost furtively, in a corner of his study, using an old golf club instead of a rifle, Edwin practised the unfamiliar drill, and at night did sentry-go round the Telephone Exchange.

The fear of invasion by Germans, in the forefront of everyone's mind, made people consciously aware of the town they lived in, and because St Andrews was now important to their survival the townspeople were convinced that it was also important to Hitler and would be the first place he attacked. I should guess that in every town or village on the east coast of Britain people thought they would be Hitler's first target. What surprised me was that the intellectuals in the town were loudest in their prophecies of doom—even the Oesers. 'St Andrews will be plastered,' they both said. 'It's only three miles from Leuchars aerodrome; of course it will be plastered with bombs. Simply plastered."

This natural fear did not irritate Edwin and me, but the arguments adduced by another intellectual did. He sat at our table proving that Britain was bound to lose the war, quoting statistics to show how many, many more front-line troops, tanks and aeroplanes the Germans had—as if war were merely a matter of arithmetic. In a revulsion from this line of talk I stood at our front door imagining a file of German motor-cyclists coming down the street and estimated how I could best hurl heavy milk-bottles at them to make sure of crashing one or two before I was myself done in.

What had happened to our gospel of non-violence and imaginative understanding? Hitler and his Nazis had happened. War had happened. One does not carry on a dialogue with a beast of prey crouched to spring. For the moment the need to survive, simply to stay alive, displaced all other considerations including gospels. The beast of prey had already sprung on Austria, Czechoslovakia and Poland; our turn was coming; the dark cloud of destruction was reaching our own country and we could not stop to parley. There had been too much vain parleying already, over Czechoslovakia.

In a way, it was a relief to know that Britain was at last preparing to resist the Nazi evil, although the prospect of war flooded Edwin and me with woe as well as personal grief. For the first time in years I remembered that by the time the casualties of Loos were published in the last war about half of the young men who were students with me had been killed. Now the Killing Times had come back and the full moon would once again be an enemy. I thought about staying alive, thankful that Edwin was too old to be called up and Gavin too young.

Edwin, too, was shocked into an immediately personal world where survival mattered more than doctrines. Our absurd gestures—Edwin's with a golf club, mine with a hypothetical milk-bottle—were symbols of our determination to resist what we knew to be a deadly evil, and in this determination we were at one with the people of St Andrews, although they were most of them less well-informed about the Nazis than we were, being instructed only by propaganda, much of which they did not really credit.

This frame of mind lasted long enough for the organization of wartime measures in the town, and, as was to be expected from excited, untrained combatants, some of them were absurd enough. A well-known character, a popular tobacconist, was made responsible for having the church bells rung should there be an invasion, and when some theorist in London decreed a mock invasion, for practice, throughout the country, our tobacconist set the church bells wildly ringing; at the same time the fire engine started circling round the town and the Home Guard were told to fire at anything they saw moving. One valiant sniper, excited by the bells, obediently shot at the fire engine every time it passed him; he missed it by yards, but he did his duty.

The invasion did not happen and St Andrews remained unplastered. The initial hubbub died down and people found that daily life went on somehow. We discovered what we might have foreseen but did not: publishers no longer wanted translations from German. Our savings, which were never large, began to run out. Had we been in London, we could have found a market for our skills, in some government department, in the Ministry of Information or the War Office, but in Scotland there was no demand for them. In the eyes of Scottish educational authorities Edwin, having left school at the age of fourteen with only a Merit Certificate to show, was practically illiterate and could not be allowed to teach English anywhere. The only job he could get was stamping papers in the Dundee Food Office, at three pounds a week, out of which he had to buy his lunches and his train fare from St Andrews. Every morning he had a long cold wait at Leuchars Junction for the Dundee train. He composed a poem about Leuchars ('The Wayside Station') which was unlike any of his recent poems in being an immediate impression of a recognizable local scene, not removed into an imaginary setting, but fitted into its actual place, related to the present world around it, as we too were finding ourselves related.

I had the bits of paper Scottish teaching regulations insisted on, and I was offered several jobs. But they were all far from home, and by the time I paid my living expenses and returned to St Andrews for weekends there would have been little ready money left. It seemed just as sensible to accept what New Park offered in St Andrews itself, which would at least keep the home intact. The school's second in command, the Classical master, had already joined the Army, and I was asked to take his place at three pounds a week and my lunches. New Park was statutorily bound to have at least one regularly trained teacher on its staff, and I would be that one. They would be getting me on the cheap, I knew, but beggars couldn't be choosers: three pounds a week, clear, was always something coming in. I should have stuck out for better pay, but I was in no condition to fight, being depressed by the war, my menopause, and the private load of guilt I was carrying for our being in St Andrews at all.

So every morning during 1940 Edwin went off to Dundee, returning in the evening, and I bicycled to New Park, where I was beguiled into supervising prep, and did not get home till about six o'clock. I liked the little boys I taught: it had already struck me on Sports Days how much nicer they were than most of their parents. Three boys in the top class had lessons in Greek, and one of these was Gavin. I was anxious not to let the class, any class, feel that I had favourites, and Gavin rather expected privileged treatment from me, which I tried not to give him.

The war was going from bad to worse. For the defence of Fife the government had sent us contingents of Poles who quite literally in many homes replaced the men at the front, so that our St Andrews doctors cynically referred to spring-time as the 'Polish lambing season'. In June, when the news came that France had surrendered, two Poles who used to visit us, highly intellectual Jews whom the Polish officers kept busy at chores like peeling potatoes, met me at the front door, crying out: 'We don't understand you at all. Don't you people realize what has happened? Are you incredibly brave or just incredibly stupid?'

'Probably both,' said I, dumbfounded at this flash of illumination into the difference between customary attitudes on the Continent and in Great Britain, its offshore shelf. Our people should have been demonstrating in the streets, rioting and smashing windows, I supposed, instead of obstinately plodding about their business with heavy hearts.

The darkness of winter then closed in on us. Edwin tripped and fell in the black-out of Dundee, hitting his head against an iron stanchion. He came home looking ill, and I made him lie in bed for a couple of days; he would not stay longer away from his daily work or wartime exercises. On some evenings he was attending a class taught by a Divinity Professor how to bayonet a hanging sack, stuffed with hay, in the proper lethal manner, with a twist to engage and disengage the blade. Why Edwin was also lugging sandbags about I do not know, but he collapsed one evening after doing so and this time on doctor's orders had to stay in bed for at least six weeks. Every weekday morning I had to go off to New Park, leaving him in bed, frail as thread-paper. Our kind neighbour next door, who kept a boarding house, brought him a hot meal in the middle of the day, and there he lay alone until Gavin and I came home. That was an icy winter. I remember the struggles I had to keep my bicycle from skidding on the frozen ruts of the road.

At the end of that term I could not afford to pay Gavin's outstanding school fees. I let them slide, saying to myself that they could wait. But when the new term began in 1941 I was informed that New Park would apply my weekly wage to paying off my debt, so that I was to teach all day for my lunches only and take no money home. Not only that, but I was asked to teach more subjects. I finished up by instructing the school in Latin, English, History, Greek and Scripture.

By the time Edwin was able to get up and go about, I was worn with anxiety and persistent belly-pains, later discovered to be the result of bowel ulcers, but I ate charcoal biscuits till I must have been sooted inside like an old chimney and went on teaching. Dorothy Douglas, meeting me in the street one day, was shocked at the look of me and insisted on an examination. Sometime at the beginning of May she kidnapped me from New Park in her car and forbade me to go back to it; I was put into a bed in the local hospital instead and remember little of what happened after that, until I came to myself and saw Edwin sitting beside me.

Before opening my eyes I had been lost in a bleak region where there was no living thing, not even a microscopic insect or a minute speck of lichen, nothing but ice, deep clefts and high ridges of bluish ice, with jagged peaks of ice rising beyond them which I knew I had to climb. This frozen landscape was still around me, yet I knew that the man beside my bed was Edwin. He saw me open my eyes and laid his hand on mine. I turned the hand over a little and looked at it; the fingers were slim, tapered and heavily stained with tobacco. It was only a hand, not very clean, an irrelevant hand, yet I told myself: But this is Peerie B's hand! And I was sorry that I had no feelings about it. Tears began to trickle from my eyes because I was sorry for being so unfeeling, and the faster they flowed the sorrier I felt, until all at once I was flooded inside with warm love; the icy peaks faded; I held on to Edwin's hand and knew that things were coming right for me again. From that moment I began to recover.

The icy peaks faded but I never forgot them. That was Margaret Fairlie's country, I told myself, and it is not for me; I cannot live except in the country of True Love. This fantasy had power over me for many years and is still not wholly eliminated.

Yet though I had been, as it were, resurrected, I found when I was allowed out that the country of True Love was difficult to fit into the ordinary world. Every experience came too sharp-edged towards me; I shrank from any encounter, from decisions, from responsibility. In my weakness I confused Margaret Fairlie's country with the world of mental action; the icy peaks, I told myself, were where the arid intellect reigned, and I must keep away from these higher reaches. It took me a very long time to become even partly able for ordinary living, so that I could meet strangers without shrinking.

One man in Scotland, meanwhile, Dr Harvey Wood, was aware of Edwin's quality and invited him to come and work in Edinburgh for the British Council, organizing programmes and entertainments for the various Houses set up to look after our foreign allies, Poles, Czechs, Free French, Norwegians.

Before we left for Edinburgh in 1942 St Andrews had its one and only bombing raid; a stick of four medium-sized bombs was dropped over some University buildings. The German plane flew very low with all lights on; we saw it not far above our roof, and the last bomb splintered our front door and its fanlight. No one was killed, by good chance, but various science buildings were much damaged. It looked as if some ex-student had indulged in a little private vengeance on the University.

Gavin had been removed from New Park and sent to the Madras Senior School, where we ought really to have shifted him sooner. To our surprise, he had absorbed snobbish ideas about status from his class-mates and regarded the Madras as a social let-down, but once he was in it he found that he liked it very much—especially the girls in his class. He did not at all want to leave them and go to Edinburgh.

Edwin departed first, to be introduced to his new job and to find living quarters for the family, no easy task in Edinburgh, where all available space was booked up. An empty flat was finally secured, on the second floor of a terraced house, bow-windowed like its neighbours. There were exactly similar bow-windows all along the opposite side of the street, as if two rows of large parrot cages fronted each other. It was no use repining; we were lucky to have a flat at all. And my sense of guilt first lessened and then vanished, now that we were out of St Andrews at last.

The new job pleased Edwin; getting up programmes of lectures and entertainments was much more to his liking than stamping food coupons; he began again to radiate that goodwill which in the years to come grew so noticeable. He was interested by the varying atmospheres prevailing in the Houses: national backgrounds did seem to make differences between one lot of allies and another. Polish House, he told me, was the liveliest in discussion; it was well supplied with senior army officers each of whom felt himself completely qualified to lay down the law on music, art, literature or architecture. The Free French were inclined to be quarrelsome, but what struck Edwin most strongly about their committee was its preoccupation with personal prestige. A Belgian merchant, a Baron feeling that he ought to be the Big Shot because of his title, was harassed by the rival claims of a Holy Roman Countess, who said she had inherited her title from an aunt, and had, moreover, the 'particule', a *de* in her name. At loggerheads about everything else, the Baron and the Countess combined to snub the Treasurer, who was a commoner, a simple M. Gateau, the most likeable and dependable of men, according to Edwin. By way of squashing M. Gateau the titled notables would spend hours tracking down alleged missing halfpence in the House laundry accounts, and Edwin used to come home from Free French committee meetings torn between high mirth and exasperation. The Norwegians were the quietest and the easiest to get on with, although the Mayor of Hammerfest told Edwin that every winter, in the long Arctic darkness, his citizens became very litigious and brought law-suits against each other for trivial causes. But he knew that when spring came they would feel differently, and so always procrastinated and put off the law-suits until the spring thawed everything out, people, law-suits and all. Edwin loved Czech House best, mainly because of the delightful man in charge of it, Lumir Soukup, and that was the first House I plucked up courage to enter. It marked a great step in my recovery when I was able to go into the evening black-out and take a penny tram to Czech House all by myself.

In daylight I was not so timorous, soon getting accustomed to standing in queues at the grocer's, the fish-shop, and the butcher's, bringing home dried egg and Iceland cod and small rations of meat. We had no food parcels from America, I do not know why. After some months, as I became a familiar figure in the queues, I got occasional extras from under the counter, but by the end of the war I never wanted to see dried egg or cod again.

Shuttling about in trams from one House to another, Edwin discovered that sitting on the top deck of a tram in rapid motion set his unconscious moving too, so that lines and snatches of poems began to come up. When the tram journey stopped, the poem stopped. In his 1946 volume: *The Voyage*, there are some of these Tram Poems, like 'Reading in Wartime'. Sometimes he took a longer ride out to Fairmilehead, where he climbed one of the Pentland Hills as far as the village of Swanston, R. L. Stevenson's childhood home, and there sitting on the turf, gazing at Edinburgh and the Firth of Forth, he composed one or two joyous songs such as 'A Birthday' and 'In Love for Long'. In general he composed more poems in Edinburgh than in St Andrews, because he was no longer turned in on himself.

Yet during his last year in St Andrews, while he lay in enforced rest in our bedroom, looking out at the tree-tops in the University Botanic Gardens, he brooded much on imaginative themes and shaped poems which appeared in his 1943 volume: The Narrow Place. Among them were some love poems addressed to me. In an article a critic called Frederick Grubb upbraided him for writing these poems to some insubstantial idealized girl: in fact they were written to an actual, middle-aged, much harassed wife. One of them, 'The Confirmation', which ended with the approving words:

But like yourself, as they were meant to be

sent me privately into a passion of tears, because I knew too well that I was only a botched version of what I was meant to be. Edwin published in all eight love poems to me. When he died I would have given every one of them to have him back, but I am more than glad now for these witnesses to True Love.

Because of the Houses, our life in Edinburgh had a strong international flavour. Edwin was lucky in cajoling friends and acquaintances to come from London to entertain our allies, including Tom Eliot, but we also had distinguished Europeans at hand, such as Raymond Aron. Louis Aragon turned up; he was too arrogant for our liking; but Paul Eluard was a delight. Neither Edwin nor I could ever quite understand how such a gentle, sensitive poet could be a Communist. Our most amusing visitor was Max-Pol Fouchet, who did not come to lecture; he had escaped from Algeria with only one ragged shirt to his back and no money at all. Madeleine Gill, whose husband lectured in French at the University, took him in charge; she had been born in Oran and was an old friend of his. The British Council generously provided money to buy Max-Pol a few garments, but he had his own ideas of what he wanted; he spent nearly all of it on tartan ties and waistcoats, a Scottish bonnet, flamboyant oddments from Princes Street souvenir shops, with which he was exuberantly pleased. War or no war, he was like a schoolboy on holiday.

The European wartime flavour can be found in Edwin's poems of these years such as 'The Refugees' or 'The Escape', even 'The Return of the Greeks'; those veteran Greeks, who

came home sleepwandering from the war

in Troy, were an image of the homeless soldiers who turned up in Edinburgh with their terrible stories.

Ever since Munich we had had sore hearts about the fate of Czechoslovakia, and when the war ended Edwin asked the British Council if they had any work he could do there. The Council told him that he could not be put on the pensionable list, since he was too old, but if he would accept that proviso, they would appoint him Director of the British Institute in Prague.

Edwin was asked to drive a car across Europe to Prague, a large car belonging to the new Representative, who was to be the head of the Council there. Meanwhile I had to dismantle our wartime flat, get our furniture stored and Gavin ready for St Andrews University, where he wanted to go. The storing of the furniture proved to be an insuperable difficulty; every furniture repository in Edinburgh and neighbourhood was already crammed to bursting point. Our very good friend, Joseph Chiari, then the French vice-consul in Edinburgh, finally offered me an empty room in his house, and I was able to save as many pieces as could be packed into it.

Gavin, now a tall good-looking young man of nearly eighteen, was despatched to the University in what was, to him, his beloved home town. I spent my last eight clothes coupons on a dressing-gown for Edwin made from a Black Watch tartan travelling rug, which he was still wearing ten years later when we went to Harvard. Then I went down to a boarding-house in London—in Hampstead, of course—to wait until the Council could book me a seat on a plane for Prague.

Here chance had a last fling at obstructing my flight to Prague and Edwin. I had already been delayed by the trouble with our furniture, and had got an S.O.S. from Edwin beseeching me to hurry for he needed me. So I went to British Council headquarters in a fairly impatient frame of mind. A pretty red-haired poppet in charge of transport took down my Hampstead address and telephone number; I assured her that I was ready to start at five minutes' notice. Days went by and no message came from the Council; I got instead a telegram from Edwin asking if I were ill, since he had been to meet the plane on which my seat was booked but I was not there. A superior young man in the Council, admitting that the mistake was regrettable, pooh-poohed my insistence that I must have a flight at once by suggesting that my presence in Prague could not be urgently required. 'Of course', he said, 'we know that wives are useful socialleh.'

Edwin had written that he was beginning to feel nervy and sleep badly. 'I *cannot* wait another ten days,' I announced, 'I shall make my own arrangements.' Our friend Lumir Soukup was now a Secretary in the Czech Embassy and to him I went hot-foot. A plane was leaving for Prague next day, and, yes, I could get a seat in it. 'A converted Dakota—you wouldn't mind that?' asked Lumir. I had never flown anywhere except in dreams, and all planes were alike to me. I climbed happily into the converted Dakota, which carried eight passengers, sat down by a window and forgot to feel scared. We left the ground smoothly and it seemed the most natural thing in the world to be airborne: we flew low enough to have the irregular small fields of Kent, the white-streaked Channel, the larger, more geometrical enclosures of northern France spread out beneath us like a map easy to read, except that at first I could not tell whether round objects in the noon-day sun were humps or hollows, corn-stacks or shell craters. By the time we came to the Rhine, where broken bridges were sticking up out of the water like blackened teeth, the clear sky to the right of us had thickened into deep cloud and we coasted along beside these white cliffs of vapour like a pleasure-craft sailing down a river, while Europe flowed past underneath, a unity, as I felt it should be, interrupted by no artificially drawn frontiers. It was a fascinating journey, and like good journeys ended appropriately in a lovers' meeting. Edwin was at the airport.

Chapter Seventeen

PRAGUE

1945-1948

(i)

We were lodged in the Šroubek Hotel on the main city square, the Vaclavské Namesti, or Wenceslas Square, which was exactly as I remembered it, except that the worn-out trams now screeched horribly. The centre of Prague looked much the same, although there was a lot of new building up and down the river valley. But the people, the one-time noisy, bustling, cheerful people, were warily silent, looking pasty-faced and ill-fed, with not a smile among them. Edwin said that when he arrived there was no food in the shops except drab packets of dehydrated carrots or potatoes. Even yet there was very little to be had. In the large ground-floor cafe of the Šroubek, where more than twenty years earlier we had drunk much coffee and read the newspapers, one could still order tea or coffee, but the 'tea' was pink, tasting of raspberry drops, or brown, tasting of cinnamon, while the 'coffee' was made from ground acorns. The British Embassy had been getting British Army rations sent by truck from Vienna, which they shared with the Council, so that we were sure of one good meal a day to begin with; presently a restaurant was taken over and we had the chance of two good meals a day. The restaurant proprietor received all the rations that came from Vienna, cooked them into excellent dishes, and kept his restaurant in the Malá Strana — At the sign of The Spinning-Wheel, or Kolovrat — as an exclusive lunching and dining club for British staff from the Embassy and the Council. We also began to get allowances of P.X. American stores, handed out personally in the Council Office: wonderful candy bars with names like 'Oh Henry!' and 'Hi Mac!' as well as canned fruit and vegetables. I became aware that I was suffering from sugar starvation as a result of the war: I could not pass a bowl of sugar-lumps on a table without filching a few, and I fell upon the candy bars like a gluttonous child.

The whole question of British hardships in the war was a matter of wonderment to the Czechs. They themselves had next to no food, yet that, they felt, was understandable, since the Germans had cleared out everything before leaving, but why should the Victorious British have no stockings for women? In vain we explained about clothes coupons and Britain's putting everything into the war effort: the stockingless legs of British women on their first arrival in Prague still provoked comment. All Czech women had drawers full of stockings and rows and rows of garments on hangers. They had never been called up, clothes had not been rationed at all, and the difference in outlook was incommensurable.

The best currency was cigarettes; as tips or bribes a handful of cigarettes procured almost anything one wanted. The lack of food and cigarettes gave one an immediate sense of dearth; there was also a less visible dearth of accommodation. The government had promised to hand over some urban palace in which the Council could house itself and its Institute, but negotiations dallied and were again and again obstructed by a hidden influence. Meanwhile the British Council was crammed into a small three-room flat, where the Institute had a share of one long table that at first had to be cleared every day to allow of luncheon's being served on it.

Edwin himself was offered immediate work in the Charles University of Prague. The Germans had closed all places of higher education to Czechs, high schools and university alike, since Slavs were being relegated to the menial slave-status thought proper for them, and Czech students, famished for learning, were crowding back into the newly reopened centres, or what was left of them. In the University the English Department's Library had been nearly gutted and there was no one to lecture on English Literature, a task laid upon Edwin, who now entered a university for the first time in his life, as a professor not as a student. At first he had to rely largely on his memory for material and kept his students busy making copies of English prose and poetry for use in the courses he was improvising; in his lectures he was so transparently dedicated and disinterested that the students gradually shed their wary formality and grew enthusiastic. When the British Institute was finally opened, Edwin's university students flocked to it in a body.

Not only the students were wary and mistrustful; most Czechs one met were on the defensive. We had more or less expected this. They had been terribly humiliated by the occupying Germans, even in small matters, like being forbidden to enter their own city parks or sit on public benches, or to buy any plates, cups or glasses but the cheapest and plainest, decorated china or glass being reserved for the superior Germans. To them, we were the Victorious British, superior even to the Germans, who might perhaps look down our noses at them. We all had to show patience and direct, open friendliness until they could feel that we were not looking down on them but meeting them on the level. This psychological barrier was even more difficult to penetrate than the language barrier that had baffled Edwin and me on our first visit to Prague in the early twenties. Although we were now in a way integrated in the life of Czechoslovakia, having a job of work to do, the sense of an alien background persisted, so that for quite a while we never felt altogether at home.

One complication was the continuing presence of Russian soldiers in Prague, not that they were much in evidence, being obviously forbidden to join in any official 'get-together' with their nominal allies. In the countryside beyond Prague stray detachments of Vlassov's army were still lurking, men who had fought for the Germans, and one midnight there was an affray just outside our hotel in which a Russian soldier was shot dead, so perhaps they had some excuse for caution. Still, they added another inscrutable element to the background. Sometime in November, I think, they were collected in large trucks at a starting-point in the Vaclavské Namesti and took their departure. Occupying troops, however friendly in theory, are usually resented by any city, and had the Russians been archangels the Praguers would still have been glad to see them go. Excited crowds gathered on the pavement and started throwing flowers and bottles of wine into the trucks. I threw them some flowers on my own account. Their departure made a definite breach in the wary reticence of the Czechs; we were now overwhelmed with stories about the Russian entry into Prague.

The first Russians to reach the city were regular soldiers, we were told, much like those who had just gone. But on their heels came hordes of less disciplined supply troops from beyond the Urals, who had driven to Prague in great straggles of horse-and pony-carts right across the fields. Perhaps they did not know what roads were for, it was suggested. Their horses and ponies ate the corn or grass growing around them and broken-down carts were mended on the spot with wood from the forests; men, animals and vehicles simply exploited the resources of the country, to the natural fury of Czech farmers who saw their crops and livestock vanish. We were assured that there were even camels among the stragglers, Asian camels, bubbling through the narrow old streets of Prague. But as our informants had not forgiven us for having left them to be liberated by Russians and wished to convey the impression that the Allies had loosed wild Asian hordes upon the civilized city of Prague, we took this story about the camels with more than a grain of salt. Czechs had, and probably still have, a natural gift for inventing satirical stories about people or situations they do not approve. I did not quite credit the camels, nor the story I heard so often about the Russian soldier who had never before seen watches or clocks and after collecting half a dozen wrist-watches on his arm exchanged them all, the little ones, for one big one, a kitchen clock. Nor did I believe that the Americans had to stay put in Pilsen because they had run short of hard liquor and, having no palates, had drunk up their reserves of petrol.

After the Russian excitement had simmered down, the next line of defence in the psychological barrier came into evidence: long disclaimers denying collaboration with the Germans, which now prefaced most conversations. We surmounted that hurdle and began to ask tentative questions about the Gestapo's behaviour which was what we were curious about, having no experience of it. But like burnt children still dreading the fire the Praguers were unwilling to mention the Gestapo, except to indicate their headquarters, with its terrible basement, in a building round the corner from the top end of the Vaclavské Namesti. What they insisted on telling us was the story of the two smallish bombs dropped near there. Bombing such as Britain had endured was as far outside their experience as the Gestapo tortures were outside ours, and these two small bombs had roused a strong feeling in them that none of us could appreciate.

Some time later Edwin and I travelled along the road from the south up which the first Russian troops had made their way, and saw the slogans that had been painted on wooden boards set up every few miles to encourage them in their advance, the kind of slogans and exhortations one might expect to find in an adolescent boys' adventure story. 'Only a few miles more, noble soldiers of the Soviets, you are nearly there!' 'Forward again, liberators!' 'Onward, glorious Soviet soldiers!' 'You have already astonished the world, and Russia is proud of you. One more corner to turn and Prague is waiting for you!' These are rough translations provided at the time by Czech friends. We got an impression of weary, homesick, dispirited children lashed onwards by the will of Father Stalin.

The Americans had reached Pilsen well before the Russians got to Prague and could easily have entered the capital city had they not been checked by the bargain made at Yalta which reserved Prague for the Russians; presumably it seemed proper for a Slav country to be liberated by fellow-Slavs, a bit of window-dressing presented by the Allies to a fellow-Ally. The basic assumption of believing that the political line of division ran between Germany, the enemy, on one side and all the Allies, including Russia, on the other, was one that Edwin and I made unthinkingly. It never occurred to us at the time that Stalin might already be deepening a cleavage, as with a sword, between America, together with her European allies, and Russia. Yet this cleavage it must have been that accounted for the baffling inaccessibility of the Russians in Prague and the hidden obstructions behind the political scene that kept the British Council so long from getting the palace it had been promised. Stalin's top men, instead of showing tact or modesty about the formal fiction that the Russians had 'liberated' Prague, blatantly advertised and exploited it to the full. They set up a Russian tank in a public square as a memento of the Liberation, a fine symbol of power. They opened offices of all kinds ostensibly for the exchange of films and trade goods, business offices that were centres of Czech political intrigue from the beginning. Because they were 'the Liberators' they saw to it that key Ministries controlling police, radio and Press were given to Communists. In short, they were making all ready for a subsequent Communist take-over. Russia was on one side of the cleavage and we Allies, including the Germans, our recent enemies, were on the other, lumped together as 'the West', satellites of that other Great, America, the rival Stalin was keeping his eye on.

The Czechs, in consequence, were being subjected to unfair political pressure from the day that the Russians entered Prague, and they were aware of it although we were not. This to some extent accounted for the opaqueness, the alien inscrutability we felt in the atmosphere of Prague, despite our friendliness and personal popularity. We put down to the deep psychological damage done to the Czech people during the German occupation any rudeness we met.

The Germans had struck with instinctive sureness at the very heart of Czech life, at that invisible emanation, made up of beliefs and traditions, heroic legends, folk-lore, art, poetry, music and vernacular songs, which surrounds a people and sustains its sense of identity and self-respect, being all the more potent because it is invisible. Today we are becoming aware of its importance; we call it the 'public image' of a personality or a people, yet it seems to be more than that name implies, to be more effectively real than many material facts. It was, for Nazis, a region they felt at home in, and they knew how to sap it in Czechoslovakia. Not only were Czechs excluded from all higher education, they were told that the national history they had been taught was false to the core and in primary school were given a simplified version prepared by German scholars, showing that any part played by Czechs in the history of Europe was the result of following German leadership or example; it was rubbed into them that they were an inferior mongrel race, born to be subordinates; that their legends were lies, their traditions fraudulent, their art and music merely derivative, their literature rubbish, their language a kitchen language unfit for higher uses.

This was the kind of damage Edwin and I expected to meet, and because it went deep we knew it would not be easy to deal with, even although the Germans who had caused it were now in their turn discredited. People who have been savagely humiliated leap too often on to the other fork of the false dilemma and strive to triumph over someone else, anyone, to make up for past subjugation. It was in this light that we explained any *brusquerie* among the working classes.

We were not mistaken, Edwin and I, in assuming that from the time of Munich deep damage had been done to the Czechs and that it might be repaired chiefly through imaginative understanding, nor were we at fault in feeling that for centuries they had been habituated to accepting the false dilemma in one form or another—Hus or the Pope? Protestant or Catholic? Czech or Austrian? Which side are you on? For or against?— since all the cleavages that sliced through Europe had crisscrossed their territory. The mistake we made here was in not realizing that the false dilemma was only a secondary instrument operated by power systems after, not before, slicing a cleavage across the people they meant to dominate. The cleavage was the first requirement in the fight for power, and we did not see that, although it represented a technique perhaps nearly as old as civilization. We had to learn that lesson the hard way, by suffering from it. At this time we were not expecting, or even thinking of, political hostility between East and West. When the British Council at last got its palace, the Kaunic Palace, and a formal, official opening was arranged, attended by President and Madame Beneš, two front seats beside the President intended for Communist Ministers were left ostentatiously vacant and we did not perceive the significance of that boycott. One or two Czech friends drew our attention to it, but our only reaction was to smile.

The damage done by Gestapo direct methods, being less devious, was easier to cope with although sometimes startling. In a Czech friend's flat, for instance, between one cup of tea and another we were suddenly shown a cardboard box, rimmed with black and silver in a parody of mourning, containing a man's white shirt neatly folded yet filthy with bloodstains and scraps of human skin. 'That's what the Germans sent me through the post after torturing my husband to death,' said our friend. Some young members of our Institute showed us the numbers tattooed on their arms when they were in concentration camps and described how they escaped from the trucks taking them (they supposed) to the gas chambers almost as the Russians were entering Prague. Edwin and I had an immediate apprehension of what life in such camps meant when we went to an exhibition of posters, photographs, wall newspapers, camp notices and other relics from Terezín (Theresienstadt), where rich Jews were segregated whose family or business connections were prepared to pay to keep them alive as long as the money lasted. These callous and cynical reminders of human degradation made us literally sick, but they were more open wounds, less hidden than the damage done to the self-respect of Czechoslovakia as a whole.

Yet we never knew when a streak of unaccountable craziness might suddenly distort any apparently normal sequence of events, like the journey we made back to Prague after attending a Summer School in the Slovakian High Tatras. We had gone there in the newly-arrived Institute car, an English postwar product, down into the increasing summer heat of the south, along roads that were all sharp stones and pot-holes. One at a time the brand-new English tyres exploded into dusty fragments; whatever they were made of, it was not rubber. Tyres were then as scarce as fine gold, and it was with great difficulty that we acquired, one by one, four makeshift specimens, and managed to reach the Tatras, sullen humps of mountains that were much higher than they looked. As the Summer School closed, a wire arrived from our son Gavin, who was coming out overland to spend the long vacation with us; his train had to be met in Prague two days later at half-past eight in the morning. One day to get back, we thought, plenty of time.

Yet at ten o'clock that night we were still a good way from Prague, what with punctures and leaks in our patched old tyres, which we had not been able to replace. We were running along a deserted stretch of road between dark forests when a hissing, a slither and a bumping told us that once more a tyre had gone. Again we drew into the side of the road, again our chauffeur looked for the jack. But there was no jack. Apparently it had been mislaid and left behind on our last mending bout; we had to sit waiting for some car to pass from which we could borrow a jack. No car came in sight.

Were it not for having to meet Gavin, we might have sat there well enough till daylight. There was a basket of fruit to nibble, including a melon, also some Slovakian cheese, half a dozen fresh eggs and a pot of honey, all pressed upon us by generous Slovaks. Yet the fear of Gavin's arriving in an unknown city with no one to meet him made Edwin and me impatient and anxious. So when powerful headlights flared in the distance and rapidly approached, both of us leaped into the road and waved our arms, narrowly escaping being mown down. A large open racing-car drew up, marked B.M.W. (Bavarian Motor Works), and the bare-headed man at the wheel sounded peremptory. Yes, he would lend us a jack, to be returned next day to a Prague address he gave us. It was now well after eleven o'clock and pitch dark among the trees. I asked the stranger what was the nearest town? He said: Tabor. Would he be so good as to drive Edwin and me to Tabor, then? Our driver could stay by the car, mend the tyre somehow by daylight and drive home. In Tabor, I thought, we could at least get a taxi to Prague, if not a train.

This suggestion amused the stranger, we did not know why, but he bade us jump in. I took the eggs, Edwin the honey-pot, for the family breakfast, leaving fruit and cheese to our chauffeur, and we jumped in. The driver bade me sit beside him, which I did, and Edwin climbed in behind with the suitcase. We roared off. I do not know what was our actual speed but it seemed at least a hundred miles an hour. We roared off all right, but not to Tabor. Uphill and down dale we raced, swooping round corners on two wheels, and every few minutes the demon driver enquired: 'Are you afraid yet, gracious lady?' I sat primly upright, nursing the precious eggs, and replied in as calm a voice as possible: 'Oh no, not at all.' The efforts to scare me were then redoubled. 'That's a wall I smashed into some weeks ago,' said the driver, waving a careless hand, and: 'A friend of mine was killed at this corner last month. Aren't you afraid, gracious lady?'

I made up my mind that the man was mad, but could not decide whether mad because he was a racing-driver (well known, he told me) or a racing-driver because he was mad. Back and forth and round again we quartered Czechoslovakia; once or twice we passed road-signs saying: Tabor, and when I called his attention to them he waved a hand and said: 'All roads lead to Tabor.' We crossed the Bohemian forest almost to the border, turned back by a different route and roared off to the north until I could have sworn we were not far from Prague. What I had to do, I felt, was to resist the madman's obsession until he got bored trying to frighten me, so I kept telling him how enjoyable I was finding the excursion. It was indeed exhilarating to rush through the dark night at such reckless speed behind these enormous headlights. At last, around four in the morning, he did get bored and decanted us abruptly in the main street of Tabor. With our suitcase we tottered to the nearest inn, where the night porter was awake.

The vibration of our headlong speed had spilt honey out of the pot in great shock waves over Edwin's trousers, which were stiff with it; the first thing was to get a clean pair out of the suitcase. Behind a sheltering pillar we washed and Edwin changed. The porter asked: 'Would you like some wine?' but what he brought was a large jug of red vermouth. There would be no taxis till the garages opened at about six o'clock, he said. He did then get us a taxi and Gavin was met at the station with a few minutes to spare; but before that Edwin made a remarkable confession over the vermouth. For the last hour or so, he said, he had been sitting with the honey-pot in his hand, wondering whether and just where he should hit the driver on the back of the head. This seemed to me the queerest of the queer happenings on that night, Edwin's even thinking of hitting a man on the back of the head. Broch's bugbear, the irrational, seemed dangerously near the surface of daily life in Czechoslovakia.

Yet we felt things were going well with us on the whole. Edwin thought himself lucky in his second-in-command. Bill Alien was a good musician—he played the 'cello and the viola —and was already intimate with the best string quartets in the city; his ear for sounds made him a genius at teaching foreigners to speak English and he was especially skilled in transmitting English idioms to his classes. His open, friendly nature made friends for him everywhere. It was thanks to the ramifications of Bill's acquaintance that two good flats were assigned to us by the National Committee, one for the Muirs on the ground floor, and one immediately above it for the Aliens. This Committee was distributing the accommodation previously commandeered by Germans and Russians. Our two flats were in a quiet street which the Praguers called 'Little Moscow', since the Russian Embassy stood at the far end of it, beside the gates of a wooded public park once known as 'The Royal Hunting Forest' and now more soberly named The Place of Trees, while at intervals all the way to the tram-stop at the other end Russian offices and quarters had been established under the Embassy's wing. We did not mind being neighboured by Russians, for the flats, once cleaned, were pleasant although they had been occupied by very dirty Russian soldiers, perhaps some of the contingent from beyond the Urals. A glassed-in verandah in our flat had been used as a latrine, and the wall of the sitting-room was pocked with bullet-holes. But there was a green garden, shared by the three flats of the house, and beside our verandah a large walnut-tree, with a black squirrel living among the scented leaves. We had our long-suffering furniture once more around us, with some extra pieces donated by the National Committee, and we were well content, especially as I had managed to acquire a very good cook.

Her name was Ella and she was a temperamental Slovak who had been cook to the Slovakian Ambassador in Berlin during Slovakia's brief term of nominal independence under Hitler. The Czechs had their usual fund of stories about that interlude; a lordly Berlin commissionaire, they reported, summoning at the end of a party ambassadorial vehicles like the American Ambassador's Cadillac, the English Ambassador's Daimler, and so on, would announce with scorn 'The Slovakian Ambassador's goloshes.' But Ella's cooking was truly ambassadorial and we began to give dinner-parties. My Czech, which was already fluent, now became adequate to any dramatic situation once I found that I had to govern my cook firmly, since, large, dark, jealous creature that she was, she refused to provide a meal for our humble weekly washer-woman except under duress from me. Even under duress she would not dish up goulash for visitors; goulash, she said, was not a proper dish for visitors; and although her goulash was incomparable and I ordered it knowing that British guests would love it, they always got something quite different, much grander, more 'suitable'.

In this matter of speaking Czech, I must admit that Edwin did not budge from his attitude of twenty years earlier; he would not learn to speak Czech, except for a few necessary phrases, such as: Where are my glasses? and: Where is my hat?, articles he often mislaid.

About the same time the British Council was given the Kaunic Palace, a small, pretty palace in a narrow street behind and parallel to the Vaclavské Namesti. Edwin and his staff moved in at once, without thinking of a formal opening. The British Council Representative, Edwin's official superior, took no interest in the way the Institute was run, probably considering it beneath his attention, teachers being small fry compared with Administrators. As far as the British Institute was concerned, he was a kind of King Log, and Edwin the poet, backed by Bill, the musician, had a free hand. With a willing staff to help, most of whom, like ourselves, had come to Prague because of a bad conscience about Munich, they invited Czechs not only to attend classes in language or literature but to sing madrigals in Bill's choir or join his orchestra; to take part in magazine programmes made up of English poetry and prose read, recited, or acted, programmes designed by Edwin on the same lines as those he had devised in Edinburgh; to learn old English dances; to join in discussions on topics like the significance of detective stories—to enjoy themselves, that is, without *arrière pensée*, to give their imaginations an airing and meet us all as friends in the Institute tearoom, which we took turns in supplying with home-baked cakes from our own rations.

The atmosphere radiated by Edwin and Bill, which spread through the whole Institute, was anything but that of political warfare, and I think that the Institute's being quite outside all false dilemmas came as a relief to the Czechs, especially the students. Without preaching the British way of life we conveyed it, of course, in everything we said and did, which seemed to us a more appropriate way of communicating it than through lectures. The Institute, gay and spontaneous, was soon regarded with affection all over Prague. I am told that even now, twenty years later, there are still people in Prague who remember us with affection.

Not only were we repairing to the best of our ability the damage done to Czech self-respect, we were also washing out the false public image of England presented by the Germans. In a bookshop I unearthed a German pamphlet about England called *Land ohne Liebe* (Land without Love), which had on its cover an illustration probably taken from an old Punch cartoon, a flat-footed, bony English spinster with projecting rabbity teeth, lank hair and a bosom like a board. Women in England looked like that, averred the pamphlet, because English men were so cold, formal and greedy that they were very bad at making love.

At the University, too, Edwin's gift of permeating the space around him, giving out an unassertive sense of benevolence, was appreciated by his students, who also much enjoyed his improvised lectures. Nearly ten years later, when we were in Newbattle, I was told that a Dundee professor had said it gave him great pleasure to listen to a man thinking on his feet, as Edwin then did when giving a talk. Not only was he beginning now to speak without notes, he was training the Institute staff to do the same. But it was at examination-times that he evoked the strongest gratitude from his students. Edwin told me that his colleague in the English Department, a philologist, in private a pleasant little man, became a terrorist when conducting an examination, trying to uncover whatever students did not know and pouncing on them for ignorance, so that they became rigid with terror and could not do themselves justice, while Edwin set himself to find out what they did know and gave them due credit for it. That marked, I suppose, the difference between an authoritarian and a poet, the one looking for rods to beat students with, the other trying to encourage the growth of a living mind. This authoritarian severity, Edwin was informed, had originated in Germany and become traditional in Central European universities.

The Charles University of Prague was grateful to him and in 1947 expressed its gratitude by staging a ceremony on his sixtieth birthday, the fifteenth of May, for the sole purpose of giving him an honorary Ph.D., which had been unanimously agreed to by representatives from all the faculties. The public oration was given by Dr Otakar Vočadlo, a survivor from a Nazi starvation camp, who had been the main instrument in prompting the University to do Edwin honour. It was a happy occasion and, although we did not know that, the high-water mark of Edwin's influence in Prague. From that time his troubles and the political troubles of Czechoslovakia together gathered momentum and moved towards catastrophe.

(ii)

1947-1948

Our King Log Representative was withdrawn, because the Ambassador had had enough of his tactless remarks at public banquets, and a new Representative arrived, a bureaucrat to the finger-tips, whom London had instructed to be a new broom. An evil chance made his first visit to the Institute coincide with an informal Evening Party for the students. The Institute, being grateful to the students, who had been its first members, staged every now and then for their benefit a Students' Evening Party, which was always noisy and gay. It was too noisy and gay for the new Representative and he was shocked by its informality. Bill, the Master of Ceremonies, was not wearing a dinner-jacket and black tie. Nor was there a Receiving Line to welcome guests. Moreover, the choir sang not only madrigals but also one of the slightly bawdy old songs the students loved:

He who would have an ale-house must have
  three things in store,
A chamber with a feather bed, a chimney
  and a – Hey nonny no!

To the new Representative it seemed that the Institute was carrying on as if it were merely a kind of night club for the young to romp in. We tried to persuade him that light-hearted romping was just what these young people needed, to counteract the stiff formality with which they had met us at first, all the clicking of heels and bowing from the waist. He was not to be persuaded. Black ties became a *sine qua non* for all social functions after that, and a Receiving Line of British Council wives, in which I stood Number Three and Hilda Allen Number Four.

The Representative also discovered that in the city at large the British Council itself, which should have been the visible centre of cultural activities, was being ignored by the public, who assumed that the Institute was the Council, and Dr Muir (as people now insisted on calling Edwin) the most important man in it. Administratively, this was preposterous, for the Institute was, and should appear to be, merely a teaching subsidiary of the Council. The new Representative felt it his duty to reorganize the whole structure of Council activities, so that British Arts and the British Way of Life might be presented to the foreign public with due dignity and decorum on the very highest level.

This high level he proceeded to achieve by means of what Edwin called Brute Administration. It involved cutting the British Institute down to size, and that meant cutting its Director down to size, a problem for a conscientious bureaucrat, since the Director was not on the pensionable list, unlike his second-in-command, Bill Allen, who could more easily be disciplined.

The bureaucrat must have profoundly distrusted the poet. He probably believed Edwin's modest demeanour to be a sham façade behind which lurked an ambitious schemer. How else could the man have attained a position of such false prestige in the city? In spite of his age, moreover, the poet appeared to be as anarchic as Bill Allen, the musician: both of them had their values all wrong. Alien's Book Returns, for example, were 'in chaos', and when this was pointed out to the Director of the Institute, Edwin seemed to think that such a shortcoming was more than made up for by Bill's inspired language teaching, not to mention his friendly connections with the music-makers of Prague and his happy relations with the students.

In return, the poet distrusted the bureaucrat, also for having the wrong values, for prizing office protocol and distinctions of official rank more than direct human understanding. He had moments of being sorry for the man; 'a timid soul,' he told me, 'who would feel lost without protocol to hold him up.'

It would have taken a large measure of goodwill to help the bureaucrat and the poet to understand each other, for the one believed in aiming at visibly high levels of information, while the other believed in penetrating invisibly deep towards a basic harmony of feeling and imagination. But I doubt if the bureaucrat came prepared for goodwill; he seemed to suspect us all of bad faith, being convinced from the outset that the staff, Council as well as Institute staff, were a bunch of miniature King Logs, thanks to the example set by his predecessor. Someone in London must have briefed him very stupidly before he came.

The new scheme of Council activities radiated, of course, from the Representative at the centre of it. His hand had been strengthened by the appointment of a brand-new Deputy Representative since he had got rid of the old one from King Log's time, and he now applied for, and got, in addition, an outer ring of specialist officers: a Music Officer, an Education Officer and a Medical Officer. Before they arrived he saw to it that a suitably formal opening of the Kaunic Palace should be arranged, a ceremony hitherto unaccountably omitted. This was on 'the highest level,' being attended by the President and Ministers of his Cabinet, the British Ambassador and other important personages from the Czech and British Establishments. Then he set himself to reorganize the Council's internal structure.

In effect, he made many of the Institute's activities redundant. The Music Officer was to provide high-level professional concerts; Bill's amateur choir and orchestra therefore came to an end. The Director's over-blown obsession with imaginative literature had to be corrected; the proper priorities were British Life, Language and Letters, in that order, with Music as a second string and Science as a third. It was a ship-shape, well-organized programme. What with weekly concerts and lectures there was sometimes no room left for the Institute's Magazine Evening, which had a lower status.

The bureaucrat prepared these schemes with a good conscience, acting on principle, quite impersonally. To show the level he wished to reach he gave a lecture himself on 'The Tertiary Use of the Preposition'. At the same time, with a view to economy and proper control, he could not avoid making cuts in what seemed to him the Institute's anarchic privileges. From the first cut, the transfer of the Institute's car to the Deputy Representative, to the last, the transfer of Bill Alien to Bratislava, Edwin set himself to put up with whatever happened and make the best of it, except for a single protest when his Czech secretary told him that she was to be merged in a Typists' Pool. The happy family atmosphere of the Institute almost vanished; even Council Staff, harassed by too much protocol, were visibly unhappy; and since Edwin felt it his duty to keep both Institute and Council staff from open rebellion, the strain told upon him. To me he said that the whole process felt like the Chinese torture of Death by a Thousand Cuts.

The one flare-up that came into the open, the Great Tea-Room Row, was the only outburst he was unable to control. We had always welcomed Locally-Appointed Staff—Czech typists, telephonists, library assistants—into the Institute tearoom, since we looked on them as part of the family. But now both the Representative and his Deputy voiced strong objections to their presence in the tea-room and imposed a ban on them. They were not members of the Institute and had no right to consume our private rations of flour. The telephone was sometimes actually left unattended at tea-time. Worst of all, it was embarrassing for senior officials of the Council to find themselves cheek-by-jowl with Locally-Appointed Staff at a tearoom table. What would the Chairman say, or some important officer from London, if he were to take tea and find himself elbowed by Locally-Appointed Staff?

The London-Appointed Staff at once closed their ranks in solidarity with their Czech colleagues and announced that they would boycott the tea-room until Locally-Appointed Staff were allowed into it again. Edwin neither instigated nor fomented this move; the two intelligent and efficient young women who organized the boycott needed no help from him or anyone; but I suspect that Edwin was blamed for it, or at least, his anarchic influence was blamed. There was a state of acute tension in the Kaunic Palace, and the tea-room boycott came as a kind of comic relief. Friends from outside, even from our Embassy, used to look in, grinning, to see how the Great Tea-Room Row was progressing. The ringleaders made illicit coffee in their cubby-holes for all the deprived victims and argued the toss fiercely with the Deputy Representative, who was no match for them. In the end, Locally-Appointed Staff were allowed to use the tea-room in shifts, for strictly limited periods, and that ridiculous episode was over.

Ridiculous it was, but significant of the change in the atmosphere of the Council Palace. We were now divided from each other by the gradings of protocol, and also from the Czechs, for we no longer belonged together unthinkingly. And at the same time as these internal tensions were making life uncomfortable in the Council, a pattern of increasing tensions was being repeated outside, as political intrigue and counter-intrigue mounted in the country, in Prague above all, on the approach of a General Election. All optimists were sure the Communists were going to be defeated, although the Communists themselves were shouting that they would get a fifty-one per cent majority.

We had begun to be aware of these external tensions, and had at last comprehended that there was a split between East and West. Our friend Lumir Soukup, whom we had first met in Edinburgh, was now posted to the Czech Foreign Office in Prague, as secretary to Jan Masaryk. He and his delightful Scottish wife set up house in a Prague flat and on the many pleasant evenings we spent with them Lumir, with due professional discretion, enlightened us about the various party factions. I was especially interested in the fellow-travelling faction of the Social Democrats because its leader, Fierlinger, passed my window daily on his way to the Russian Embassy. I had got to know his foxy nose very well and did not like the look of it.

We learned a lot, too, from our dinner guests, who relayed political gossip. Even the most intelligent of them were optimistic about the election. We were told that the Social Democrats were going to vote down Fierlinger's faction, and that this was a gleam of light after a long tunnel of darkness and uncertainty; the Communists certainly would not get more than thirty per cent of the votes, if that.

But the real body of our information came from the Writers' Circle which met every week in our flat. The lively young people in this circle were writing poems, plays, film-scripts, short stories, novels; they were very much aware of the political intrigues in Prague. They also trusted us and opened their hearts to us. At first we had tried to head them off political discussions, following our own theories of avoiding all false dilemmas, but as the political scene grew murkier we were thankful to have it elucidated. The cleavage between East and West became shockingly evident.

One of the chief wedges used in widening it had been Munich. 'We were always hearing about Munich,' said our young friends. 'Czechoslovakia isn't strong enough to stand alone; look at Munich! We can't trust Britain and France; look at Munich! And now they say; Czechoslovakia needs a strong Power to back her. The two strong Powers are America and Russia, but America is too far away while Russia is just next door.'

The playwright pointed out what a vast, anonymous fog of fear is generated by modern city life, among industrial workers, clerks, and other small people. Their lives are governed by faceless impersonal forces, great factories, blocks of tenements; somewhere unknown to them sit unknown men causing unemployment or employment, wage cuts, rent increases, shortages, directing everyone's life, so that they are filled with vague anxiety, an insecurity which drives them to join for protection any visible body that looks like Power. Besides all that, he said, in Central Europe political life is dominated by parties, by party tickets, rather than by known individuals. The average voter doesn't know the deputies on the list he votes for; he simply votes for the list. They are just names, not human beings; functions of their party, not persons. Government by intrigue is what we have here, he said, and many bewildered people may vote Communist, simply because they are told that Russia is strong and has a clear programme.

He was not optimistic about the future, nor was Lumir. We could see that Lumir had things on his mind; he could not keep us from knowing that he was troubled, although he never betrayed his secrets. Then in the late summer of 1947, in Marienbad, where we were running a Summer School, it was hinted to us that the Communists would do anything rather than risk defeat in the election. Agit-Prop, it was rumoured, was stacking rifles in some of the factories.

Agit-Prop, the Communist Bureau for Agitation and Prop-aganda, had long before been called to our attention by the Writers' Circle, who told us to have a good look at the shop-window in the Vaclavské Namesti that Agit-Prop had set up. The first day I stopped to look at it, the window was filled with an enlarged photograph of a British soldier on horseback with a severed head swinging at his saddle-bow. 'This is what the British Imperialists are doing in Greece,' said the caption. It was an actual photograph and the soldier was certainly wearing British khaki battledress, but his head and face had been blacked out; the head swinging by his saddle was just as certainly a plaster head hacked off some statue of Tragedy, and the runnels of blood on it were streaks of paint. This was a cynical fake crudely prepared for people who would not see that it was a fake. The stolid, peasant-like Czechs staring into the window were not likely, I thought, to reject it instantaneously, as I did, nor would it outrage patriotic feelings of theirs as mine were outraged. After that, I kept an eye on the Agit-Prop window and reported to Edwin what I saw. The cartoons usually showed fat capitalists ill-treating workers, types more repulsive even than those of Georg Grosz. This anti-bourgeois campaign went on right up to the Putsch in February 1948, but a day or two after that take-over the line was suddenly changed: the villain was no longer the gross capitalist but the Demon Drink. A Front against Alcoholism was proclaimed and Czechs were enjoined to drink less beer. The Czechs, I supposed, must surely now perceive how cynically they were being manipulated.

In this supposition I was not much at fault. When the working people of Czechoslovakia discovered that Utopia was not at hand, that they were being made to work harder, often for less pay, and expected to drink less and be more obedient to directives, even those blared at them from loud-speakers on lamp-posts, they began to grumble and fret. I suppose everyone knows how the Putsch was organized and that the populace was helpless because police, radio, Press and army were all under Communist control, but perhaps everyone does not know how the mood of the country fluctuated during the next few months between despair and irrational hope, fluctuations which the Government met with increased severity, sacking or jailing those who had not joined the Party or signed the form pledging loyalty to it.

The unrest, the flurries from pessimism to optimism, which ravaged the country ravaged Edwin and me as well. To begin with, there was disbelief and weeping, everywhere. In our kitchen the cook's niece sat sobbing; she had been sacked from her typist's post in a factory office because she was, like her father, a Socialist. All the workers in the factory, she said, had been given rifles and told to march to the Vaclavské Namesti or lose their jobs. That was on February 23rd, the day the new police swarmed everywhere in pairs, boys in their early twenties with the snub black noses of rifles showing over their left shoulders, even in our quiet street. I saw also one of the armed workers' processions making for the city centre; many elderly men in it trailed their rifles with the look of dogs who know that tin cans have been tied to their tails. In the Kaunic Palace, since the members of our Institute were partisans of the West, there was more weeping. People poured their distress into our bosoms, some of them wildly asking: Why did the Great Powers like Britain and France allow it? So many people were openly crying as they walked through the streets that no one found it odd. In our Writers' Circle the first alternation between fear and hope appeared. If only, they said, if only France would go Communist, as was being forecast, it would do a lot for Communism and modify the Russian model; one might get a better future out of it. Czechoslovakia was too small, too exposed, to make anything original out of Communism.

The rumour about France I had already heard from our landlord, who lived in the top flat of our building. He said that the Russians were forming Action Committees in their zone of Austria, but that the Americans would never let the Russians swallow Austria, it would not mean war; yet if France and Italy were to go Communist we might have war in the next three or four months. This was what he was hoping for.

Edwin and I went down with influenza, of a recurring kind, and our nerves grew ragged. Then on March 10th Jan Masaryk committed suicide. There is no doubt that it was suicide; he told Lumir Soukup that he was going to do it. On this same afternoon there was the first meeting of Parliament under the new Government, and he had been programmed to make a speech in the evening in the biggest hall of Prague, the Lucerna. He threw himself from a window of the Czernin Palace, and the whole country was convulsed with grief, a deep, human grief that came up against the impersonal, cold, synthetic system of Communist doctrine but could not overcome it.

Our friend, Lumir Soukup, had been appointed the executor of Jan Masaryk's papers, and although being followed round by a Communist watch-dog thought he would be safe enough until he had finished that job. His wife had been summoned home to Edinburgh where her father was mortally ill, and would not now be coming back. Lumir did not want us to communicate with him at all: better not, he said.

The Writers' Circle told us about the Communist League of Czech Youth, who were strongly pro-Zhdanov, all for 'Social Realism', arguing that they knew girls who could work twelve hours a day in a factory and then write good poems. Party pressure on writers was beginning to be severe; on painters, less so. Our playwright said that his play would never be put on now. A friend of his had written a drama about a murderer, but made him a murderer for Nietzschean not Marxist reasons, and so had been severely reprimanded by the Party. All dramas and novels had to be on strict party lines. One might, for instance, write a play about Agriculture, but first one would have to work on a village farm for three years to be sure of getting it right. Then his deep distress burst out. 'But this is my country and Czech is my language. I could go to Paris, yes, but there I'd only be a tenth-rate journalist. I cannot write well except in Czech.'

A wind of panic began to blow through the Council; some of the wives insisted on going home to England, as did also some of the British wives in the city who had married Czech soldiers during the war. There was a general feeling that wives and children should clear out, and Edwin suggested that perhaps I should go too, a suggestion I resisted. I did not want to go until circumstances forced me out. Besides, too many of our friends were imploring us to stay as long as we could. The French Institute, they said, was doing little or nothing, and the British Council was their only link with the West. But my real reason for staying was that I would not desert Edwin.

The Council was carrying on activities arranged long before the Putsch: an exhibition of British Books in one of the market halls and a Cultural Convention to be signed by Czechs and British, which Edwin as well as the Representative was called to attend. As a result the Education Officer sent two young poets on scholarships to England, but one of them called Blatny asked for political asylum and broadcast from the B.B.C. Czech service. The Moravian Creative Writers' Block greeted his defection by issuing this statement:

'We are convinced that not even in proud Albion, whose agelong understanding for honourableness in human character is expressed by the progressive creations of her subjects, will Ivan Blatny be accepted as a pure human being.'

Progressive creations were being composed by at least one of Albion's subjects in Prague, for Edwin had begun the fine series of poems called 'The Journey Back' which appeared in his volume of 1949 (*The Labyrinth*) as well as two short poems that were inspired by all he had been hearing: 'The Bridge of Dread' and 'The Interrogation'. Many of the other poems in that volume, some of which were directly concerned with the situation in Prague, were written during April, May and June of that summer. He was tired, but he was keyed up, and the burst of poetic activity kept him going. Yet he became rather evasive about day-to-day routines. One of the Council staff said to me that Edwin was turning into a will-o'-the-wisp.

The fluctuations of mood among our friends may have been partly responsible for this. Nothing was clear or crystallized, and being suspended in a to-and-fro of feeling became wearisome. An evening we spent with the Havraneks, Czechs we were fond of, was characteristic.

Havranek was a Civil Servant in one of the Ministries. Unlike others, he had refused during the German Occupation to divorce his Jewish wife; when she went into a concentration camp, he went too. They were idealists, disliking tyranny of any kind as much as we did, full of goodwill, and still full of hope in spite of the political situation. He told us that in Europe all moral standards had fallen low; not even in writers like Čapek was there anything one could identify one's aspirations with; yet the Czechs' genuine love of democracy would never be lost, he was sure, although they had no chance of real independence. Socialism with freedom, a new form of democratic Socialism, was what they longed for. People were now beginning to settle down a little and hoping for the best. International tensions in Europe were too much for the Czechs, but they would never lose their desire for the West as well as the East. They were and wanted to be Europeans. The Poles who used always to look down on the Czechs treated them now as equals, and that was a straw showing how the wind might blow. (This odd facet of the Czechs' sense of insecurity we had already noticed: the friend who had shown us her husband's shirt in the cardboard box always insisted that Poles despised Czechs.)

The desire for the West as well as the East was strong in the Charles University, said Havranek. In making arrangements for its sexcentenary celebrations, interrupted by the Putsch, the University, to the astonishment of the French, had not cancelled its invitation to the Chancellor of the Sorbonne, who was to give the main oration. The Charles University did not want politics to interfere with what should be a European, international event, and after all, the Sorbonne was in a way the mother of the Charles University of Prague. The attitude of the British universities who had refused their invitations was a bitter blow to Prague University. It looked as if they were under the thumb of the British Government, didn't it?

Edwin denied that. He said that British universities might be timid, in a way, but they saw the Communist take-over as an interference with academic freedom, since professors had been dismissed for political reasons. But with a look of masterly mild regret on his face he agreed with Havranek that it was a pity. Neither he nor I betrayed that it was Edwin himself who had advised Edinburgh University to refuse its invitation. When he did so, he had been asked to represent Edinburgh at the celebrations, and I had had a stab of unwilling regret that he had opted himself out. On the way home he said that he had been swept away on a tide of indignation at that time, but, on the whole, was still inclined to the same opinion, only he didn't want to hurt Havranek's feelings.

Jiři Mucha, another friend, said at luncheon one day that he had a hunch July would be the decisive month, and he hoped that by then the tension would have relaxed, after some crisis or other, without war. If there were a war, that would be the end of politics and politicians, Communist or Capitalist; the survivors would be crawling to hospitals, doctors, Red Cross nurses, instead of to political parties, trying merely to go on living. He looked on politics as on a poker hand; the weaker the hand, the stronger you play. Things that look particularly strong, he suggested, are often on the point of being swept away. As for the idealists among the Communists, they had no power at all. Power centred on the Party Secretariat, grey eminences from Hungary and Germany who could not make public speeches in Czech but were the real masters pulling the strings, directed by Moscow.

From some idealists we heard what might have been expected; that the Iron Curtain was a kind of safety curtain between them and the chaos of Capitalism; that now Czechoslovakia was going to have a really sound government; all abuses would be cleared out and all needful things done for the good of the whole country.

To and fro, from this starry-eyed innocence to panic and hysteria, the moods of people fluctuated. A poet called Holan who had once been a disciple of Rilke published a vulgar yell of vituperation against the West: our Writers' Circle opined that he was drunk when he wrote it. There were days when my heart withered up and I felt a *scunner* at the Czechs, mere grumblers at a *fait accompli*; there were other days when I was filled with remorse, especially when my friend Jiřina, who was being threatened with the loss of her small widow's pension if she did not join the Party, said one must never lose faith, never give up hope. Edwin then produced his poem: 'The Combat', which steadied both of us with its reminder that the armoured Killing Beast could not kill humanity, humble and battered as that might be.

I have selected these samples of behaviour from a diary I kept during and after the Putsch, the only diary I have ever kept, and I hope I have conveyed the nature and intensity of the strains and stresses to which we were subjected. Their after effects, once we got back to England at the beginning of August 1948, were devastating. Edwin had a bad nervous breakdown and my back began to be disabled by alleged arthritis.

Meanwhile, Edwin went on lecturing at the University as if there had been no Putsch; he was an independent agent with a British passport and could ignore the two Communist spies who took down every word he said, even when he lectured on John Stuart Mill's idea of Liberty. The other professors, some of whom had already been sacked, had no such protection. Edwin's classes lost their supple responsiveness; he was now met by closed faces, he said; the students were listless, wary, reticent; it was heart-breaking.

The students, of course, were all being subjected to pressure by the Committee of Action set up in the University. One member of our Writers' Circle described her interview with that Committee; she was examined by a youth of nineteen who said: 'Why are you not a Party member? What proof can you give that you are progressive? Produce two signatures to guarantee that you are reliable.' Those who were not accepted as reliable were refused permission to sit for degrees.

In the streets, in the trams, one saw the same closed faces. People no longer talked to each other; the fear of spies and informers was in the air as thickly as in the time of the German Occupation; no one, it seemed, trusted anyone else. The one-time Minister of Justice had tried to kill himself; the one-time independent judges were being eliminated; an edict forbade jokes about the wife of the Prime Minister, Gottwald, on pain of prison. In Edwin's language, the roads were twisting wrong all through the land. A distressed Czech said to me: 'We are a nation of cowards again, a nation of Schweyks.'

Yet, such is the instability of human feelings, we enjoyed respites from the prevailing tensions when we managed to get away from Prague for an occasional stay at Dobřis is, the tomato-red rococo country palace bestowed as a centre on the writers of Czechoslovakia. We were permitted to use this Writers' House because Edwin was accepted as a writer. One very gay evening occurred there when Professor J. B. S. Haldane and his young wife were guests of honour at a dinner. Edwin and Haldane, who had never met before but were both high-flown with wine and sentiment, embraced each other as brother-Scots and sang Scottish songs together, the words mostly provided by Edwin. We had also, about Easter, a fortnight's holiday at Piestany in Southern Slovakia, a spa with hot springs and mud baths which relaxed us considerably.

But the strain was wearing us down, the double strain of life in the Council and under the Communist Government in the country. Edwin decided to leave, for he felt that he was becoming incapable of doing good work where he was. The Chairman of the British Council, Sir Ronald Adam, arrived on a visit; with some difficulty Edwin secured fifteen minutes alone with him and asked to be allowed a transfer on the score of his health. This decision came as a deep relief to both of us.

Shortly after this, I finished a piece of Kafka I had been translating through and between everything. With the end of that task, my ravaged nervous system began to make itself more felt: I found myself shivering and sobbing for no reason at all; anything could make my eyes overflow. Edwin became more of a will-o'-the-wisp than ever, except when we managed to take off an hour or so for walking in the Place of Trees, which put us both right again for a while. Our Writers' Circle still continued to meet, although sometimes only two people turned up, but the meetings tended to be gloomy rather than pleasant. Then an unexpected emergency arose, caused by Lumir Soukup, who had made up his mind to flee the country.

The telephone in the hall rang one evening when I was busy with flower pots, and Edwin, after a little prodding, answered it. He was beginning to withdraw himself from taking action of any kind, but this evening's happenings brought him back to earth again. He returned puzzled, giving the name of a British Embassy attaché who, it appeared, had rung up to ask if we would both be at home, saying he would ring again later, before he came in. We were not intimate with him, and it seemed odd that he should have referred to me as 'Willa'. When the telephone rang again, I answered it, and recognized Lumir's voice as he gave the false name. Would we open the outside gates, he said, in about five minutes' time? When Edwin heard that it was Lumir, he roused himself and went out to the gates. Presently they both came in, but Lumir would not sit down until he had made sure that all windows were shut and all curtains drawn tightly across them. He did then sit down and told us he was going to escape in the coming weekend, when there was a holiday of two days for all government offices, thanks to Saint Cyril and Saint Methodius, whom the Government had forgotten to abolish. The route he proposed to take, across the south-western frontier into Austria, was dangerous, patrolled by men with rifles and police dogs. About one man in five got through, said Lumir, but he was going to take his chance. On this evening he had thrown off the man who was tailing him and had come to say goodbye. We weren't to worry about him; he would get across the frontier. His mother, who was psychic, had told him he would, when he went to say goodbye to his parents.

Lumir looked as if he had been shrunk and bleached. Sheer lack of sleep, he said, working all day and more or less conspiring all night. His job was ended now, and it wouldn't be safe for him to stay; he knew too much. Once he was across, the young British attaché, whose name he had used, would tell us, sending a message about the edition of Shakespeare having safely come to hand, or something like that. He would make his way somehow to the sea and get to England.

Lumir thought it would take the country sixty or seventy years to recover. Then we asked if he were going to send a suicide note to his parents? This was done in the days of the German Occupation, to save an escaper's relatives from the Gestapo. Lumir began to laugh. 'I suggested it to my father, for his sake and my mother's, and do you know what he said? That it would be telling a lie! My father wouldn't accept any protection that meant telling a lie. I had to promise him that I wouldn't escape with a lie on my conscience.' He was still laughing about that promise when he slipped out, begging us to pray for a deluge of rain on the night he was due to escape, to keep the guards from ranging too far.

He did get across the frontier, was rescued from the refugee camp by an English General living near it, and arrived safely in England. That evening with Lumir brought Edwin back from the remote Muir Limbo in which he seemed to be losing himself; there was plenty to do before we could get away, and Edwin stayed on deck, as it were, until we reached Cambridge.

At our last meeting with the Writers' Circle we discussed the depersonalization of modern society, and Edwin read his poem: 'The Good Town'. This was a pleasant, frank evening. It was followed next day by an extraordinary happening that helped to send us away feeling less depressed.

We had persuaded the Council and the appropriate Czech Ministry to let us put all our furniture and household goods into a van which would be sealed and sent across Europe without further examination. The Ministry insisted on being shown receipts for any purchases made in the country, since it was not going to allow the wealth of Czechoslovakia to be drained away. Only one piece of Czech glass, for instance, would be allowed, receipts or no receipts. I had to make a list in Czech of every item we proposed to put in the van, and the list had to be in triplicate. Similar lists were demanded for each suitcase in our hand-luggage. We were going by train, since the hand-luggage would be too much for an aeroplane. Besides, among other panicky rumours, we had heard that officials at the airport sometimes tore fur coats off their wearers, shouting that the wealth of Czechoslovakia was to be left in the country; it seemed not improbable that the rumour might be true.

The van waited in the courtyard and two Customs officers arrived to check my lists. The Ministry had carefully sent two men who spoke no English; they had closed, unsmiling poker faces. I was not quite at ease, because among our books were some of Lumir's, volumes about Masaryk that were now taboo, and I feared they might be confiscated. But we started at the kitchen end of our possessions, counting coffee spoons, cutlery, towels, china and glass, item by item, checked by the Customs men on the lists they held. It was a dreary process, which Edwin was lucky enough to miss, since he had gone to the Kaunic Palace.

Then a glass tumbler turned up, with the first verse of a patriotic poem by Jan Neruda painted all round it in white, with red ornaments and capital letter. One of the Customs men picked it up and began to read the poem. His face broke into a smile, a very human smile, and he said: 'Jan Neruda is my favourite poet.' I smiled back and we began to discuss Neruda's poems. The whole atmosphere was altered in a trice. I sent for some lemon tea and biscuits from the kitchen and the three of us sat down to a friendly survey of Czech poetry, with a disquisition from me on Halas, my favourite. After that, there was no more separate checking of items. The Customs men waved their arms, comprehensively taking in everything of ours, signed all the lists without further ado and wished me a good journey. Such was the humanizing power of poetry in Czechoslovakia, in 1948. I still have that glass; it is a precious souvenir.

Chapter Eighteen

STRANGE INTERLUDE

August–December 1948

(i)

By the time we got to Cambridge where we had been recommended to try a quiet boarding-house called 'The Hermitage' that had associations with the Darwin family, we were both exhausted. The exhaustion took us in different ways. My back seemed broken in two but I was still more or less myself; Edwin's back stayed unbroken but he was hardly recognizable as the same man.

I had long known him as a person who gave out exciting radiations, which I thought of, especially those he shaped into poems, as rising into the air to become elements in future climates of belief. Now he was giving out nothing, much as if the sun had withdrawn its corona and hidden away all its heat and light. His true self which had emitted the radiations was apparently inert. He seemed almost dumb and although neither deaf nor blind heard and saw things without attaching meaning to them. His eyes went to and fro following, as if by compulsion, any small movement within range, a tortoise walking along a garden path or a golf ball being putted across a lawn, but they might as well have been camera eyes; he watched these movements with the vacant stare of a shell-shock case after a modern war. In response to suggestion from me he reacted with mechanical politeness, sitting down to food and eating it, accompanying me for a walk, undressing and going to bed, but he initiated no conversation, no action. Left to himself he merely sat and stared. Remembering my own small attack of indifference in the St Andrews hospital when I had looked at Edwin's hand and for a moment seen it as an irrelevant hand with no meaning, I was sure that he too had lost touch with the feelings that give immediate meaning to life, and I took it that he would recover from this effect of sheer exhaustion. Yet I could not help thinking that there was frustration as well as exhaustion in him which might not be so easily recovered from.

In Prague all he had striven to accomplish seemed to have been blighted. I could not believe that the blight would be permanent, but there was no doubt that the University students, for instance, whom he had cherished until their natures blossomed into friendly confidence, had now been left with faces once more closed up, while the members of our Institute were weeping in despair. The bureaucratic system imposed on the Institute, he had once confided to me, made his flesh crawl on his bones with revulsion, but he had strongly repressed that revulsion, and it might now be causing havoc within him for all I could tell, since his conflicts had vanished beyond reach. I suspected that he might be in a state of despair about the whole human race and was refusing to belong to it. But I was also reminded of The Enchanted Knight lying stricken in a field who appeared so unaccountably in some of his poems.

The other people in the boarding-house were not of the kind to help us in any way. Employed in university offices or laboratories they were closed in their own parochial round and talked their own shop, giving out no human warmth to us and very little, I think, to each other. The liveliest conversation I ever heard them have was an argument about who legally owned a cheque once it was handed in and cashed at a bank. Edwin, anyhow, was unaware of them. He was nearly unaware of me but not quite; he went on accepting suggestions when I made them. His formal politeness was heart-rending.

When the weather was fine we strolled along the Backs, slowly, and sat in the riverside garden of Clare College, looking at the water and the punters. On wet days we sat in the back verandah of the boarding-house, looking at the grass and the trees. During one of these verandah afternoons Mr E. M. Forster was announced. We had never met him before, but Edwin was very friendly with his cousin, J. R. Ackerley, who had probably passed on the information that Edwin was to be at The Hermitage. Mr Forster sat down and gently tried to talk to Edwin but could get no response; after a little while he went quietly away.

Gradually, as Edwin showed willingness, we extended our strolls, crossing the river, and so discovered Clare Fellows' Garden which seemed the very place for both of us. No one queried our entry and we went there daily to sit beside a lily pool with busy birds and green, growing plants around us. Edwin now began to give signs of coming back. He noticed that I moved with difficulty because my back hurt and he said he was sorry. We actually exchanged a smile or two. When a letter came from the British Council suggesting a post in Coimbra, Portugal, he managed to answer it briefly, saying that would be all right. Once or twice we took a punt along the Backs. Yet his reviving awareness of the world had little warmth in it. He was quite indifferent to the next letter from the Council which told him that the Coimbra post was not after all available. To Edwin that seemed not to matter; he did not mind.

About this time we found a little pub at no great distance from The Hermitage and went in, tentatively, one evening, taking Gavin with us. It was a usual kind of small English pub, but it had cushioned benches as well as the usual piano, a dreadful instrument which Gavin could not resist trying. After producing some lively jazz from it he launched out on a Polonaise of Chopin's which pleased the few customers. When more people came in, he was urged to play on, and a warm feeling spread in the air. Every evening after that we dropped in at the pub and were welcomed, because of our son's piano performances, with a simple friendliness that I think did Edwin good.

Presently we started to explore Cambridge and visit the colleges. On the King's Parade one day Edwin told me that there were more pretty girls with neat features and trim figures in Cambridge than one would ever see in Prague. Little by little his interest in the things around him was growing stronger; it was not eager but became perceptible. We left Cambridge then and went for a while to Edinburgh, then to stay in London, latterly in Hampstead, and when the Council appointed him Director of the British Institute in Rome he was able to look forward to his new post, without enthusiasm, with a certain aloofness, but with reasonable interest.

This strange interlude took time; it was nearly December, I think, before Edwin set pen to paper to do writing of his own, and we went to Rome only at the beginning of January 1949. My back had not improved meanwhile, but after some unauthorized shots of penicillin which I persuaded a young doctor to put into me I was able to climb into a plane and fly to Rome. During our stay in Rome Edwin made a complete recovery. What he says about that in his Autobiography gives a good clue to the kind of trouble he had been suffering from. In Rome, he says, he became deeply aware that Jesus had been born in the flesh, since there were so many images of Jesus in shrines, street niches, churches. One could not but be aware that Jesus had lived on earth in a human body, with all its limitations and yet had lived the good life and conveyed the gospel of Love to mankind. A wave of loving feeling for the incarnate Jesus brought Edwin clean out of the limbo in which he had still been partly lingering. He was now able to feel as well as to know that Jesus had lived in a man's body, and that one should not even think of shrugging off the very humanity that Jesus had accepted.

Edwin was joyously released as from imprisonment. He was able to come out of himself spontaneously again and meet the spontaneous Italians around him with a positive affection which they returned more than generously.

In his autobiography Edwin rather plays down this strange interlude, but it gave me much to brood on which I want to record here. Troubled as I was by the queer state he was in, I could think of no way to find direct clues to it except in the poetry he had been composing in Prague. There was one Prague poem called 'The Intercepter' which I had felt at the time to be faintly ominous, since it stirred up old anxieties of mine:

> *Asleep, awake, at work or play,*
> *Whatever I do, wherever I go,*
> *The Intercepter bars my way,*
> *And to my 'Yes' says 'No'.*

This 'Intercepter', who, in another verse,

> *... lifts his hand*
> *And closes up my side.*

represented, I thought, the influence that had led him in earlier years to shut doors so often on his feelings, giving rise to fits of absentmindedness, or 'Muir-family remoteness'. Edwin used to reassure me about them, saying that these lapses into remoteness were as nothing compared to the absence of mind he lived in nearly all the time he was in Glasgow, where, he said, he was mostly sleep-walking. Now, in Prague, long after he had apparently abandoned the habit of shutting himself off, so that he seemed to me to have become a whole man, he had reacted to the Putsch and his difficulties in the Council by again showing signs of withdrawal, turning into a will-o'-the-wisp, as someone mentioned to me, being evasive, as politely indifferent as a changeling to the stresses of daily life. This poem, 'The Intercepter', had made me a little anxious fof him, yet I told myself then that he was in no danger from The Intercepter's negations since he was able to shape a poem about them. How wrong I was became evident in Cambridge, where he vanished into a remoteness farther away, more unreachable than ever before.

It could not be caused exclusively by his revulsion from bureaucracy or from the impersonal machinery of Communism, although these extra factors very likely made his withdrawal more complete. The Intercepter had plagued him off and on for many years, although not given that name. In *Variations on a Time Theme* one of the poems had been about The Intercepter, whom Edwin had then called Indifference. 'My homespun fiend Indifference', he had said. And: 'If I could drive this demon out I'd put all Time's display to rout. Its wounds would turn to flowers and nothing be But the first Garden.' In Prague he had composed a much better poem, a lovely poem, precisely about that process, 'The Transfiguration', in which he journeyed back through Time undoing human aberrations to reach a primal innocence transfiguring the whole world. That was an attempt to rid himself of something which had apparently long troubled him; one would have said a successful attempt, driving his demon quite out. What was this demon? Who was The Intercepter that harassed him and cut him off from his true self?

Sitting in Clare Fellows' Garden I had plenty of time to brood over the problem. The conclusion I came to eventually was that the demon Indifference, The Intercepter cutting Edwin off from natural feeling, was his own defence against the doctrine of Original Sin. It was sin he had tried to by-pass in 'The Transfiguration', all-pervading human sin. It was the Fall of Man and the consequent inherited guilt of the whole human race that kept haunting his imagination, and, I suspected, at times had paralysed him like his own Enchanted Knight.

Ever since the beginning of our marriage I had been aware of his preoccupation with the Fall and with Original Sin, and had thought that it burdened him unduly. I disliked the doctrine of Original Sin, at least the version of it I had met in Scotland. For Calvinist Scots, only the Elect were forgiven their share in Original Sin; Jesus died to save only the Elect. Everyone else had to face an unforgiving final reckoning on the Day of Judgment. As no one could be certain of Election, Calvinists spent much of their time on earth in rehearsing Judgment, censoring their own and other people's conduct, showing up others as less likely than themselves to be counted among the Saints. My instinctive objection to the doctrine arose from my belief in True Love, which presupposes an open, trusting attitude to other people, not expecting them to be perfect but not too concerned with their failings. I think I should have disliked Original Sin in any country, not only in its peculiarly gloomy Calvinist guise, but in Scotland I had found it a detestable doctrine. Edwin was well aware how I felt about it.

So irrational an obsession, I thought, must have taken root in his unconscious at an early, very impressionable age. I inclined to believe that another obsession, the arbitrary death of his two brothers, had also something to do with the operations of the Demon, Indifference. The more I looked at this idea, the more it seemed to explain much.

If the whole human race inherits guilt, life among orthodox Calvinists is regarded as a penance for that; every little pleasure has to be paid for, and all human suffering is part of the payment. But supposing the young Edwin could not agree that his brother Johnny deserved his sufferings because of inherited guilt—and these sufferings were slow and agonizing, resulting from a brain tumour caused by a fall off a bicycle—if Original Sin were barred out, the sufferings seemed not only intolerable but unjustifiable. I could see that this dilemma would ravage Edwin in his vulnerable adolescence, and that after Johnny's death he might put up Indifference as a defence, finding that it could shut off his anguish. I knew that he had actually practised shutting off his feelings until he became adept at intercepting any he wanted to be rid of, a habit that grew upon him in Glasgow and was reinforced by Nietzsche's rejection of 'sympathy'. Eventually the strain, the extra strain, of life in Prague after the Putsch must have sent him right back behind his old defences. And these were too strong to be merely masks, or to provide a technique of self-possession: they cut him quite off.

This seemed to me to make sense. I did not try to discuss it with Edwin because he was fighting his own battles in his limbo where remarks of mine would not help. In any case, he was in no condition to discuss anything. I thought vaguely that when he was himself again we might talk it over, but by the time he was his own man in Rome we were too happy and busy to rake up the past, and my simplified guesses had become irrelevant.

When Edwin was released by his warm, new love for Jesus I looked up his Prague poems again and discovered in 'The Journey Back' this statement:

some day
I know I shall find a man who has done good
His long life-long and is
Image of man from whom all have diverged.

He was then already on the way to find Jesus. Still earlier, in his 1946 volume, 'The Voyage', he had written about Jesus as a

Child in body bound
Among the cattle in a byre,

and in this poem, 'Thought and Image', a recognition of the Incarnation was already dawning. It looked as if The Intercepter had broken into and temporarily stopped a process already under way.

I did hope that The Intercepter would never, never come back.

(ii)

Rome 1949-1950

Having had more than enough of politics in Prague, we went to Rome with the unpolitical open-minded tolerance we had once brought to Vienna, prepared to appreciate whatever we found and to by-pass anything we did not like. We expected Rome to be impressive; we did not expect that we should come to love it, as we did.

The love for Rome began, I think, in the Rome Institute of the British Council, where Edwin found already in being the happy atmosphere he had tried, with some success, to create in the Prague Institute. When Laura Minervini, the Institute Secretary, who may have been fearing that the new Director would be an official tied up in red tape, told him that Italians would do anything for love of their friends but could never be driven, Edwin felt that this was an ambience to which he naturally belonged. His predecessor, Roger Hinks, had been on the best of terms with everyone and Edwin carried on the friendly human tradition in that office. The Representative in Italy, Ronald Bottrall, was also a poet and likely to behave humanly rather than as a bureaucrat; this judgment was confirmed by Ronald himself, who held up to our ridicule, with loud guffaws, London's warning to him before our arrival that Edwin was a trouble-maker and Willa a dangerous woman. We laughed too, though not quite so whole-heartedly; we thought we knew where that assessment of the Muirs had come from, even if Ronald might have embroidered it a little.

The friendliness of the Institute members was as spontaneous as that of the Institute staff and naturally coloured our feelings about Rome from the beginning. Not that we were unaware of other social layers in the capital. There was, for instance, a double contingent of diplomats, those accredited, as usual, in Embassies to the Italian Republic and those accredited to the Vatican, so that the round of diplomatic cocktail parties was twice as large as elsewhere. The only thing to do, we were told, was to attend them all at first, until we discovered for ourselves which we could omit. We found it easy to decide on omissions. In general Edwin and I followed up introductions only to people we personally liked.

The fashionable sets, representing 'la dolce vita', we simply avoided, having been scared off by the glimpses we had of Parioli, one of Rome's fashionable quarters, when we were looking for a flat to live in. I remember one Parioli living-room with tomato-red Pompeian walls diversified by alcoves in which white porcelain nymphs simpered; the chairs, upholstered in magenta plush, were ranged round a large table where a huge spiky glass fish leered at us, a most sadistic-looking fish. Our dismay was probably comical;

it was certainly not comprehended by the letting agent who had taken us there.

The finding of a flat was our most imperative task, since the hotel where the Council had put us, near the Pincian Gate, was too noisy. After Parioli we suggested to the agent that Old Rome might suit us better than New Rome, and he took us through the narrow Via Giulia where rooms were to be had in old palaces. They were large but sombre rooms, usually looking on interior courtyards and needing artificial light all day; although we liked the numerous fountains jetting their water from lions' mouths we did not want to live in semi-darkness. By good luck we then saw a small penthouse on top of a solid apartment block beside the Tiber, in the Gampo Marzio. Once we stood on its wide terraces we knew that this flat was ours. The east terrace looked towards the Quirinal, over some of the oldest roofs in Rome; the west terrace faced the Tiber and the Palace of Justice. These terraces covered most of the space which the apartments beneath used for grandiose suites of rooms; the flat itself was merely a small habitation constructed round the lift-shaft, but it was big enough for us since we meant to live as much as possible in the open air on the roof.

We moved in at once, and I sent a telegram to Hilde who was marooned with her Italian husband, Luigi Riva, and their small son Mario in a remote village at the top end of Lake Como. A Fascist ordinance still in force forbade Italians to apply for jobs outside the region where they were born, and Luigi had been stuck in his native village, Cremia, ever since he got back from the German Labour Camp where he had been put during the war. Luigi was a high-class waiter, Hilde had told me, earlier accustomed to wait on the King of Italy, no less; but within reach of Cremia there was little demand for a man of his training, nor any demand for a woman of Hilde's accomplishments.

In two days' time she appeared at our door, so thin and haggard that I wept over her as she wept over me because she had not known that I was hobbling about on a stick; I think also that we wept for the sheer joy of seeing one another again. She had left Mario in another part of Rome with a relative of Luigi's, and confessed to his being there almost as if she had committed a crime; but I sent her to fetch him at once. There was just room in the flat for him as well as Hilde, although I regretted that we had no room for Luigi. 'Oh, Luigi,' said Hilde, 'Luigi has his mother and two sisters in Cremia; he'll be all right till I find him a job in Rome.'

Little by little Hilde told me most of what had happened to her in the war. Before Munich was intensively bombed, things weren't so bad there, she said. Being in charge of all the wine in one of Munich's famous hotels, she found it easy to get in touch with British prisoners of war, who were sent from a nearby camp to load and unload beer and wine casks; she began by emptying their water-bottles and filling them up with Marsala. Two of them had sent field postcards to Edwin, telling of her marriage and of Mario's birth.

Later on she was bombed out of three separate flats in Munich, one after the other, and Luigi was directed to a Labour Camp. Hilde decided to make for her mother's inn down in the Pfalz. So she loaded up a pram with Mario and as many Army boots as she could pack in——

'Army boots?'

Oh, her mother had reported that good strong boots were urgently needed in the Pfalz, and as she was now the unemployed wife of an alien, she wouldn't get German ration cards, and would need something to bargain with.

No wonder, I thought, that she looked haggard and waif-like. She had joined Luigi after he was repatriated to Italy, but then there was the constriction of living in Cremia, mostly without work or money, dependent on Luigi's mother, whom Hilde could not approve. The realism of old Signora Riva was too much for her.

'Only think,' said Hilde, 'when her husband's body was dug up in the churchyard——'

'But *why* was he dug up?'

'They always do dig them up, after so many years, is it ten years? The coffins are put in a common vault—there's never any room in the churchyards. But just think, there was a large marble slab over the old man's grave, and Luigi's mother brought it home to set her cooking-stove on! Her husband's tombstone! In the kitchen, with a new gas-cooker on it!'

However shocking she might find Italians, Hilde knew how to get on with them. Her foraging among Roman shops and market-stalls was highly successful. In about six wine-shops she sampled the draught wines—her taste in wines was professionally excellent—and having found a good red *vino aperto* in one of them she laid it in for us by the litre. She managed to get on friendly terms with the restaurant keepers of the neighbourhood, always with an eye to getting a job for Luigi, until one day she found him one, in a restaurant famous for its spaghetti, where Americans always went and the tips were large. The proprietor's son-in-law was ill and a man to replace him for a while was needed: just the thing for Luigi. He would board with the family. And it was a *high-class* restaurant; Luigi needn't think it wasn't good enough for him.

Luigi certainly had an air and a presence when at last he appeared, and our parties, which he insisted on attending in his best white coat, for love, not money, gained an enormous cachet from his services. So the Riva family was rescued from its village exile, and we once more had the benefit of Hilde's housekeeping. She ceased to be waif-like; her eyes were no longer sunk in her head; she even grew merry again. Luigi, of course, objected to the job she had found for him. As a replacement for a member of the restaurant family, he was supposed to do as the family did every morning, sitting round various buckets in the yard peeling and cutting up vegetables, which did not consort with his dignity. He found himself another job in the Ambassadors Hotel, where the tips were smaller but the prestige greater and he did not have to do kitchen chores. In due time, the Riva family acquired a flat of their own and became lawful citizens of Rome.

The penthouse itself was another basic element in our wellbeing. We could welcome the sun on either terrace or avoid it by shifting to the other as seemed convenient. Sitting beside tubs of geraniums, oleander and Beautiful Ladies of the Night, on top of the Roman world, we were deeply content, having found, to our astonishment, that this was a world which seemed familiar although neither of us had been in Rome before. It was not simply that we had a wide view on either side in a spacious setting of air and light; after all, when we first went abroad in the twenties, to Prague, we used often to sit on airy heights above the river Vltava, also looking over mediaeval roofs made up of curved tiles, the colour of wallflowers, amply overlapping old palaces, there as here, yet we had never felt at home in that panorama as we did in this. Prague had a fairy-tale unreality then, and though it had become real enough to us during the last few years there was an alien harshness in its reality. But that Rome seemed neither harsh nor alien did not arise wholly from our favourable penthouse setting.

Favourable it was. Sitting at ease on our roof-top Edwin was moved to write occasional poems. Conversations there with visitors were gay and free. Wystan Auden, for instance, turned up one evening and over litres of *vino aperto* (seven litres, Hilde swore; she kept bringing them like a sorcerer's apprentice) argued the case for the resurrection of the body while Edwin argued for the immortality of the soul, in a happy antiphony that went on for hours. The roof-top was a liberating place. But much of its comfort came from our recognizing what we were looking at, buildings and features already loaded with associations. The Tiber was a known river as the Vltava had not been; we had never heard of the Prague Hradčany before seeing it, but we had heard of the Quirinal; a hill outlined on the sky from our western terrace had been long known to me as Horace's Soracte, *nive Candida*, a piece of knowledge now shared by Edwin. In the same way all through the city the many great buildings that witnessed to the ambitions and aspirations of the men who had erected them were already familiar to our minds. What we had known as concepts or pictures now became actual, daily realities. We recognized that the layers of history visible in Rome were layers from the history of European civilization, our own history.

It was not the larger show-pieces, St Peter's, say, or the Coliseum, that moved us most deeply, but less obtrusive buildings, like the church of San Clemente. This typified Rome for both of us. The basilica entered from the street, a twelfth-century basilica with a great apse on which the Living Vine branched into countless mediaeval symbols, was, one learned with some surprise, the modern church on the site. Beneath it was the ancient church, still intact, a fifth-century basilica. Beneath that again was part of an old Roman villa, the original meeting-place for Christians, flanked on one side by a temple of Mithras. This continuity of centuries made visible, all on the same site, appealed strongly to Edwin and quite capsized my own rickety time-sense. Enlightenment also came from seeing so-called Anglo-Saxon attitudes pictured round the portico of San Lorenzo, angular knees and elbows that were by no means peculiar to England, one discovered, but a mode of illustration fashionable in its day all over Christian Europe. Much that had been left out of our education was thus filled in, and we became better, because more understanding Europeans.

This process went on during the year and a half we spent in Rome and I do not propose to enlarge upon it, except to say that out of it came our sense of belonging to the historic Rome. Yet even more exciting was our sense of belonging to the Rome of here and now, which was what we most inordinately loved; that is to say, the Rome of living people. Our awareness of that began in the British Institute but did not stop there, if only because both staff and members of the Institute had friends all through the city. Even in Vatican circles we had our acquaintances, since Laura's assistant, Sabina, had a brother in the Pope's Noble Guard, so that we were sure of seats at any ceremonial in St Peter's, while Joe O'Brien, Edwin's second-in-command, had a close friend who was a Monsignore and introduced Edwin to the Scots College. Edwin gave a talk on literature to the students there; he appreciated the mediaeval College which still owned a vineyard in the middle of Rome and bottled its own wine. Later on a body of us from the Institute went there to see an excellent production of *The Mikado* put on, with great brio, by the young Scottish priests.

As in Prague, Edwin was lucky in his nearest assistant. Joe O'Brien was a lovable and beloved personality, with a large acquaintance among Roman teachers. Like Edwin he felt that the Institute should reach the middle layers of the populace, especially school-teachers, who were beneath the reach of the British Embassy. Yet the Institute membership was not large, and Edwin and Joe set themselves to extend it. Edwin persuaded the Council to open a tea-room in the Institute, which proved a popular innovation. Luckily, the young women on the staff were all good-looking as well as intelligent, one or two very pretty, and their presence in the tea-room was a draw.

A class of Italian naval officers—I think about eighty of them—came to the Institute to learn English; there was little reason why the Italian Navy should love the British at that time and on their first arrival the officers were cold, formal, even hostile in manner. In less than three weeks they were captivated by the friendliness of the tea-room and became enthusiastic admirers of our young women. The fame of the tea-room spread and it became a favourite rendezvous for Romans. They did not bother to say 'The British Institute Tearoom'; they told each other simply: 'I'll meet you at The British.' Because the atmosphere of the whole Institute was friendly and welcoming, the response from Romans was instantaneous, and the membership went up by leaps and bounds. When a General in the Italian Army presented us with a box of our own at the theatre we felt that we had become a popular success.

Our affection for Romans was no one-way traffic; it was reciprocated. We had been taken, as it were, right into the family. One thing that struck us was the frank anarchy of the family life we now shared in; people did anything at all on behalf of friends and completely ignored troublesome laws or edicts. Our Roman friends were wonderfully obliging and not at all law-abiding, and as we identified ourselves with them we too became happy-go-lucky in our attitude to the Law. Even Edwin smoked without demur the smuggled English cigarettes, Players' No. 6, which had found their way to Rome from Switzerland and appeared at our door punctually every week— punctually, because we bought them not from a smuggler whose supply might have fluctuated precariously but from a Customs officer who could guarantee regular deliveries.

This open disrespect for constituted authority, this Roman irreverence, seemed remarkable in a city which had been for so long a centre of ruling powers. The river of human feeling apparently flowed along quite unaffected by the legal grids straddled over it, and we wondered how long it had been flowing like that. At its best, it was essentially humane in the actions it inspired; during the war the hill-farmers sheltered and succoured any soldier or partisan in distress who came to the door, whatever his uniform, while Laura told us that the Germans could never keep Romans from rushing with drinks of water to parched Jews in horse-trucks. At its worst, when it erupted into abusive quarrels, it was still frank and its gestures were still graceful. Both the good and the bad in the people of Rome came out into the full light of day, without inhibitions, apparently straight from the unconscious.

The frank, anarchic, family feeling extended from our middle-class Institute members down to the populace that filled the Corso every evening as they promenaded in what they felt to be *their* street, *their* family centre, where vehicles of any kind were outsiders and groups would not move an inch away from a honking motor-car until it actually nudged them. I have used the word anarchic, but the anarchy appeared as such only to outsiders, to external authorities; the family had its own personal laws of conduct, which, by their own standards, were usually considerate and humane.

Few Romans could resist expressing themselves on a blank wall-space, so that *graffiti* abounded, but I never saw any that were obscene. They were mainly political and went in for no compromises, no half-measures; most inscriptions were a matter of Life or Death to so-and-so, a big W for *Evviva* or a big M for *Morte*. On a stretch of the Tiber embankment, opposite our western terrace where we breakfasted, an inscription suddenly appeared one morning in white letters about eight feet high, which some craftsman must have spent the small hours carefully painting, for they were beautifully shaped, and which announced to the world: 'Scelba Assassino'. Scelba was then the equivalent of our Home Secretary and had been organizing squads of riot police in the city. The Thames had never been embellished with such a description of a Home Secretary, and as members of a reputedly law-abiding country we should have been shocked, instead of which our Roman sympathies inclined us to the craftsman, and we frankly relished his handiwork.

In the Pantheon one day I found and showed to Edwin a Latin inscription on the floor which supplied a clue to this feeling of human kinship we were aware of among Romans. It commemorated an old priest from Dacia who had come to Rome as a pilgrim, died there and been interred in the Pantheon, under the care of Roma, Mater Gentium. There it was, the recognition of a human family; Roma, Mater Gentium, Mother of Peoples, even of far-off peoples in Dacia, nearly beyond the pale; an aspect of Rome that my text-books had said nothing about. I was moved by this testimony that people in Rome so long ago had passed on a mothering tradition. Apparently some Romans had long known that the human race needs mothering as well as fathering, although the patriarchal structures of their governors provided only a surfeit of fathers, many of them celibate. It must have been an ancient tradition, I thought, inherited from earlier Mediterranean societies, since in its religion it had preserved the essential Feminine Principle, the Mother, the Madonna, as did no other branch of the Christian Church.

So we lived in Rome surrounded by what Edwin calls 'the free environing warmth' of human kindness. On official visits to other towns such as Siena, Perugia, Assisi, where Edwin gave talks, we had not the same intimacy with the populace, but carried away from them an almost awe-struck admiration for the innumerable lovely things produced by the Italian genius during so many centuries. These journeys were made in the Institute car and I managed to include myself in most of them. But when it came to a tour of Sicily Edwin was asked to do, with a programme of lectures to be given in Palermo, Messina, Catania, Syracuse, I found that merely as a wife I had no claim to be officially included. The British Council, perhaps rightly, would not pay for the satisfaction of my passionate desire to see with my own eyes the quarries at Syracuse where the Greek prisoners had suffered incarceration, and all the other scenes of The Sicilian Expedition. Yet if I would agree to give a lecture in Italian, I could accompany Edwin, I was told. I prepared a lecture in my best Italian and off we set together to see as much of Sicily as an official programme allows.

Neither Edwin nor I then knew anything about the Mafia, and our tour round the island brought us into no contact with the realities of Sicilian peasant life. We saw it only from the windows of a car; that is to say, we saw the beautifully-painted carts on the roads with plumed horses finding their own way home while the supposed drivers slept in the cart-bottoms, and we rejoiced at the sight of acres of golden wheat already, in May, being harvested. Edwin, who loved islands because of Orkney, wrote a poem about Sicily ('The Island') that conjured up an entirely romantic image. But in a later poem ('The Desolations') he remembered our unforgettable ascent of Etna, with the town of Catania at its foot, where the houses were trimmed with black lava 'like a pleasant street in hell' and the soil was pure black slag, growing seven crops a year. At the time, Catania reminded us of Doré illustrations and gave us rather a grue.

In the semi-tropical heat below Etna on ground level, among the sooty fields, everything seemed to turn into yellow or amber colour, lemons, thistles and goats alike, but halfway up the mountain one reached pear trees in white blossom and clumps of violets, in the cooler air that was like a Scottish summer. Farther up still, one came to desolate billows of lava, thirty feet high, stopped in mid-career when their red fires died; they were like nothing we had ever seen or imagined.

Then we ran south into limestone outcrop, on our way to Syracuse, into goat-herds' country. The enchantment of Syracuse was all I had looked for, and more, although it was daunting to find the fountain of Arethusa imprisoned in a tank. Our guide, a Syracusan poet, Luigi Guido, was himself a delight. He escorted us to the widespread ruins of ancient Syracuse, which had been a huge city. Crowding together in outsize cities was apparently a much older habit of the human race than I had suspected. Then, very unwillingly, we left Syracuse because we wished to make a dash to see the great temples at Agrigentum before giving back the car to the Council officials at Palermo who had lent it to us. These temples provided another unforgettable experience, sited as they were in such harmony with the landscape and the sea. The Greek temples and theatres I saw, either in Sicily or on the Italian mainland, all seemed to suggest a relation with infinite spaces beyond them; they were built and placed in such a way that they led the imagination out into the sky, the sea, or the mountains; unlike modern buildings they never stopped dead just where they stood.

In the worst heats of our first summer, when the towers rising from Roman roofs seemed exact copies of the thunderheads above them, Hilde wiled us to Lake Como, to Cremia, for a holiday, in a large house which an acquaintance of hers wished to let. There we discovered that the village lived mainly by smuggling goods from Switzerland. Any young man in Cremia inherited his father's share in a smuggling gang as if it were a family business. Besides being smugglers, the friendly people we met were free with personal information about Mussolini's capture, at which some of them had assisted. Hilde said darkly that no one would ever know what happened to the money and Clara Petacci's jewels,but a man in the next village had unexpectedly set up a hotel and his wife was wearing a diamond sun-burst. The pleasant youngsters who rowed us up the lake to Dongo and picked bunches of wild cyclamen for us did not look like murderers. Yet Hilde professed to know that some of them were. Cremia, as Holms might have said, was 'not without merit' as an interesting holiday centre.

Besides holidaying or giving talks and lectures, Edwin was kept busy producing magazine evenings at the Institute and training his staff to lecture without scripts. Meanwhile, Holy Year came upon us and Rome was overwhelmed with waves of pilgrims. Thinking to avoid the crush, we took coach at Easter for Florence, but we ought to have foreseen that Florence would be crowded too; the pilgrims on their way to Rome or on their way back inevitably stopped there. Florence itself had grown enormously and even its central Piazza was thronged. In San Marco we could hardly glimpse the Fra Angelicos, so many solid German shoulders and rucksacks made a barrier in front of us. We solaced ourselves by driving out in a pneumatic-tyred carrozza, especially round the Cascine, where the scented poplars were filling the air with small clouds of woolly down. In a fashion that most of our countrymen would think heretical we decided that we liked Rome better than Florence. What the Florentines would have said to that, we could guess, for their interpretation of S.P.Q.R. was: Sono Porchi, Questi Romani.

It had been somehow understood that we were to spend at least three years in Rome and so we had no sense of urgency in our explorations of the city, thinking that we had plenty of time. With the same spacious feeling Edwin walked daily through the Piazza della Rotonda in front of the Pantheon to his office in the Palazzo Doria, ten minutes away, where the affairs of the Institute were progressing merrily. Then an axe wielded by the British Government fell upon us. The Council's subsidy was cut, and its head directors decided to shut down most of the Institutes in Europe, on the theory, which we thought mistaken, that the United Kingdom was close enough to Europe to need little help from the Council in establishing good-neighbour relations. The money saved would be better used, it was thought, in setting up centres farther away, in India, say, or Africa, or South America.

The decision to close the British Institute in Rome was felt by Romans to be an outrage, almost a national insult, but the popular outcry against it had no effect. The day inevitably came when we had to leave. Meanwhile, Edwin had been asked to accept the post of Warden of Newbattle Abbey College, beside Dalkeith, in Scotland, which was to be restarted as a centre of Adult Education after having been taken over by the military during the war. This would be the only Adult Education College in Scotland, and Professor John Macmurray, a friend of ours, who was on its Executive Committee, strongly urged Edwin to take the job. The more Edwin reflected on it, the more he was inclined to do so. He, if anyone, should know what it felt like to be a young adult hungering for education and enlightenment without knowing where to turn for help. He became enthusiastic, so that although I had misgivings, since Scotland reminded me of St Andrews, which was still a bruise in my memory, I was persuaded to fall in with the plan.

We expected to be seen off at the station by a fair crowd of people, but when we reached it and saw the hundreds milling around our train we looked at each other in amazement. Surely this mammoth send-off couldn't be all for us? It was not. Laurel and Hardy were travelling in the next compartment, and the crowd swarming on the platform were fans of Stanlio and Ollio. The weather was very hot, and one could not help seeing poor Ollio, a fat, suffering baby in very short shorts, sitting whimpering on his seat, all doors and windows open, while three blondes curved over him saying: There, there! and bringing cold drinks. Stanlio, on the other hand, full of grit, was doing the hard work of coping with the fans. He stood wisecracking at the carriage door, signing innumerable autograph books, an indomitable little man. When the train reached Turin the same situation repeated itself.

Our own fans were numerous enough. We had just shaken hands, warmly but correctly, with three friends from the British Embassy when our chauffeur, Gildo, burst through the crowd, flung his arms first round Edwin's neck, then round mine, and kissed us each fervently. The Embassy young men made no comment; their eyebrows merely rose a fraction. But it was a real Roman goodbye.

Chapter Nineteen

NEWBATTLE ABBEY COLLEGE

1950-1955

(i) *Preliminaries*

Unwilling as he was to leave Rome, where he had been brought back into the human community and learned to live more kindly with himself as well as others, Edwin was eager to start work at Newbattle Abbey College. What he had been told about it, chiefly in letters from John Macmurray, had fired his imagination. Newbattle Abbey would be attended by students coming not under compulsion but of their own accord, because they felt a need for more education than chance had given them and now had the opportunity of getting it through money grants from Local Education Authorities. For a whole year they would be in residence, learning to live in a wider context, sharing experience with their lecturers and with each other. The Executive Committee, said John Macmurray, had settled what courses were to be offered: Literature, Philosophy, History and Economics. The Literature course Edwin himself was going to conduct, and this prospect delighted him, but he would have to appoint staff for the other subjects, as well as a Bursar. Much would depend on the quality of the lecturers, who should, he felt, themselves be young and in sympathy with the aims of the College; he would need time to find the right people. He wished also personally to interview each applicant for a student's place, if possible,before acceptance. The College was due to open in October, and the sooner he was in residence the better. There was a flat for the Warden, he had been told, and residential accommodation for the staff. A housekeeper was already installed.

All these sensible conclusions, exchanged in letters between Dr Muir and Professor Macmurray, met with approval from me, but I had an extra, a private interest in Newbattle Abbey College, because the prospect of living there stirred into action a foible of

mine which I had for years been trying to ignore: my secret wish
for a permanent home. I had ignored it because a more powerful
voice within me said that my home was in Edwin's bosom. The
foible took its revenge every now and then by compelling me to
read through the pages of British Sunday papers which advertised
houses for sale or to let, but I had managed to keep it under cover.
I cannot be sure that Edwin did not know about it; I think he did
not. Now it began to assert itself, telling me that Newbattle Abbey
might prove to be a permanent home for our old age.

Edwin was sixty-three and I was sixty, yet we were still young
enough in spirit. Edwin found it easy to re-live his own young days,
when he had been astray, bewildered, needing help, and to see in his
mind's eye students coming to him in the same predicament. His
eagerness was more than official goodwill; his concept of education
was not limited to the providing of subjects in separate categories;
for him the proper concern of education was to encourage in each
student an ultimate harmony between Story and Fable. This idea
was not confided to Professor Macmurray or the Committee in
the letters written by Dr Muir, but it was lighting up Peerie B.
inside himself all the way from Rome to Newbattle Abbey.

Shortly after reaching Edinburgh the pair of us went helter-
skelter in a taxi to Newbattle Abbey without even ringing up the
housekeeper beforehand, an excursion with which Dr and Mrs
Muir clearly had nothing to do, Peerie B. and Peerie Willa being
in charge. The sun was shining as we turned in at the main gate
and the lions couched above it, in blurred stone, were cosy-looking.
The river behind the lodge was the Esk, Edwin thought. Between
trees the drive led up to a handsome portico. I had been told that
Newbattle Abbey was a family seat of the Kerrs, handed over by
Philip Kerr, the late Lord Lothian, to be an Adult Education
College, yet I had not realized that it was a country house more
impressive and spacious than any I had fallen in love with among
the illustrations in the Sunday papers.

The glass door at the top of the steps stood open and we walked
into a lofty stone hall quite empty except for a large empty staircase
leading to upper rooms. At that moment we heard footsteps
coming along a passage to the left of the staircase and a smallish

man and a tallish woman came in sight. The woman's manner was distant as she denied being the housekeeper; she added that the Abbey was not open to visitors for the present. Then who were they, and how did they come to know their way about? We did not voice these questions, but we did not like being eyed as if we were intruders. 'Oh, here is the housekeeper,' put in the man as another tall woman with apple-red cheeks came briskly along the passage. Her eyes rounded in amazement when Edwin said that he was the new Warden. We were made aware that our unauthorized arrival was a breach of decorum that had to be overlooked.

The presence of the two strangers, which had surprised us, did not surprise us less when they were introduced as a Glasgow Bailie representing the City of Glasgow and the Head of a Glasgow Pre-Nursing College, who had come to make the last arrangements for a Summer School in the Abbey, due to begin next day when the pre-nursing students would arrive. No one had told Edwin that such activities were going on in the Abbey, just as no one had told the housekeeper that the new Warden was proposing to come into residence as soon as possible. We suggested that things would naturally sort themselves out, but the housekeeper was still ruffled. Most unfortunately the Warden's flat was locked up, she said, and could not be inspected. The caretaker who had the key had gone into Fife for the day. Certainly, the rest of the College could be inspected, but not the Warden's flat. It was most unfortunate.

So it was, especially when conveyed in such formal language, which struck a little cold on us. It served us right, I supposed, for coming without warning. We had forgotten that Scotland was not Rome, where our childish impetuousness would have been accepted with indulgence and very likely someone would have picked the lock of the Warden's flat for us. One could not suggest such an operation to these three dignitaries who now escorted us over the College. They were formal enough to be on the defensive, but if so, it was a challenging defensive, not like Czech defensiveness which had shown itself merely in reticent wariness. Here we were not foreigners; we were being challenged to prove that we were reliable members of the same tribe as our escorts. Something more positive was expected of us than the patient, receptive kindness which had sufficed in Prague, some gesture to set us right with our tribal fellows. But what gesture?

As we went through the College we were able to praise whole-heartedly the magnificent proportions of the great drawing-room and the attractive look of the library. The thin film of social ice began to thaw; apparently we were doing the right thing. The Bailie was quickest to thaw; he grew facetious about the State bedroom that had once been prepared for Queen Victoria. Indeed, its maroon carpet deserved facetious comment; the whole floor seemed to heave as one looked at the blue-ribboned bouquets of lily of the valley that ran diagonally from corner to corner. It began to dawn on me that what was expected of us was the Bailie's kind of jocular facetiousness, to show that we were neither superior nor censorious. Edwin was laughing pleasantly at the facetious remarks; that was his social gift, radiating kindness; he had no gift for retailing jokes, but surely, I thought, he was conveying assurance. In the students' bedrooms, adequately if sparsely furnished, we then approved everything, and when we reached the ground floor again to see the long dining-room with a billiard-room opening out of it we were urged to join the others in having afternoon tea in the crypt.

The crypt was not really a crypt; it was a 'dortoir' of the ancient Abbey incorporated in the Kerrs' mansion, giving a faintly monkish ambience to that part of it. The roof was vaulted; the walls of grey stone were historic-looking; some worn, squat columns made of small pillars clustered together had perhaps suggested the idea of a crypt. As in all the public rooms the fireplace was impressive; here , not marble, with a huge coat-of-arms carved above it. Before the war, said the housekeeper, the crypt had been the students' common-room.

By this time the ice had vanished. As the Bailie handed me sandwiches he handed me also the remark that no woman could keep a secret, and I was prompted to reply that any woman could keep a secret for nine months—a jest perhaps as old as Noah. Yet it seemed welcome to the Bailie who shouted with laughter. After that we were all on more than friendly terms. When tea was finished we were escorted into the delightful knot garden at the back of the house so that we could see from the outside the windows of what were to be our drawing-room and the Warden's study.

This odd experience of learning how to overcome Lowland Scottish defensiveness served us well later, since there were always some Scottish students who arrived at Newbattle curiously on the defensive. The Scots we had met abroad had not been on the defensive at all; indeed, we had noticed that they got directly on human terms with strangers more easily than the English. An Englishman meeting a stranger abroad seemed first to cross a small no-man's-land around him in which he probed anxiously for hidden mines; once he was through the no-man's-land he could be a good and loyal friend, but he took longer to reach that secure relationship than the average Scotsman.

Englishmen abroad—those we met through the British Council, at least—were more on the defensive socially than they ever were at home, where their accents and manners at once established their status. In a foreign country, meeting foreigners, they could not be sure of being recognized and their social antennae rather quivered with apprehension. The Scotsmen seemed to have fewer social antennae and consequently a more forthright approach to foreigners. Why, then, so much defensiveness at home in Scotland?

Might it not be a hang-over from the censoriousness of Calvinism, the habit of rehearsing Judgment Day? There was certainly an element of challenge in Lowland Scottish defensiveness, a hint of self-righteous disapproval, a suggestion that one's pretensions might need correcting, that one was not above reproach, as Edwin and I had been made aware that our first incursion into Newbattle was a breach of decorum. But this challenging defensiveness seemed not so much social as moral, and was more easily conjured away than social defensiveness. The challenger only had to discover that one was not pretending to be morally superior at all.

In our varied adventures in Europe Edwin and I had been, as it were, trained to cope with this kind of situation. Edwin's great gift of benevolently permeating the space around him, which I have already mentioned as comforting to his Prague students, was even stronger, now, because of Rome, than it had been in Prague.

The atmosphere, or ambience, or whatever one may call it, which Edwin diffused is difficult to convey in words, and I am aware of the risk that in trying to convey it any words of mine may be taken as presenting a figment of my own imagining. But I have evidence from Dr Harvey Wood, which I have his leave to quote. In March, 1962, after he was appointed British Council Representative in Rome, he wrote to me:

'I must tell you that when I arrived here first I got the impression that you and Edwin had been here for years and years—because you had both left such a warm, affectionate, imperishable memory behind you. When I realised how short a time you had had here, I knew it was another Muir miracle, like the time I walked through the Charles University with Edwin and saw how *everybody*—students and staff alike—beamed with pleasure at the very sight of him.'

This was true. To the unimaginative, Edwin may have appeared as a friendly, likeable, unpretending man with an odd lack of self-assertiveness which they sometimes mistook for weakness, but to the imaginative he was a living delight, and to some an inspiration. There was no one in Newbattle Abbey College, from the daily cleaners to the lecturing staff, who did not more or less feel his pervasive influence, although it was not deliberately exercised. It was something he could not help giving out; he radiated it as he walked and breathed, and the whole College benefited.

(ii) *The College*

During the first year rather more than twenty students turned up, and every year we were there the numbers fluctuated between twenty and around thirty. Not all were Scottish; an Englishman or two usually came from the south; one year an Australian journalist was a lively addition; we were never without foreigners from Europe, Africa or India.

In the very first term a coffee-coloured man appeared, from French Togoland, sent by the Colonial Office. His mother tongues being Somali and French, he had been directed to train as a teacher at Moray House, Edinburgh, where he did not understand a word. The Colonial Office then had the bright idea of sending him to Newbattle for a term, to 'learn the language'. It did not take us long to become used to the colour of his skin and the different map of his features, but we did have to get used to them and were naively astonished to find that getting on friendly terms with him was easy. His first name was Bonaventura and in no time everyone was calling him Bona. He was a gay young man and was taken immediately under the protective care of Bob, a heavy-metal worker who had been making the great pipes that carry oil over deserts.

Bob was a big man with strong shoulders and glowing brown eyes rather like Robert Burns's. From him Bona learned the language all right; after about a fortnight I heard him saying confidently: 'Gie's a fag, Bob!' Once he was able to talk, he became a great tease, especially of those students he liked, and most especially of Frytschek, a Dutch Trade Unionist, who had come to Newbattle to brush up his English and learn the workings of British Trade Unions, with the intention of becoming a liaison officer between the two countries. To Frytschek, lazily stretched on a couch in the crypt, Bona would advance, pin him down by the shoulders and go on repeating: 'Your Queen is a very Ogly Woman,' until they were tumbling over each other like puppies.

When Bona left at the end of the term to go to Moray House (where he then understood every lecture he heard) we were all sorry. Foreigners who came singly, like him, from Europe or wherever, were easily assimilated. Some of them became wildly popular, like a French Trade Unionist from Lyon, Joe Jarru. Volatile, talkative creature that he was, he could read English but spoke hardly a word of it when he arrived, and his sufferings for lack of conversation were pitiable. Before he left, he had the whole student body shouting French songs: one heard

> Buvons voir, oui, oui, oui,
> Buvons voir, non, non, non,
> Buvons voir si le vin est bon

all over the Abbey. He had himself photographed in a kilt, and invited everyone in the place to make his home in Lyon a port of call if they should go hiking through Europe. Two of our students accepted the invitation and later reported that no wonder Joe felt suffocated for want of speech on his first arrival; the Jarru household, Joe's parents, brothers and sisters, sat down more than a dozen to table every day, all talking away at the very top of their voices. Later, when some Yugoslavs came in a bunch one did not get to know them so intimately; they hived off into a group of their own; they were not really assimilated, although friendly enough and hard-working.

People with a secret passion for literature are rare in any walk of life, but Bob, the heavy-metal worker, was one of them, and he responded at once to Edwin's ambience. Before coming to Newbattle he had conformed to the life his mates led; a trade union meeting on Friday, a football match on Saturday afternoon, and the pub on Saturday evening. He kept his trade union minutes; I think that was the only writing he had admitted to. But during his second week at Newbattle he brought Edwin a poem, saying: 'I dinna ken what my mates would say about this.' Edwin was so pleased that he came hot-foot to tell me.

Bob committed himself whole-heartedly to the literature Edwin presented in class. *Paradise Lost*, to use his own words, knocked him end-ways, and he was knocked end-ways again by the Book of Job. When his year was up, Edwin abandoned a principle he had set himself, never to put pressure on a student, and put pressure on Bob to come for a second year. After the summer vacation, which Bob spent working in his home town gas-works, he did come for a second year and, yielding to more persuasion, agreed to write an essay for the Cambridge Extra-Mural Delegacy. A miner from Newbattle had already secured a place at Cambridge by an essay on Kant, and Edwin hoped that Bob would get to Cambridge too. An essay on *Paradise Lost* was written and sent away; neither Edwin nor I saw it until it came back with the information that Bob had won a place in King's College. That essay was a naked confrontation of John Milton and Bob, no other critic being mentioned. I think Bob rather astonished Cambridge, he was so patently 'the real thing'. I was later told that the Provost of King's College, offering him sherry, asked 'And what do you think of Cambridge?' to which Bob replied that it wasna very like the gas-works in his home town. He is now the head of an English department in a Scottish high school, transmitting to the younger generation his own enthusiasm for imaginative literature.

During our five years in Newbattle Edwin had no less than five other students with literary gifts, including two poets, Tom Scott

Newbattle Abbey

Edwin Muir, Louise Bogon, James Merrill,
Mount Holyoke, 1956

and George Mackay Brown. More students of exceptional gifts, a good handful of them, finished up in Ruskin College, Oxford, doing economics and politics, including one argumentative young man, born for politics, who is now an outstanding Labour M.P. Among them was a brassfounder, P., whom I mention because he was an example, when he first arrived at Newbattle, of the ferociously defensive Scot. At social gatherings in the crypt or in our drawing-room P. stayed in a corner, glowering, with his back to the wall. He was also ferociously independent. His Local Education Authority had offered him a grant to pay his way at Newbattle and he refused it, saying he had saved up money to pay his own way. Economics were his main interest, and Kenneth Wood, the Economics lecturer, reported that he seemed intelligent on paper yet could not be got to utter.

Had Newbattle Abbey been only a male college, I doubt if P. could have blossomed as he did, but, following the Scottish tradition, it had women as well as men students, and some of the girls simply took him in hand. He was lured to dance in the crypt and given special lessons in the management of his steps; he was neat on his feet and became a good dancer. He was well chaffed until able to keep his end up. He deserted his corner and turned out to be one of Kenneth's best students. He even joined my voluntary Latin class which was held for anyone who might be interested. Presently I was enchanted to learn that P. had been declaiming 'Da mi basia mille' to his roommates. He won a scholarship to Ruskin College, and before he went there the girls escorted him to Edinburgh and helped him to buy a new suit, ties and socks. Apart from becoming an authority on Economics and Social Work, I think P's most satisfactory achievement as a man was proposing to and being accepted by one of Ruskin's junior matrons.

The less exceptional students had their aspirations too. Some wished to become teachers, including one frail, pretty girl who was fascinated by Gerard Manley Hopkins and his inscapes. One wanted to do art work and has become a fabric designer. An older man, about forty, twice the age of most others, had a passion for historical research. A whole book could be written about our students and their half-stifled longings which found room to breathe in Newbattle. Besides what they absorbed in lectures and discussions they learned that their interests could not only come out into the open but could be shared with others. There was a strong sense of companionship.

One fact strikes me as curious now, although at the time I took it for granted; there was no sex trouble between the men and women students. They treated each other in the brotherly and sisterly way to which I had been accustomed in my own student days at St Andrews. Being all in residence together they felt like a family, with the little extra zest that came from their not really being brothers and sisters.

The life of the College, one might say, was founded on good faith as between staff and students and among students towards each other. Edwin was content with the way it was working out. In his dream of a better order for society he felt that he was tackling the problem from the right end, helping frustrated individuals to realize themselves by bringing Fable and Story into closer harmony.

Yet the first symptom of bad faith came from inside the College, not from outside. The Philosophy Lecturer, an attractive young man of strong personality, had been a fellow-student and friend of Gavin's at St Andrews. On our way through London we had given luncheon to him and his wife, since he had applied for the post, and liked them enough for Edwin to appoint him. Their flat was above our drawing-room and we could hear the rumble of lively discussions often going on overhead until the small hours, which we thought all to the good. But during the second term of that first year a deputation of students came to see Edwin, complaining that the Philosophy Lecturer was slanting all discussions towards Communism. Our most solid and reliable students were on that deputation and they accused the Lecturer of being an under-cover Communist trying to make converts. Their disputes with him, they said, were now threatening to spread through the College, because the Bursar, apparently under the Lecturer's thumb, had begun canvassing all the students, asking them if they were for or against the Lecturer.

For or Against—the old False Dilemma. It was a familiar technique, stirring up in Edwin's mind reverberations from his experiences in Prague. As he told me later, he was not going to have the College split by politics and a false dilemma! Despite this echo of past disturbances, despite the fact that an accusation of bad faith is heart-sinking as well as difficult to disprove, in his dealings with the deputation he kept his self-possession. The Intercepter showed no sign of coming back. Edwin investigated the evidence, patiently, allowing for the possibility that the Lecturer, being young and inexperienced, might simply have been trying to stimulate his students by throwing pro-Communist arguments at them. His subsequent interview with the Lecturer was none the easier for that young man's being an intimate of Gavin's, whose presence hovered invisibly in the background. But he was aware of the Lecturer's inclination to domineer and have recourse to other false dilemmas in shrugging off blame for the Bursar's foolish action. He thought he sensed an itch for power.

When Edwin described this interview to me I had the impression that the Lecturer had mistakenly assessed him as a weakly tolerant person who could be manipulated. As it was, Edwin decided that the Lecturer and the Bursar between them were creating an intolerable situation in the College, and could not be trusted not to do the same again. He sacked them both, for that reason, leaving aside the question of whether the Lecturer was an under-cover Communist or merely a fellow-traveller.

The whole episode was a strain on both of us, especially as Gavin resented his friend's dismissal. But once both young men were gone, a tension went out of the College. Then came the spring, heralded by great drifts of snowdrops, followed by wood anemones. Edwin and I strolled along the woodland paths listening to bird-song. Among the Newbattle beeches more chaffinches sang every year than I had ever heard elsewhere, and the pattern of their song had a peculiar triumphant trill at the end of it that uplifted one's heart.

By this time I was sure that Newbattle Abbey was our home, and would be our home for the rest of our lives. The Warden's study and our drawing-room were even pleasanter than they had looked from outside when we first tried to see them through the windows. Our own furniture fitted the light drawing-room well, and the fireplace, of red marble with an interlacing of ivy leaves and roots carved round it, warmed my heart even when the grate was empty. We had perforce got into the habit of discarding most of our papers, but now Edwin had room enough in his study and could begin to keep track of his writings and arrange his books in order. On one side, the study opened on to the square landing at the top of the main stairway, accessible to students and visitors, on the other it opened into a wide passage leading to our bedrooms which I had turned into a private dining-room, since we had come to the conclusion that we could not bear having every single meal downstairs among the students: it was enough, we thought, for us to have luncheon daily with them. I engaged a maid of our own, an eager, cheerful little person who slept in our spare room and cooked light meals for us on a gas-cooker beyond the far end of the dining-passage.

Newbattle Abbey made a pleasant and spacious setting in which Edwin, devoting himself to imaginative literature, was happy and at one with his environment. He talked rather than lectured about literature to his students; nearly every week he wrote a literary review for the *Observer*; every day he waited for his own imagination to send up into his conscious mind the premonition of a poem, or some lines of a poem already begun. He always waited for his poems, never saying to himself: I am going to write a poem about such-and-such. Sometimes a line 'came up', as he said, that proved in time to belong to the very middle of a poem rather than the beginning, and he simply waited until he knew what the poem was going to be. Once it was composed and written down he would revise it, again and again. His revisions were written in smaller script—the poems were written out in longhand first—and the revisions of revisions in smaller script still, which sometimes he was not able to read. Edwin's handwriting remained secretive all his life: it was the kind of script that sends compositors in printing-works round the bend; that was why he had to teach himself to type. But he could not set down a poem straight off the typewriter; he had an intimate affinity with his pen which he could not feel with the machine.

In the summer of 1949, while we were still in Rome, two books of his had come out: *Essays on Literature and Society* published by the Hogarth Press, and a volume of poems, *The Labyrinth*, mostly written in Prague, published by Faber & Faber. For these he had had more recognition, more praise, than for anything he had yet produced, and that made him very content. Now the young J. G. Hall, also a poet, came up on a visit to Newbattle in order to persuade him to let a Collection of his poems appear. He was persuaded, on condition that John Hall should edit the volume, and in June 1952 the Collection was published by Faber.

For Edwin, his poetry and the College were not divided from each other but belonged together. The poems he wrote mostly at Newbattle were published separately in 1956 with the title: *One Foot in Eden*, and that title was a true one. Only one foot in Eden, the other firmly on earth. In a little poem called 'The Emblem' he describes his 'Scant-acre Kingdom':

> ... *enter, (do not knock; it keeps no state)*
> *You will be with space and order magistral.*

His kingdom kept no state at all, in accordance with his own simplicity. But its scant acre on earth reached far up and down into timelessness.

Outside the College, there were more contracted minds which distrusted such kingdoms of the imagination—the Scottish Trade Unions, to begin with. Kenneth Wood, having taken on the job of Bursar as well as his own work in Economics, had written to the Trade Unions suggesting that they might give a subsidy to the College. Only one small Union sent a small sum; the others refused to contribute a halfpenny. Kenneth asked why, and was told that Newbattle was of no earthly use to the working-classes. It only spoiled good trade unionists, giving them 'ideas'—sending a miner to Cambridge, for instance! A nest of the bourgeoisie, nothing else.

Edwin and Kenneth were surprised and puzzled. Surprised, because this blind, belligerent, class-restricted attitude of the Unions belonged naturally to the Thirties, when men were workless, hungry and uninterested in educating themselves, yet the Thirties were long past. Puzzled, because the General Secretary of the Scottish T.U.C. was a member of the New-battle Executive

Committee which had voted to re-start the College, and must have known from the beginning what kind of place it was.

The Abbey was of course a gentleman's seat, donated by a gentleman to provide a liberal education for adults. Lord Lothian had included in the gift a lavish equipment of pictures, books and fine pieces of furniture to make a cultured setting for the College. The best of the furniture had disappeared somehow during the war, yet the pictures remained and many of the books. How could the Executive Committee be unaware of all that? It looked as if the Trade Unions' representative on the Committee was an embodiment of bad faith.

This was a conclusion Edwin did not like, since he preferred to take good faith for granted. But it did now strike him that the Executive Committee was showing no interest in the actual running of the College. No one from the Executive had put in an appearance to find out even what standard the lectures reached, although nearly every educational body in Scotland was represented on it.

One member of the Executive had indeed been turning up from time to time, a Director of Education who had been a fellow-member of the Glasgow Guilds Group in Edwin's young days, but he apparently came in the spirit of 'auld acquaintance' not being forgot rather than as an emissary from the Executive. He ate with us in our private dining-passage and never saw or talked to any of the students or staff. He was very shortsighted and gently garrulous, conveying the opinion that New-battle was doing quite well but would, of course, do better yet; it needed, of course, more money and at least twice as many students. He seemed rather like a stray old man from a Greek chorus, quite outside any dramatic action, uttering the commonplaces of the collective.

What we did not know was that he was now a power in the educational world of Scotland, a member of every committee in the country. He, if anyone, could have told Edwin directly what no one had mentioned and what I learned only a year ago: that the vote to re-start the College had been taken after heated debate and was carried by a narrow majority. He knew that a section of the Executive, including the Chairman who was a financier, insisted that the College's ability to pay for itself must determine whether it were to continue or not. He knew very well how precarious was the existence of this College which Edwin believed to be firmly rooted in Scotland's need for and interest in Adult Education. It would never have occurred to Edwin that financial costs could be the sole criteria for the running of the only Adult Education College in the whole of Scotland.

Edwin's 'auld acquaintance' did not tell him any of these things. Perhaps he did not want to be discouraging. But towards the end of summer in 1951 when the whole country was heading into a financial crisis and all Government departments were anticipating a squeeze, he had already begun to change the drift of his conversation. He told us at length about various short-term Adult Education Colleges in England he had been visiting, where students streamed in only for the weekends, getting half-day courses in Literature or Economics and so on, with local history thrown in and a game or two for relaxation before they streamed back to work. They were very popular and well attended, these short-term colleges. How would Edwin like to run Newbattle in that way? All the woollen mills along the Border could send plenty of week-enders to the College, which was near enough to be convenient for them. Students would roll up in fifties, or maybe hundreds, and so would their fees, and everybody would be pleased.

The look in Edwin's eye said: 'Over my dead body'; but he merely remarked, mildly enough, that weekend snacks of information were not his idea of education.

The threat of a financial crisis in the country simply passed Edwin by, nor was he troubled by John Macmurray's retirement from the Committee, although regretting it, since he was quite unaware that the removal of Macmurray's strong influence spelt danger for the College. He felt that things were shaping well. Bob, for instance, who was very near his heart, had agreed to come for a second year and our vacation trip to Orkney had secured a promising Orkney student, a shy young man with a soft Orkney lilt in his voice and eyes as blue as periwinkle flowers.

But on our return to Newbattle something happened that disconcerted Edwin entirely. A Glasgow youth, whom he had already seen and accepted for the second year of the College, sent him a panic-stricken letter to say that he had heard Newbattle was to be closed down in October and what was he to do? Edwin answered at once, denying the rumour as nonsense and telling the student to secure his Local Authority grant and come to the College as arranged, but he was shaken to find that a whispering campaign against Newbattle must be going on in Glasgow. If the hostility of the Trade Unions was the first symptom of obstructiveness, this was the second.

From the Executive Committee itself he then learned, a little later, that the Scottish Department of Education in St Andrews House, Edinburgh, was getting restive about the College's finances and suggesting that it might have to close down unless the student members increased. The Committee was considering what measures should be taken.

This came as a knock-down blow to Edwin; he was stunned to realize that the College was not being backed, as he understood backing, by the Committee or the Department, or, presumably,by the Treasury. Yet, as Scottish affairs seemed to have the knack of doing, it roused his fighting spirit. His old acquaintance, the Director, was now urging upon the Committee the scheme for turning Newbattle into a week-enders' short-term College, and unless he did something to prevent that, a short-term College it would most likely become. As happened in St Andrews when he wrote *Scott and Scotland*, all his hackles rose up; he was again ready to hit out, despite his own theories, but with an important difference. In St Andrews he had been resenting a general attitude,here he was prepared to fight for a concrete embodiment of what he valued, his beloved residential College, which, as Warden, he was responsible for and had to protect.

At a Conference held in Dunblane by the Scottish Institute of Adult Education Edwin took the floor and, as Kenneth told me, ridiculed the short-term partisans with such wit and energy that they were routed. Kenneth added that he had never been aware of so much cold determination as Edwin gave off in the car all the way to the Conference. After their Dunblane humiliation the short-term party in the Executive had to lie low for a while, but a personal animosity against Edwin now became evident. At about this time someone reported a comment publicly made by one of them: 'What can you expect of Newbattle, run by a bloody poet?'

This comment lit up very well the difference between one mental climate and another. It appeared that, in any case, Orkney and Lowland Scotland found it difficult to understand each other, for when our young Orkney student came to the Abbey, after his first journey in a train, and began investigating his surroundings he was more than disconcerted. Having explored the Abbey grounds, he went to look at Dalkeith, just outside the gates, and came back in distress, saying: 'What's the matter with the folk in Dalkeith? Not a single smile on any face! In the street they all had tight mouths and worried foreheads. What's wrong with them?'

The continued uncertainty about the future of the College naturally upset the staff, especially the two married young men, Kenneth the Economics Lecturer and Donald the new Philosophy Lecturer, and their wives. Unhappiness filtered into all our lives. We tried not to let it affect the students, but could not tell how far we succeeded.

Not that a certain wry comedy was absent from the actual situation. A meeting of the Executive was held in the College Library, for instance, instead of in Edinburgh as usual, and three or four members lost their way trying to find Newbattle Abbey; they had no idea where the place was and turned up very late in very bad tempers.

By April 1952 a compromise solution had been found. Part of the Abbey was hired out to the managers of the Lothian mines who arranged that resident weekly courses for batches of mining foremen or deputies would be held by their own officials. The miners would use the students' common-room, the crypt, for recreation, and the housekeeping staff would feed them and look after their bedrooms. The rent to be paid for this accommodation would suffice to keep the College going.

Edwin, formally and informally, made the miners welcome and begged our students to do the same. The students rose to the occasion. The good atmosphere in the College proved its worth; although they were overcrowded in their common-room, the students showed great goodwill. The miners' courses began on

Monday and every Thursday evening they gave a concert in the crypt; every Thursday evening Edwin and I, in two special chairs, sat out the whole programme. Our students attended the concerts too; there was general friendly feeling and the miners enjoyed themselves hugely before dispersing on Fridays.

Newbattle Abbey College was saved. But that was by no means the end of hostilities. I suppose the short-term partisans had not forgiven Edwin for holding them up to public ridicule at Dunblane, and a fog of denigration hung round his name from this time on. Edwin was not the man to plume himself on supposed status or position; it would never have occurred to him that he was to be seen as a successful figure strutting on the battlements of Newbattle, a triple, soon to be a quadruple, Honorary Doctor, making all he could out of a very undeserving Wardenship. But that is how his image was projected. When he was presently made a C.B.E., an honour paid, as we thought, to his poetry, his enemies were convinced that he had collected the honour only because he was Warden of Newbattle. They made up their minds that Muir Must Go.

Somebody or other always conveyed to Edwin what was being said about him, and he grew very tense at times. I persuaded him one afternoon to drive into Edinburgh with me to see the film *Whisky Galore*, thinking it would lighten his mood. We had already heard many stories by word of mouth about what had allegedly happened in the Hebrides after a whisky ship was wrecked offshore. The film was nothing like so good as these stories, he said irritably, as we emerged, and he drove our car out of its side-street straight into a Newington tram running downhill. I could see that tram coming down on us; if Edwin had backed a little it would have missed us, but he did not back. He felt the need of hitting out at something bearing down on him, as it might be the Treasury, and so he bashed the tram. He was repentant afterwards; the endorsement on his licence was a stain on his conscience.

But the strain on him proved too great. He began to have acute pains in his chest, which we thought were nervous pains, but which killed him in the long run. I got so anxious and worried that by 1954, in spring, I was carted off to hospital in Edinburgh to have non-malignant lumps removed from me and was even more near dying than I had been in St Andrews. I was still very weak when I got back to Newbattle.

From Edwin I learned what had been happening. The Executive Committee were now openly conspiring to get rid of him. They had called their last meeting without letting him know, although *ex officio* he was bound to attend. The Director of Education, our old acquaintance, was canvassing in support of a certain able young man, the successful head of a short-term college in the north of England, the very man, he said, to make a good Warden of Newbattle instead of Edwin.

Yet fate was inclined to thwart the Executive, for they discovered, to their chagrin, that as the Governors had appointed Edwin only the Governors could dismiss him, and the Governors were disinclined to do so. Also the able young man turned down the Director's provisional offer of Newbattle, despite all cajoling.

None the less, Edwin and I, both of us worn down and depressed, decided that we had better pull out. Edwin had hung on as long as he could because he was afraid of what might happen to the College as soon as he left it, yet the pains in his chest were becoming too troublesome. We had to think where to go, our usual predicament, but Providence, as so often in the past, pointed the way for us. An invitation came out of the blue from Harvard, asking Edwin to be the next Charles Eliot Norton Professor for the year 1955-6. He would have to give only six public lectures during his tenure of the Professorship. Edwin accepted the offer, with gladness, and began preparing his six lectures, which had to be typed, since they were to come out in book form as well as by word of mouth. In August 1955 we set sail for the United States.

Yet, in Newbattle, Edwin wrote some of his best poetry, turning towards life on earth, although with the light of Eden still filtering down.

> *Strange blessings never in Paradise*
> *Fall from these beclouded skies,*

he said. Also, when he wrote:

> *This is a difficult country, and our home,*

he did not mean only Newbattle, or only Scotland.

Chapter Twenty

UNITED STATES

August 1955– May 1956

Our despondency at leaving Newbattle Abbey was much eased by the manner of our going. To be invited to Harvard, an honour, instead of straying into uncertainties was like taking a child's revenge on the Executive Committee, leaving with a bang instead of a whimper. On our last night in London we fell into an impromptu party that transmitted in heightened form the sense that we were heading for a fresh adventure, so that Edwin and I dropped Newbattle into the back of our minds and indulged ourselves in London gossip and amusing speculation.

Yet the excitement had fizzled out and we were tired all through as we went on board the Cunarder at Southampton. We lay inert on day-beds spread out on a deck, glad of the rest and the mid-morning cup of broth, thankful, too, that we had opted for a sea-voyage instead of flying across the Atlantic. We scarcely bothered to think at all, not even about what kind of set-up we might find in the States. We had always met Americans as individual persons, in Europe or in Britain, without considering that they were transients in a setting not their own or that their native set-up might not resemble ours. This visit to the States, we felt, was just a long visit to far-out cousins, quite unlike going to a foreign country. We had a lot of impressive book-information about American life and had yet to learn that it did not reach very far into actual knowledge. One instance of our ignorance is that a great deal of room was taken up in our trunk by thick woollen winter underwear; white elephants they proved to be, every single garment.

We were not expecting to be surprised; we were going to take New York and the States for granted. All the more bemusing was it when we were decanted at our hotel and entered its reception hall, a vast arena more like a Continental railway station than our idea of a hotel. Around us were many shops, a hairdresser, a book-stall, a jeweller, a beautician, even a bank and a post office; we had difficulty in finding the reception desk. And when we had identified it we were both nearly knocked down by a hurrying phalanx of women in tricorne hats, sashes and badges announcing them to be Drake's Daughters. Our far-out cousins, it appeared, could be startling.

In the morning our breakfast trays presented each of us with a Hottle. The Hottles were full of hot and excellent coffee; they were rather like elaborate thermos flasks and their absurd names were round their necks. Hottles! Drake's Daughters! We might as well be on the moon, we told each other.

This moon-feeling persisted in the train all the way to Boston. Two long rows of swivel chairs ran down the length of our coach with a gangway in the middle; the States apparently did not agree with the English idea of separating people into exclusive compartments. There was no restaurant car and no luncheons would be served, for this was Labour Day, we learned. No labour because it was Labour Day? We resigned ourselves to starve, but no! Halfway to Boston a gang of vendors invaded the train with baskets of hot dogs and other instant foods, and we picnicked instead of starving.

Then we were told that we must go to the club car at the front of the train to finish our cigarettes. The club car had small tables and an observation window; Labour Day or no, it provided drinks, though not eats, on request; naturally, we stayed there and looked at the scenery. A succession of inlets from the sea ran past us, with pleasant wooden houses among stretches of young scrub, much of it birch. There were no woods as the English understand woods, with well-grown trees and a deep look of permanence, only these provisional stretches of spindly young trees and random wooden houses, which also seemed provisional. Every now and then one came to a town apparently full of parti-coloured beetles. It was not at all like England.

Yet our hotel in Cambridge, when we reached it, looked so like a family hotel that our travelling-on-the-moon feeling vanished. We had booked 'a housekeeping suite' without knowing what that was and found a sitting-room and bedroom which might have belonged to any plain English hotel, with a small kitchenette and a shower. The shower suited me; it was easier to get under a shower than to climb into a bath.

Cambridge, although surprisingly joined to Boston by dull lines of factories and business buildings, must have been enchanting in the horse-and-carriage age for which it had been designed, with large old trees and a biggish common still surviving. Harvard University was made up of Georgian-style houses in warm red brick with white trimmings and a few stately pillared structures in its Yard. The Yard itself, with its genuinely ancient trees, was a pleasure to stroll in. We took Harvard and Cambridge to our hearts at once, and presently took them for granted.

This taking places and people for granted was a curious process that had to penetrate various levels. On the surface of daily life, in what Edwin called the Story, it meant accepting whatever was different in manners or language; this we had been accustomed to do in Europe. The real difficulties began when one came up against deeper-lying assumptions which reached down into the Fable and were not even easy to identify, much less accept. After we had spent nearly a year in the States we were still not clear in our minds why we did not want to stay longer. Our unwillingness was not for want of having made friends there whom we loved; we had enjoyed ourselves and been hospitably welcomed; we had been offered jobs if we would only stay; but we did not want to stay. By that time the one thing Edwin wanted to do was to make a bee-line for Orkney as fast as possible.

The initial surface adjustments were amusing and often surprising. New England in its beginnings had been prim, and traces of this primness survived even in Cambridge. Every day the chambermaid in our hotel pulled our window-blinds exactly halfway down and left them like that. As I pulled them up again I noticed that all house windows within sight had their blinds exactly halfway down, giving them an extra prim look. An unskirted window, it seemed, was not decent.

Not only naked windows were taboo; some words were as indecent as if they were naked. The word 'cock' was very indecent. Although one could say 'cocktail' one could not possibly use cock to describe a fowl or a water-tap. Cocks had to be chickens or roosters, water-cocks were faucets. The word 'nigger' was also taboo. An Irish girl fresh from Donegal told me she had asked for a nigger jumper in a Boston store and the shop-girls were cast into such dismay that she now supposed they had taken her to be asking for a black coon leaping to the ceiling. At table, too, there was some kind of taboo on knives, which had to be used as little as possible and then laid aside. Small tea-knives were made respectable by being called 'butter-spreaders', which removed them from that dangerous category: knife.

Some of the usages novel to us had come over with the Pilgrim Fathers. When I went into our hotel waving a frying-pan from a hardware shop I learned, in pure Elizabethan English, that I had gotten a skillet. And we were told, on being offered a picnic by the sea, that we were to be taken to the Ocean. The word 'ocean' at first struck us as faintly pompous (Britannia the pride of the ocean), but its matter-of-fact American use may have pre-dated the Victorian sea-side. The respectable English word 'solicitor', too, had retained its older, raffish meaning, so that one saw warnings outside house doors: 'No Solicitors', as in England one might find: 'No Hawkers'.

These old words gave one a sense of continuity, contrasting with innovations like 'motorcade' or 'Jumboburger' and other hybrids without lawful parents. Naturally enough the road-signs beside the modern turnpikes were also unknown to us although not hybrids; along the intricate fly-overs, clover-leaves and mergers spreading widely outside Boston one learned to accept 'soft shoulders' followed by 'squeeze left', to understand that 'oil-spraying' meant the road was being tarred, and to cease wondering, when one came to a notice: 'Live Parking Only', what on earth 'Dead Parking' might be.

The hair's-breadth precision of American driving on these roads gave us a sense of awe. Fortunately, neither of us ever had to drive a car in the States, so many willing hosts transported us everywhere, controlling their huge cars in the dense traffic lanes as if they were darning needles. Compared with these monsters our old fifteen horse-power Austin in England dwindled to nothing. 'What horse-power is your car, Ted?' I said casually to a friend beside me, who was driving us about a hundred miles to a luncheon party, and was made nearly speechless by his equally casual reply: 'Oh, I think two hundred and fifty.'

The deeper-lying assumptions in American life dawned on us more gradually, but our very first social occasion, when Archie and Ada MacLeish invited us to tea, taught us something about ourselves and about Harvard. People in Cambridge lived, delightfully, within reach of one another on foot, and we strolled along to have tea with the MacLeishes merely supposing that we should have a pleasant afternoon. All we knew about Archibald MacLeish was that he was the Professor of English who had invited Edwin to Harvard, that, like Edwin, he was a writer who had published both poetry and prose, a man of our own world. Yet this was only part of the truth about him, as we kept on discovering. Just as American railway coaches were not divided into exclusive compartments, the men of Harvard were not to be divided into exclusive compartments either. At this tea-party we became aware that we had been making assumptions about academic people which did not apply in Harvard.

We were the only guests; the tea was excellent and the atmosphere friendly. But no sooner were the cups cleared away than trays of drinks arrived, other people dropped in by twos and threes, hot little savouries were handed round, and we were launched on a cocktail party, except that the long tumblers we were given, full of ice-chunks and a straw-coloured liquid, contained a drink more potent than martinis. My tumbler never got empty, however much I sipped; every time I set it down it filled up again, until at last I realized that Archie was supplying me whenever I was not looking. What we were drinking was Bourbon on the Rocks, our first introduction to that stimulant, which lit up Edwin and me until our tongues wagged very gaily and we laughed a lot. Edwin was already calling Archie 'Archie', as everyone else did; it took him only a little longer to get round to calling Ada by her first name. Small and beautifully finished, Ada seemed unaware of her own elegance, like the other women in the room. American dons clearly enjoyed the company of women and expected them to join freely in the talk, so that there was genuine social intercourse at this blissful party.

Edwin Muir, 1955

Going back to our hotel, Edwin and I babbled about the party to each other. Our Bourbon-illuminated minds saw these Harvard people as less restricted than their English counterparts. American academics, we decided, sat more loosely to themselves than the English; they could not be thought of as drilled in any conventional routine. We were reminded of American soldiers in the war whose loose-jointed easy gait made our soldiers look over-drilled. Here we stopped to laugh at the memory of the mushroom-pink American trousers that used to go gangling along wartime Princes Street, and how our men with their drilled shoulders and staccato movements used to scorn what they called 'the American slouch'. None the less, the American 'slouch' was poised for a quick take-off in any direction, and so were these Harvard dons.

The odd thing was that Edwin and I had not anticipated such academic freedom. Considering how unorthodox Edwin's own road to professordom had been, there was no excuse for us. We had stupidly taken for granted that Archie, being a professor, had always been a professor or on the usual way to becoming one, yet he was no more to be labelled Professor MacLeish than Edwin to be labelled Professor Muir. Later, by chance, we learned that among other activities he had been Librarian of Congress and before coming to Harvard had been famous for the brilliant speeches he prepared in an influential politician's campaign.

We never got so tipsy again, once having learned what Bourbon could do, yet our highly-coloured impressions were not inaccurate. We had discovered one of the basic assumptions underlying American life, that it was one's duty to be a Good Mixer, unfettered by protocol, free to take off in any direction.

This was an assumption we accepted and enjoyed. Edwin and I still had enough youthful naïveté to welcome and respond to vibrations of goodwill, and among Harvard people the goodwill was genuine. Edwin was transparently free from any intention of exploiting the friends he made, and in return he evoked good will equally disinterested. Having found friends to love, we were happy in Cambridge and felt almost at home there. Only small things reminded us sometimes that we were in a relatively foreign country, the sudden harsh, slightly plaintive squawk of an unknown bird in a tree outside our sitting-room, for instance; it might have been a jay, larger and plainer than an English jay.

Robert Frost dropped in to see us fairly often. During the winter months Amherst College kept a room ready for him, and whenever he was there he was likely to be in Cambridge of an afternoon. Rosy and twinkling he sat at our tea-table, telling incidents from his life and assuring us that once a man is over eighty he is practically indestructible. All his many nervous ailments had left him, he said. His mother had been an Orkney-woman, he insisted, and he would tease Edwin gently by repeating: 'We Orkney-men'.

Robert Frost had an affection for England. Perhaps he enjoyed our company because it reminded him of past days in England, when Ezra Pound helped to publicize his first volume of poems. In our experience, Cambridge and Boston were more Anglophile than not, despite old memories of the Revolution. Bostonians in our time drank tea out of tea-pots instead of throwing it into the harbour. Charles Eliot Norton's surviving daughter, an old lady nearly in her nineties, invited us to tea on Beacon Hill and the tea she provided might have come out of an Oscar Wilde play, even to the wafer-thin cucumber sandwiches. The most fashionable men's shop in Boston, Brooks Brothers (the Man in the Brooks Brothers shirt), sported a large portrait of Edward VII on its wall. We went there, for fun, to buy a pair of braces for Edwin, and he bet me that if he asked for galluses they wouldn't know what he meant. But the gentleman behind the counter did not blench; he produced braces at once. Galluses, as Edwin had forgotten, was an Irish word imported into Glasgow, and the Irish had imported it into Boston too.

Boston we liked. Parts of it, not the best parts, might have been taken from London, and its streets were humanly irregular, not right-angled in a grid pattern as in New York. We were told that New Yorkers professed to get lost in the quirky Boston streets and complained that it was not safe to move out of sight of one's Underground station, but we appreciated what they deplored. There was a feeling of tradition in Boston, especially round the harbour and the T-wharf. We were taken to a favourite old eating-house, Locke-Obers, and discovered that planked swordfish, cooked and served on a slightly charred thick oaken slab, was delicious, despite its sinister-sounding name.

Harvard, we were warned, was an enclave of its own kind, hardly typical of New England, let alone the United States. Nathan Pusey, the President, a man of firm principles, had stood out against Senator McCarthy's blackmailing campaign, for instance; the Senator had loathed him and all that he stood for, but it was Pusey who survived, not McCarthy. When we met the President we noted that he had a wary face, looking younger than his years because it was singularly unmarked by lines betraying emotion, a poker-face, a mask of some kind, a defence against a multiplicity of stresses. Poker-faces were more usual among business-men involved in the fiercely competitive money world, but it was moral stresses, one felt, that Nathan Pusey was vigilantly involved in. His wife, Anne, had no defences of any kind in her face, which conveyed sheer goodwill and understanding.

The men of Harvard who liked feminine company were rewarded by having attractive and efficient wives. Any professor's wife, with the minimum of domestic help, was capable of cooking and dishing up a first-rate dinner and yet not having a hair out of place or withdrawing her attention from the conversation. Outside Harvard itself we became very friendly with Richard Wilbur the poet who was teaching in Wellesley College nearby, and his wife Charlee. No poet could ever have had a better wife than Charlee. Men who came over from England and grumbled that American women had too much say only betrayed their own domineering bias, I thought, poor things. These delightful women in Cambridge were neither bossy nor subservient and they were uncommonly competent.

Edwin did not have to give his first lectures until December and we had plenty of time for our pleasant social life. Meanwhile, we were beginning to explore New England, visiting Concord to begin with. We felt faintly resentful at the anti-British bias of an inscription about the Minute Men. Hawthorne, Emerson, Thoreau and Lousia M. Alcott came into the picture, as did also Emily Dickinson when we went over her quiet house in Amherst. About this time we became aware of our shrinking from the vast spaces of the United States beyond New England.

To suggestions that we should take a trip to New Mexico, or Arizona, or California, we put up an instinctive resistance, saying that we should be content if we could only get to know something of New England. I was reading about the education of Henry Adams, and a friend told me I should try *The Country of the Pointed Firs* by Sarah Orne Jewett, if I wanted to get the real 'feel' of New England, so I read and loved that little book, yet was queerly daunted on hearing that Maine, Sarah Jewett's beloved, backward state of fishermen and farmers, was bigger than the whole of Scotland. But Scotland, I protested, has ten times as much history behind it!

That protest showed up our unwillingness to venture into what we thought of as relatively empty regions, with no Fable that we should recognize. Edwin began to point out that he had a peasant unconscious; he preferred countries that had been patiently tilled and worked over for generations, like Italy, rather than newly broken territories. For much the same reason, he had always refused to consider going to Australia or Canada. His sense of the human past needed a denser ambience than these sparse new countries could provide.

Our shrinking from too great space and size might have been a symptom that we were ageing. Had we reached the United States thirty years earlier we might have gone merrily into Arizona. As it was, even the size of the Sunday papers put us off. Their mammoth dimensions, mostly advertisements, reflected the dominating importance of buying and selling in this new American world, and here we were coming up against a basic assumption we could not accept: the belief that everyone had a duty to keep on selling or buying something in order that the great wheel of industrial life should not slow down or look like coming to a stop. Not that this assumption was peculiar to America; we were aware of its workings in our own country; but the over-riding importance it had, the intensity with which it was believed, the large scale of its operations were peculiarly American. Buying or selling was more important than friendship among the dollar-hungry, we felt, when it came to business being business.

Here I am compressing into a couple of paragraphs what took us some time to recognize. We began by noticing small failures in human communication, not among the Harvard dons but in our dealings with purveyors of personal service, like the messenger from a valeting company who came to take Edwin's old dressing-gown away for cleaning. Edwin, who loved his Black Watch dressing-gown, boasted, naively enough, to the messenger as he handed it over that he had had it for ten years and the man looked at him with contempt and pity, saying: 'How come you could never afford a new one?' As for showing friendliness towards a hairdresser, that was to lay oneself open to insistent exploitation amounting to emotional blackmail.

Much later, we became indirectly aware of the giant corporations that made up Big Business. These, powerful and impersonal, loomed in the remote distance, beyond the periphery of our actual experience, but what we read and heard about them disturbed us. They were already beginning to use the word 'global' in their planning, and Edwin instead of delighting in the idea of 'global' operations making for some kind of unity, lumped them together as 'machinery' and was horrified at the prospect.

Yet we were in fact privileged in being able to look on at the expanding competitive world from the outside, and this privilege we owed to the dollar-world itself. Time and again it had come to our help when no help could be found elsewhere. American dollars, having first taken us into Europe and rescued us from bankruptcy on the Sunday Mountain, had rescued us again from Newbattle by providing our pleasant interlude in Cambridge, Mass. We were grateful. All the same, we could not agree that the only way to live was to sell and the only way to enjoy living was to buy.

Meanwhile we did not yet venture far from Cambridge, far, that is, in the American sense of the word. We haunted the Lament Poetry Library, where Jack Sweeney made us welcome. It was a small building, separate from the Harvard complex, a sunny place for lovers of poetry, with reading-desks and quiet alcoves, stocked, it seemed, with copies of all the poetry ever written and records of poets reading their own poems. Edwin was begged to record some of his poems, which he did rather unwillingly, so that Jack then begged me to read another one or two of them. Here something curious happened. Ever since my last operation my sympathetic nervous system (I suppose it was) had escaped my control, so that when I was moved by any work of art, Mozart's G minor symphony, say, or a new poem of Edwin's, I could not help crying. I used to say to Edwin: 'My lamb, I'm going to cry', and he would hold my hand and say: 'Cry away, my lamb.' On this occasion I began to read a poem Edwin had published ten years earlier, a poem I thought I knew well: 'In Love for Long'. Suddenly, in the third verse, two little lines rose up and hit me in the midriff and my eyes filled with tears; I could not go on and had to apologize to Jack Sweeney. These were the lines:

> Being, being, being,
> Its burden and its bliss.

All at once I felt that in celebrating his love for 'Being' Edwin had been experiencing another version of what I once called 'Belonging to the Universe', and for ten years I had not noticed this correspondence—not to be aware of it, anyhow. Edwin's poems I usually took as total wholes, in the round, not separating them into individual lines.

Another attractive institution in Cambridge was the Poets' Theatre, which held about eighty people. It was a jewel of a small theatre, with a proper stage, wings, footlights and all. The actors were students and the performances were put on of an evening. Here, one evening, we came upon T. S. Eliot and Djuna Barnes, at a performance of Dick Wilbur's translation of Molière's *Misanthrope*. Djuna Barnes, who had known Eliot since he was a very young man in Paris, was treating him with easy, affectionate camaraderie and he was responding with an equally easy gaiety that I had never seen in him before. As I put it to myself: Tom Eliot is much more human here than in England. He was less deliberate, less cautious, smiling more easily, spontaneous in repartee, enjoying the teasing he was getting from Djuna. Neither Edwin nor I had met Djuna before and we were both drawn to her on sight: a tall, gallant, high-spirited woman with a faint suggestion of rakish adventure and fun about her, difficult to define but very likeable. In her company Eliot seemed to have shed some English drilling and become more American. This impression was only confirmed when we met two aunts of his, little old ladies who told us: 'Tom is so good to us, he has taken us to Schrafft's and given us steaks.'

The time came for Edwin to deliver his first three lectures, in a fairly large hall, and Archie MacLeish and the electricians had a problem, since their usual microphone was not geared to cope with a soft unemphatic Orkney voice. After much flurry and rearrangement of wiring Edwin was made audible in the preliminary rehearsal, and I took my seat in the middle of the hall at half-past eight that evening without being unduly nervous, although the hall was full. Edwin looked impressive on the dais, with the cloud of silvery hair that made his face smaller and more delicate by contrast; he was an appealing figure. He was a little excited, with a faint flush on his cheeks, but managed to read his script without keeping his nose too close to the paper; every now and then he glanced directly at his audience; and, to use his own laconic formula, it 'went well enough'. So did the other two lectures; they 'went' better than he admitted.

In the New Year we visited New York, where Edwin gave a Poetry Reading at the Metropolitan Museum, on January 5. We were staying this time not in the daunting Grand Central Hotel but in the charming flat of the van Dusens, belonging to Union Theological College, which gave us the chance of feeling more at home. The audience for Edwin's Poetry Reading was appreciative—'went well' his engagement book says—and the van Dusens welcomed us kindly, yet we could not feel at home in New York. Moving from numbered avenue to numbered street was too like walking about on a squared-paper graph. We saw the sights, yes, but once we had looked at the Empire State Building we had finished with it, and it was the same with the other skyscrapers; for us they stopped dead where they stood. Little holes and corners, upstairs and along passages where pleasant people were to be found in offices or studios, cheered us, like oases in a desert, yet even in these we sometimes felt that the over-riding business of New York was Business, and that our merely friendly call on old Ben Huebsch of the Viking Press, for instance, seemed to his secretaries an unwarrantable waste of his time. It was a strange city to us.

As a mart for merchandise from all over the world it was incomparable. Edwin, who thought of buying clothes for himself only when the suit he had on was out at elbows, looked with a cold eye on the windows of Fifth Avenue, but they went to my head. I needed a dinner-dress for our Cambridge engagements, to vary the solitary black silk outfit from Rome in which I had been appearing,and on an afternoon when Edwin went to see Djuna Barnes about her play *Antiphon*, which he wanted her to revise, I vanished into Lord and Taylor's to buy that dress. When I came out again and met Edwin, I said, with apprehension as well as triumph: Peerie B, I've bought three dresses!' Edwin burst out laughing for such a thing had never been known to happen in the course of all our years together, and, indeed, never happened again. That was the effect of New York, which sold frocks off the peg in half-sizes as well as sizes to fit every conceivable figure, as London did not. Elderly women in London were then fobbed off with shapeless dowdy garments, and I had secured, besides the dinner-dress, two becoming summer frocks in a fine, drip-dry fabric. Edwin's engagement book has only one exclamation mark in it, where he recorded my unique feat of derring-do: 'Willa bought 3 dresses!' After that, it is not quite fair of me to say that New York seemed a hard-boiled place compared to Cambridge.

Ever since coming to Harvard we had noticed that the sun was much higher in the sky than in the south of England and so did not expect the winter climate to be as severe as it now showed itself. The blizzard season had begun. House interiors grew hot and hotter. We had to turn off one of the radiators in our sitting-room. But we acquired the American habit of layering ourselves under coats and scarves as we made a bolt for some waiting car, well heated inside, and our Scottish woollens stayed in their trunk. The blizzards interfered with what was to have been our joint flight to Chicago, where Edwin was to lecture and read some of his poems at the University. The journey had to be made by train, and when we discovered that it would mean nineteen hours in the train I cried off, for my back was intermittently giving me more trouble. Edwin had to go alone and came back disgruntled and depressed, having loathed Chicago. The University itself was all right, he said, but it stood in the middle of a dreadful Negro slum. As for the famous lake shore, that was only dirty snow all the way with large, ugly houses facing dirty-looking water. This was possibly true, yet I felt that had I been there I might have mediated between Edwin and the unattractive environment, that being one of the things he depended on me for. To depend on each other for this and that had long been a habit with us; we used each other's nervous energy through a kind of osmosis whenever the need arose. This process was a fact neither of us could, or ever attempted to, explain.

Luncheons, teas, dinners, an occasional excursion to hear the Boston Symphony Orchestra, does our social life sound very small beer? We enjoyed it. After all, we were having tea with Herman Melville's granddaughter, or William James, son of William and nephew of Henry, and his wife Alice, in the James family house, with mirth and good talk, or we heard contemporary music superbly played by the Boston Orchestra, having been escorted there by an upright legal authority who once took another man's car, the exact replica of his own, on coming out of a concert and drove us halfway to Cambridge before he discovered his theft. We even enjoyed sitting in the middle of a traffic jam in Boston while a police helicopter overhead decided how it could best be loosened out. At the Puseys' we met unexpected people like the chieftainess of the Macleods, touring the world, splendid in Macleod tartan, or Tillich and his fun-loving humorous wife. Besides, we were getting to know two remarkable Englishmen: I. A. Richards, if one can call that elfin Welsh phenomenon an Englishman, and W. G. Constable, then the Director of the great Museum of Fine Arts in Boston. W. G., with warm kindness, pushed me round his Museum in a wheel-chair, so that I was able to see the wonders it housed. In the evenings, as often as not, we had a gay meal with the Wilburs over *coq au vin* in some restaurant.

Yet what we enjoyed most were visits to the Pickmans in their unusual family estate on the other side of New Bedford. Unlike those Americans who shared with neighbours the lawns and gardens in front of their houses, as Good Mixers might be expected to do, setting up no railings or sundering walls, the Pickmans had withdrawn themselves into the privacy of an extensive wood; their house was tucked into the heart of it, and they were parking their married children in other houses within the wood, where the trees, though not ancient, were fairly well grown. Their house included a large old barn which made an impressive hall for friends to gather in, and they were devoted lovers of poetry, so that poetry sessions were frequent. The Sweeneys used to drive us there and we would find the Richardses already arrived with Ivor willing to let us hear some of the poems he had now begun to write. The atmosphere was serene and welcoming, at once restful and stimulating. The dinners were sumptuous, served by old family retainers, on an old table dressed with magnificent silver pieces. To visit there was like moving into a bygone era.

But Mr and Mrs Pickman had contemporary interests, and one of these concerned the cows in their dairy farm which, to our delighted surprise, were being given the benefit of the Good Mixers' gospel. Instead of being fastened each into a separate stall, these contented cows strolled at large in a little courtyard of their own, conversing amiably with one another and feeding themselves out of communal hay-racks in an adjoining barn, where they chose their own stalls as they pleased. Edwin was fascinated, for he loved cows. The Pickmans' cows were obviously happy in their freedom. The Pickmans' daughter in charge of them told us that this open access treatment was the latest theory in cow-keeping.

With so much poetry in the air Edwin found himself composing a poem now and then, although he had been warned that he would not be able to make poetry in America. From the first days in our sitting-room we saw a new church being built outside; day by day it grew, until one day the skeleton of its spire was set up, delicately pencilled against the autumn sky with a small gilt cross on top. Edwin was moved to write about it. That it was, as he knew, a Mormon church was a matter of no moment to him. Catholic, Orthodox, Protestant, all ecclesiastical structures made by 'ingenious theological men', for him only cribbed

> *in rusty bars*
> *The Love that moves the sun and the other stars.*

It was a bare shell of a church, and as a bare church he made it welcome. Later one day in spring we went to Salem with the Wilburs, following the 'Witches' Trail'. Edwin wrote another poem about that, an unwelcoming poem this time. It was a clear, sunshiny day in Salem and the wooden houses with their handsome pillared porticos looked what they were, dwellings for rich burgesses. We had got past our early feeling that wooden frame houses were somehow provisional, like booths at a fair, and we could not but admire Salem.

Our peregrinations in New England did not take us as far as Vermont or Maine. Edwin's chest pains tended to recur when he was tired and my back was not good, so we rationed our energies to visiting the colleges he was booked to lecture in. Bryn Mawr was the first of these, where he entertained a roomful of young ladies with a disquisition on Jane Austen's Villains. Whether it was due to the Victorian Gothic buildings, or the restraint of conversation and manners at table, we found this college surprisingly formal. Edwin succeeded in making his audience laugh and discuss Jane Austen's villains with liveliness but even squatting on the floor the students stayed, somehow, ladylike. A small group of the English Department staff, on the other hand, with whom we had drinks, was anything but formal. It included Laurence Stapleton, whom we had last seen in the Carswells' sitting-room in Hampstead, and perhaps that was why its atmosphere was friendly and gay from the start.

After Edwin's next batch of three public lectures, which were given in March, this time in an even bigger hall than before with correspondingly greater trials for the microphone electricians, we visited the University of Connecticut, at Storrs, a State University. Here a breath of New England austerity was still perceptible. On this one-night stand we occupied a set of rooms designed for two students, a study with an adjoining bedroom. The study contained everything that could help students to work: comfortable revolving chairs at comfortable desks with good reading-lights and shelves for books, but the bedroom was strictly for sleeping in. There were no bedside lamps and not even a rug on the cold floor. Next morning we had the prospect of tramping across half a mile of open campus in the rain to get breakfast at the canteen, but a saviour appeared in the nick of time; a friend of ours on the staff turned up in his old car and carried us home with him for breakfast. These trivial discomforts seemed more than trivial at the time; we were not young and limber enough to ignore them.

All the more comforting was our next stop, Mount Holyoke, not a State college, where we were lapped in luxury; carpets, rugs, bedside lights, ashtrays, even, if I am not mistaken, breakfast in bed. The Head of the English Department, Dr Anna J. Mill, had been a student a little my junior at St Andrews, and she made us very much at home. Besides giving a talk, Edwin acted as one of the three judges of poems sent in by students: the other two judges were Louise Bogan and James Merrill. It was a merry, lively occasion.

In Harvard and Radcliffe, the neighbouring women's college, we talked to a good few students. At one Harvard evening party students sat jam-packed on the floor and sang ballads from the Appalachian hills and the old Wild West; the range of their repertoire delighted and surprised us. We went on an afternoon by special invitation to a seminar on translation, which was not so enjoyable—at least, I remember being bored by the abstract analytical quibbling. I would rather do translation for two hours, I felt, than attend for one hour to an intellectual dissection of its problems. I suppose I was a 'natural' for translation, since I never thought of theories when translating; as I had once been a 'natural', in the same way, for playing golf.

One thing we noted, with some sorrow: the burden of reading laid upon young students of English Literature. It was assumed, with what justice I do not know, that students on their arrival from school had read little, and a very broad syllabus of reading was prescribed. Harvard students were worked hard, and so, I think, were the girls at Radcliffe. There was also strong pressure on junior members of the staff who had not what was called 'tenure', that is to say, who were not 'established'. To be sure of keeping their jobs they had to publish something at least every two years if not every year, were it only a learned pamphlet, to show their quality, since the competition for junior posts at Harvard was intense. It struck us, although we did not say so, that showing off in print to keep one's job was unlikely to result in first-rate work. Professors, who had tenure, could take as long as they liked to produce their books; there was great advantage in having tenure.

The Harvard Medical School, we were told, was very up and coming; why should we not consult it about our disabilities? An organization called 'Blue Shield' was open to us, because of Edwin's academic status, and would considerably reduce the medical fees. We joined 'Blue Shield' and consulted the Harvard Medical School. Edwin had the arteries of a young man, they said, and his pains came from a false angina. The angina might be false, he objected, but the pains were real. The report on his arteries, however, was a relief to us both. As for my back, a cheerful young man patted my bottom and said I had a cyst at the foot of my spine which would clear itself up in time; anyhow, I should be pleased to know that it was usually a young woman's affliction. But my hip-joints should be attended to. I ought to be put on crutches for a while to rest them, and then they could be hung on wires.

The emphasis on youth in the reference to Edwin's 'young man's arteries' and my 'young woman's cyst', gave us some rather sardonic amusement. I refused to be put on crutches and to be wired. How could I possibly go on crutches to New York where we were due again, since Edwin was to lecture at the Young Men's Hebrew Association, or to Washington which was next on our programme?

Washington was a surprise to us. Edwin was to give a talk at the Arts Centre run by Maida and Robert Richman and they put us up at their own house in Georgetown, in R Street. Georgetown must have been built at about the same time as Hampstead High Street; it was so like old Hampstead that it was at once familiar and dear to our hearts. To be living in R Street amused but did not alienate us; we had disliked streets named only by numbers in New York, but streets named by capital letters were at least literate. We saw all the buildings and memorials one is supposed to see and were taken to Mount Vernon, Washington's estate. The early background of the South, which had an authentic English look, came vividly alive; the landscape of Virginia was more like an English landscape than anything farther north, and had it not been for seeing the blocks where slaves used to be put up for auction we could have loved the old Southern towns. We were taken over the Blue Ridge Mountains and gazed on the valley of the Shenandoah, the home of a favourite song of Edwin's, which in his younger days he always contributed to festal parties. In the city itself we appreciated the deep, shady ravine that cleft it, and the wonderful gardens of Dumbarton Oaks.

Impressed as we were by the way American Colleges and Foundations looked after poets—besides Robert Frost and Richard Wilbur we had met Donald Hall, Richard Eberhart and Robert Lowell—Edwin was passionately resolved to light out for Europe. Offers were made which we took so little seriously that I hardly remember them. Some literary organization I cannot now identify, for instance, offered us a house erected in memory of some literary man, I have forgotten which, if we would only come and live in it. The daftest offer came from a Boston corporation lawyer, who had influence in a company running the Saudi Arabian oilfields and was apparently fascinated by our conversation. He wanted us to go to Saudi Arabia and start a cultural centre there for the benefit of the American staff marooned among the oil wells. He was prepared to pay us a large fee in dollars, enough to keep us in lifelong comfort after a couple of years or so, if we would only take our stimulating presence to the Saudi deserts and enliven the listless young Americans who did not know what to do with themselves, he said, they were so bored. We had taken him seriously until then as an authority on the Arabs; when he told us that Arabs could always be depended on to quarrel among themselves and would never become a unified menace under Nasser or any other dictator, we listened to him attentively; but when he made us this offer we could not help laughing. He dwelt on the size of the fee we should earn; we dwelt on our inability to stand great heat and insisted that we would never survive the fiery Saudi deserts. What we did not tell him was that we should never be acceptable to American oil technicians, however bored, because we were too old, too literary in our interests and, above all, too European.

By this time we knew that as between America and Europe our background was unshakably European. This fact we had surmised years earlier but it now stood clear in our minds, sharply outlined against our surroundings. The precipitating agent had been an afternoon spent with an elderly Austrian couple called Weisskopf, who treated us to coffee and Guglhupf in their Cambridge flat. We did not know, until someone later told us, that Weisskopf was a nuclear scientist of distinction; what we did know was that with him and his wife we spent one of the most comfortable afternoons we had had for a long time.

It was comfort in depth, arising from a background of common feeling and common knowledge among the four of us. Naturally enough, we talked about Hitler, and there we were at one. Hitler led on to mention of Broch, and we did not have to explain Broch to our hosts, for they knew about him. They agreed with Broch's conclusions as far as Austria was concerned; Austria, they said, had been shaken to pieces. Remembering Prague, and how Czechoslovakia had been shaken to pieces, we knew what they meant; they did not have to explain it to us. I think that was the key to the rare understanding of the afternoon, we had to explain very few things to each other; we did not have to spell out meanings. We all knew that old systems in Europe were collapsing, and that new systems were being painfully imposed on unwilling people or painfully groped for among uncertainties, or altogether renounced. We met each other somewhere in the same Fable, which reached back into the history of Europe. That did not make the Story less delightful, as for instance when we discovered that every one of us had enjoyed *Cosi fan Tutte* in the small theatre of the Vienna Hofburg.

All this happened too confusedly for me to be precise about what was said, except that I know we talked also of Mozart and Mahler. When Edwin and I came out into the street we felt dazed for a moment to find ourselves in America instead of Vienna, and that was when we realized that we had had to come to America to find out how European we were.

Chapter Twenty-One

ENGLAND

May 1956–January 1959

Standing at lunch-time by St Martin's in the Fields and watching crowds of people walking towards Hyde Park as they came out of their offices, we felt that England was much the same as ever. During our stay in the States we had never seen so many people on foot, walking as if walking somewhere were the most natural movement in the world. But when it came to finding a place to live in, England began to look different.

It was long since we had looked for a house and prices had soared meanwhile. Hampstead, we learned, was out of the question, being now full of City men instead of poets and writers and we were not drawn to any other part of London, especially not to the outer suburbs. Yet we had believed that a cottage might turn up within reach of London, a little better than but not unlike our Penn cottage. We found that the cottages we could afford to buy we disliked, and those we liked were beyond our means, so we had to decide on some other part of England to live in. We shrank from going back to Lowland Scotland, while Highland Scotland seemed too remote for earning a literary living unless one could have a small helicopter (vain dream) as well as a telephone.

Edwin, impatient with our lack of success, was all for going up to Orkney immediately; we could get a cottage later on, he said, and meanwhile summer in Orkney. But we had trunks and books parked near Victoria, furniture stored in Edinburgh, where Gavin also was, and our old Austin car laid up at Newbattle Abbey under the care of Webster, the general factotum: this dispersal bothered me like a dispersal of our personalities, and I wanted to make sure of a sheltering roof, or the promise of a roof, before going off to Orkney. Edwin was not thinking of settling in Orkney: he was having too much trouble with chest pains, with what he called his 'tubes and glands', to find the damp dark Orkney winter suitable for his old bones.

We were then urged by Kathleen Raine in Girton and John Holloway in Queens' College to try finding a cottage near Cambridge; there were still good cottages to be found in villages outside Cambridge, they assured us. We went to Cambridge, looked around, and found the freehold cottage our hearts desired in the village of Swaffham Prior. After committing ourselves to buying it, entry to be made on August first, we went off to Orkney, collecting Gavin on the way.

Orkney was an extreme contrast to the United States. Our experiences in the States were only half digested, if that, and Edwin needed the comfort of getting back to the sources of his Story and Fable. Ernest Marwick, an ex-Newbattle student, took us in a hired car round farmhouses where people sang and played fiddles, accordions or tin whistles, but we spent much of our time just sitting, watching seals on the rocks of a bay or watching people in the main square of Kirkwall outside St Magnus Cathedral. An old man, Magnus (Mansie) Flaws, whom Edwin had known in Wyre as a child, was now living in Kirkwall with his wife, and he used to keep us company on our bench, saying little. Sometimes we looked in on some lively second cousins of Edwin's in Kirkwall, or went out to a cousin's farm at Skaill, Deerness, where he used to holiday as a young clerk, or to see Stanley Cursiter and George Mackay Brown at Stromness. Edwin was thoroughly at home. He was, I think, serene by the time we went down to our cottage.

Our biggest problem was Gavin. He had, to us inexplicably, gone deaf, and no one knew how to cure it. We had had him several times examined in the Edinburgh Royal Infirmary, which professed itself as much baffled as we were. The career of a concert pianist, on which his hopes had been set, was now impossible. He had enrolled himself at Moray House, Edinburgh, to train as a teacher, but after a while they rejected him. For the time being the bottom was fairly knocked out of his universe.

When we moved into Priory Cottage, Swaffham Prior, he attended lip-reading classes in Cambridge. Otherwise he occupied himself striding over the countryside, especially over the great old dyke to the east of us which was made to keep out the Danes, or to keep them in, a wild irregular earthwork. That part of East Anglia had been overrun by the Northmen and one still met occasional sturdy-legged red-heads, like a neighbouring milkman who needed only a Viking helmet to fit him out as a Norse raider.

On our first journey along the eight miles from Cambridge to Swaffham Prior, Edwin and I had been vaguely pleased to think that we might be the spearhead of a new Norse invasion. What induced us to feel like that was our coming to a hamlet called Quy, a purely Norse name for a cow-farm that reminded us of many Orkney quoys, such as Grimsquoy and Quoydandy. To see Quy announcing itself on a road-sign was almost an omen that we might belong to this district. The charming appearance of Priory Cottage did the rest.

It was very like us to ask no questions about sewage, water mains, walls or roofs. From any outside angle the cottage looked attractive. It had a walled garden behind it, as well as a garage; its front door was on the main street of the village and we walked straight into a spacious sitting-room, made out of two original small rooms which gave two different heights to the ceiling. Most old English cottages are cursed with very small rooms, and as soon as we walked into this large room we nodded to each other and said: 'This is it.' The front casement windows looked out on two parish churches, one on either side of a hill. The left-hand one had a dilapidated octagonal Norman tower, but its nave had been roofed over in the nineteenth century and except for the tower it was weatherproof. The right-hand one was in Perpendicular style; it had a fine tall belfry, quite whole, and a clock-face, but its nave was a ruined shell. These incongruities could be explained later: the immediate consideration was that the cottage faced a view which could never be vulgarized by any development company, for the whole hill was sacred ground. An unspoilable view, a large sitting-room, a delightful garden; we booked the cottage at once, asking no questions.

Luckily for us, Priory Cottage provided the right answers. It had been constructed for his own use by a local scapegrace when his finances were depressed in the great crash of 1929. Three old cottages which he owned had been combined into a small gentleman's residence for himself and his wife, so that he could let his manor house at the other end of the village. As it was for his own use, Priory Cottage was well finished; the walls were double—what if the interior ones were merely wattle and daub?—the doors were of a polished red-brown wood, perhaps a kind of mahogany, the window casements fitted, there was a good bathroom In the village there was then no sewage at all, but Priory Cottage had its own cesspool. The cottage stood on the verge of the fenlands: the soil at the foot of the garden was deep and fertile fen soil, good for roses, while at the top, just beside the back door where it was already climbing towards the little hill, it was a chalk and flint mixture, poor for anything except lavender, which grew there in a fine hedge. The village shop stood next door, within my reach, in an ancient little building whose roof was tiled in the right wallflower colour with an old storehouse behind it, of a pattern common to the region, very like a dovecot. The whole lay-out was a delight to the eye. As if that were not enough there was a small crab-apple tree so symmetrical and lovely that it might have flown to its place from some mediaeval Book of Hours. It was beautiful in autumn with its small bright scarlet apples, and when spring came it was fairy-like with blossom. We could see it from our beds in the ground-floor back and Edwin loved looking at it—a very radiant tree.

We settled down to become villagers *de luxe*, with a study upstairs lined with books and downstairs a piano, a big radio-gramophone and plenty of records housed on a home-contrived arrangement of shelves. Edwin passionately enjoyed listening to music. His experience of it had not been entirely through listening, for he could sing many songs in a true, tenor voice and as a youngster had played the accordion, which he had tried playing again in Orkney this summer, tucking his feet under the chair and rocking to and fro in the locally traditional manner. In Dresden I had taught him to read music and play it on the piano. But Gavin became such a brilliant pianist that neither of us thought of performing while he was at hand to do it so much better, and now we also had the joy of listening to orchestras and operas on our radio-gramophone, which had a first-rate sound chamber.

One unexpected pleasure was added, the excellent peal of eight bells in the tower of the right-hand church opposite our

Willa Muir, 1967

cottage. When the Fens used to be flooded, the little hill was a place of refuge well above the waters, and the bells had sounded over the countryside as a guide. They were such good bells that the champion bell-ringers of the district, in the neighbouring village of Burwell, used to spend a whole Saturday afternoon every now and then practising on them. We listened with delight to the intricate patterns they played, as the bells wove in and out; this was a new experience to us, for that art of bell-ringing is found only in England and we had never before lived beside a peal of such bells.

We did not lack for company, from Queens' and Girton. One afternoon when Kathleen Raine and Muriel Bradbrook were in our sitting-room Edwin came downstairs with his finished version of 'The Brothers', that last successful statement about the deaths of his two brothers, and read it aloud there and then, his face illumined.

At that time Kathleen was a Fellow of Girton and under her influence the college was very friendly. On our first arrival it staged a welcoming reception for us, and Bob whose college career at King's had just finished, stayed over for some days in order to attend it. We were inordinately pleased to meet him again. After that we were often at Girton, sometimes seeing friends like the Richardses, who returned to Cambridge, Eng. every summer, from Cambridge, Mass. We reached a height of magnificence when Edwin gave a Poetry Reading there one evening and we were put up for the night in a suite specially kept for the bishop who was the College Visitor.

John Holloway's college, Queens', was also friendly; we had the pleasure of being taken through its historic old rooms and attended some afternoon parties. Edwin was made a Member of it, so that he could borrow books from the University Library. The rest of the Cambridge Colleges mostly kept their distance. St John's invited Edwin once to dinner at the High Table. It was like Edwin to set off to that dinner expectantly, looking forward to an evening of conversation as High as the Table; he came back disappointed and rueful, saying: 'Kens thu what they talked about? Trams!' David Daiches, then at Jesus, invited us to a sumptuous luncheon in his rooms there, with the College speciality, *crème brulée*, to crown the feast. I got the impression that dons lived very comfortably by our standards, for they could entertain people well without much effort. Our standards were, I fear, conditioned by my having to be the cook and housekeeper. As I had to do everything while hobbling about on a stick, entertaining people to any meal but tea was quite an undertaking.

Edwin's digestion had always been delicate and was now more so; our cooking had to be carefully selective, and that was a compelling reason for my being the cook. It was impossible to find even a rough daily cook in the village. I was lucky to have a daily help for the heavy work.

Shortly after settling in we completed our household by adding to it an enchanting tabby kitten with all the necklaces and bracelets a tabby ought to have. Neither Edwin nor I would have been able to exercise a dog sufficiently. But a kitten could, and did, exercise herself. After being trained to come down tree-trunks tail-first instead of head-first she became a notable climber of walls, roofs and trees. From the garden foot she had the freedom of open fields and the Vicar's woods. Edwin spent a lot of time arguing with her about which of them owned his bed. She is now in London, a lithe and still beautiful cat, and still has to be argued with, nowadays about whether she is to sit in the middle of any paper I happen to be using.

One had always been led to believe that in backward English villages (and Swaffham Prior, an agricultural village on the edge of the Fens, was backward) people had to live for twenty years in the place before being accepted, but this proved untrue in Swaffham Prior. We met with great kindness from all our neighbours.

Professed Europeans, why had we imprisoned ourselves in a backward English village that maintained its self-respect chiefly by despising people who came from the Fens lower down? The answer is simply that we did not feel imprisoned. There was more to Edwin and me than was visible from the crowns of our heads to the soles of our feet, and that 'more', whatever it was, reached well beyond the village. The same might have been said about other people in the village. The influence of the Bottisham Village College, an offshoot of a Cambridge educational scheme, penetrated into our High Street; across the road from us play-readings went on which we were glad to attend and take part in. Edwin himself, sitting in his study, was in living communion with the Fable that recognizes no frontiers between people or countries. To write a review for the *Observer* on Hofmannsthal's work ('Austrian Genius', July 21, 1957) he did not need to be in Austria; to compose a poem like 'The Desolations', remembering the frozen slag on Etna and Catania's 'black house-rows like a pleasant street in Hell' he did not need to be in Sicily. But perhaps he needed to be in Swaffham Prior to reach the conclusion of that poem,

> *'The roof-tree holds, and friends come in the evening'*
> *What saves us from the raging desolations*
> *And tells us we shall walk through peace to peace?*

The desolations, as he felt them, were gigantic impersonal forces threatening all mankind; to face them he needed the peace of home. As for me, scrubbing pots at the sink, communion with the Fable I found less easy, but even at the sink I had flashes of awareness that I was doing this work for my True Love.

At times we were impatient of our disabilities, at times very tired, but we never felt imprisoned. We had a constant source of joy in each other's company. It did not need even the comfort of laying hand in hand or cheek to cheek; it was enough to be sitting in the same room together, in contented wholeness.

From this central core of home peace we lived in and through the village, in accordance with our gospel of imaginative understanding, as we should have tried to live in and through any ambience in which we found ourselves.

There was, of course, a more obvious reason for our settling in England rather than on the Continent. Manuscripts written in English find their easiest market in England, and Edwin had to consider markets. He had no pension but the Old Age Pension, a scheme to which we had become Late Entrants while still at Newbattle, and in Swaffham Prior we benefited, though we drew less than the standard rate. We had to depend on Edwin's writings for the rest of our income, and this sometimes gave him, as he said, a sinking feeling. I was proposing to do translation again although I had been out of the running for years and was doubtful whether work of mine would now have much market value. While Edwin was earning a good salary in the British Council and at Newbattle

I stopped translating partly because the British taxation system treats a married woman earning money as if she is a catspaw for her husband and taxes him for what she brings in, on a cumulative scale, which would have burdened Edwin a lot. Our reduced income now would not lead to such crippling taxation and I was willing to begin again. Edwin was unwilling; he thought I had already enough to do.

Kathleen Raine, who knew more than we did about possible grants, here suggested that Edwin should apply to the American Bollingen Foundation for a grant to write the book on Ballads he felt should be written. After some hesitation he did so and was awarded a grant for three years, amounting to three thousand dollars a year. At the end of May 1957 he went to Edinburgh for a week to consult the School of Scottish Studies about Ballad material and had a grand evening with old Newbattle students. I was relieved not to be doing translation, although I enjoyed translating worthwhile texts, because the modern language I knew most intimately and could best translate was German and I was still rather bedevilled by a revulsion from it that overcame me when I found out what the Nazis were like.

Yet the trip to Edinburgh was an effort that brought on Edwin's chest pains again and he had difficulty in breathing. He kept on reviewing for the *Observer* and the *New Statesman* and wrote his dreams down in notebooks, but he was growing less able to concentrate. I knew that he was far from well but believed, wishfully, that with rest and care he would recover. At the beginning of 1958 we called in a local doctor, who prescribed a regimen of tranquillizers. At first these improved Edwin's condition. On the invitation of Professor Lionel Knights he went to Bristol University in the middle of February to give the newly-founded Churchill Lectures, stayed there for a month, rested a good deal in bed and reported that he was feeling better. His lectures played round the theme of Imagination and the human need for it; he gave them, as he preferred to do, without a script and almost without notes, and it did not occur to anyone to take them down on a tape-recorder. Lionel Knights told me later that they made a lasting impression on the students, but that a still stronger impression was left by

Edwin himself, just as he was, a living embodiment, said Lionel, of what courses in English Literature are supposed to be all about.

That summer I bought two long garden chairs and laid them out at the back of the cottage, one for Edwin and one for me, to be occupied every afternoon. In this way I hoped to keep him from over-exerting himself. He was no longer able to drive our old car without chest pains, so we sold it. Edwin was glad to be rid of it; the care and effort needed to drive it round our drive into the main street were too much for him. I had given up driving while we were in Newbattle since I could no longer trust my legs; although they looked like quite good legs they were not.

On June 5 we had a day of excitement and, perhaps, undue stress, when Edwin was given by Cambridge University the honorary degree of Doctor of Letters. Cambridge gave only one of these each year; in 1957 they had chosen Robert Frost for the award, and Edwin felt greatly complimented in being Frost's successor. An array of distinguished people was receiving other doctorates, and when the procession was marshalled Edwin found himself paired with Dag Hammerskjöld. As these two passed me in the street they were talking eagerly together, apparently getting on very well with each other; as usual when animated Edwin looked less frail. But once we were inside and his turn came in the ceremonial he was a very frail figure as he stood in the light of a nearby tall window in front of Lord Tedder. I wondered if he were going to be able to see it through. Lord Tedder looked down at him very kindly, beaming approval and encouragement, and this gentle kindness visibly heartened Edwin; he became more at ease. That was the first time I noticed how thin his neck had become.

Then we had a luncheon in Trinity College, which, I had been told, was famous for its feasts, yet provided nothing like a feast on this occasion. But the British zest for spit-and-polish had full play; all the College silver was on the tables; the wines were first-rate; after a bad luncheon three different kinds of fragrant snuff in a massive old silver casket were solemnly handed along. At last Edwin and I could get together and support each other. Edwin told me that Hammerskjöld had been talking mainly about Djuna Barnes, whose work he admired and was setting out to translate into Swedish, although he found the exactions of public life so great that his private interest in literature was being nearly crowded out and he had time for reading only after going to bed at night.

The strain of the ceremonial was now relaxed, but we could not yet go home; we had a satisfying tea in a college cloister with the Holloways. That was Edwin's second last public appearance. His last appearance was later in the same month when he had booked himself to give a talk at the Bottisham Village College. He got only halfway through when he felt he had no breath left. In obvious distress he stopped and excused himself: the only thing to do was to get him home and into bed. The doctor diagnosed water on the lungs. I was so ignorant I did not know that this accumulation of fluid might mean a failing heart. Because I did not know, I could still hope. What I hoped for was to keep Edwin going along gently until the healing forces of the unconscious could get him right again. In my experience the unconscious was a great healer, for something that was not my conscious self had resurrected me twice from the brink of death. I could not believe that Edwin, so closely in touch with unconscious forces, should not also be brought back to health.

He would not stay in bed at first; he liked the long chair in the garden beside the lavender, facing the crab-apple tree. After the district nurse had 'dehydrated' him, as he said, he felt well enough to take an occasional little walk. These walks shortened, until we went usually only up the small hill between the churches, each of us leaning on a stick, to the plateau behind it where the modern cemetery was laid out, with a bench on which one could sit, under a great round of sky.

He grew weaker. Finally he had to stay in bed. The district nurse came several times a week to give him injections which encouraged him to rid himself of the fluid clogging him. My hopes and belief in healing were now almost over-borne by anguish.

People who came to see Edwin sometimes had to be sent away. E. suddenly turned up one day from London, where she was making a visit. Mam had died some years earlier and E. had moved from Glasgow to Edinburgh, to a pretty cottage left her by an aunt. From there she used often to turn up at Newbattle, a hollow shell of a woman re-hashing Mam's anecdotes and harking back to holidays she and Mam had spent in Brittany. (E. is dead now, too.) When she arrived on that day in Swaffham Prior, I was weeping into the semolina I was stirring for Edwin on the stove. I asked him, did he want to see her? Very firmly, he said: No. When she went back to Edinburgh she told everyone she knew that Edwin must be seriously ill, for Willa was crying, 'and, you know, Willa never cries'.

I could have sworn that we wore no masks, Edwin and I, yet ill-fitting masks were often wished on each of us, like this one. Edwin had more of them to suffer than I did, having so many reviewers commenting on him and his works, from the early reviewer who denounced him as 'a blue-nosed Scot' to the recent cartoonist who has portrayed him as a clumsy, shambling 'primitive', naked but for a girdle of leaves. Time, one hopes, will discredit the false and leave the true.

Two incidents in these last weeks I keep in the forefront of my memory. One day, Edwin, troubled about the fate of the world, suddenly sat up in bed and said to me, urgently: 'There are no absolutes, no absolutes.' I was able to reply with conviction: 'No, darling, no absolutes at all.' He was comforted and lay down again.

The other incident happened not long before he was taken to hospital in Cambridge. I was leaning over the foot of his bed, smiling to him; from his pillow he smiled back and said, in a glad voice: 'My lamb, how *nice* thu looks.'

I was haggard and exhausted. Only the eye of love could have seen me as looking 'nice' at that moment.

Dozens of scilla bulbs were planted beside the lavender and the crab-apple to please Edwin in the spring. They all came up and flowered but he never saw them.

He died on the third of January 1959, just after answering the doctor's morning greeting.

That was the end of our Story. It was not the end of the Fable, which never stops, so it was not the end of Edwin's poetry or of my belief in True Love. But any story about human beings is bound to have an end, like this story about us, a pair of ingenuous people who fell in love and went journeying together through life, blundering by good luck in the right directions so that we came to a lasting wholeness and joy in each other. It has happened before; it will happen again; it happened to us. We belonged together.

In reaching this personal harmony we made at least a start, we took a step or two along the road towards that greater world harmony which haunted us like a dream from the Fable. Edwin believed that it *was* a dream from the Fable which would ultimately come to pass, and he felt himself to be a spokesman for it in his poetry.

Index

Lightning Source UK Ltd.
Milton Keynes UK
UKHW01f0630250618
324740UK00001B/45/P